DATE DUE

NOV - 4 1996	
FEB - 7 2002	

THE PSYCHOTIC
Aspects of the Personality

David Rosenfeld

THE PSYCHOTIC
Aspects of the Personality

David Rosenfeld

Foreword by
Otto Kernberg

Karnac Books

London   1992   New York

Chapter two reprinted with amendments from the *International Journal of Psycho-Analysis, 67* (1986), 53–64.

Chapter seven adapted from the *International Journal of Psycho-Analysis, 61* (1980), 71–83.

Chapter eight reprinted with amendments from the *International Journal of Psycho-Analysis, 65* (1984), 377–387.

Chapter ten reprinted with amendments from the *Analytic Psychotherapy, 9* (1982–83), 435–446.

First published in 1992 by
H. Karnac (Books) Ltd.
58 Gloucester Road
London SW7 4QY

Distributed in the United States of America by
Brunner/Mazel, Inc.
19 Union Square West
New York, NY 10003

British Library Cataloguing in Publication Data.
A catalogue record for this book is available from the British Library.

ISBN 0 946439 96 6

Printed in Great Britain by BPCC Wheatons Ltd, Exeter

CONTENTS

PART TWO
Psychosis, technique, and body image

PART THREE
Drug addiction, impulsions, and linguistics

FOREWORD

Otto F. Kernberg

The recently renewed interest in the psychoanalytic investigation of psychosis stems from several sources:

First, the assumption that the psychopharmacological treatment of schizophrenia would render psychotherapeutic approaches to this illness obsolete has proved illusory. We have learned that psychosocial interventions in schizophrenia are crucial to consolidating the achievements brought about with medication and in preventing relapse, and that indeed a toxic psychosocial environment may precipitate a relapse. The importance of psychoanalytic psychotherapy for psychosis becomes evident when we consider the effectiveness of ordinary

Dr Otto Kernberg is Associate Chairman and Medical Director at the New York Hospital–Cornell Medical Center, Westchester Division; Professor of Psychiatry at Cornell University Medical College; and Training and Supervising Analyst at the Columbia University Center for Psychoanalytic Training and Research.

psychosocial interventions in the aftercare of chronic schizophrenic patients and further consider that these interventions
are a far cry from what skilled psychoanalytic treatment might
do in selected cases. In addition, we are accumulating clinical
evidence to show that certain schizophrenic patients who do not
respond to psychopharmacological treatment may be receptive
to a psychotherapeutic approach, if they present at least a certain degree of integration of their personality, a capacity for differentiated object relations within the psychotic regression, at
least normal intelligence, and an absence of antisocial features.

A second reason for the renewed interest in psychoanalytic
psychotherapy of psychosis is our deeper understanding
provided by the pioneering work of Edith Jacobson, Herbert
Rosenfeld, Harold Searles, Wilfred Bion, and Piera Aulagnier.
We can now be more effective in dealing with psychotic regression and psychotic transferences, as a result of our ability to
analyse the psychological structures of psychosis.

The third reason is perhaps clinically the most important: we
have found that psychotic transferences and mechanisms also
make their appearance in patients with borderline personality
organization, narcissistic pathology, the perversions, addictions,
as well as patients with impulse disorders and antisocial tendencies.

Lastly, the psychoanalytic investigation of psychosis dramati-
cally provides us with insights into the functioning of the early
and the primitive mind, which is a source of direct investigation
of the dynamic unconscious that enriches psychoanalytic understanding in theory and practice.

The Psychotic: Aspects of the Personality, building on the
work of the pioneers mentioned, expands the psychoanalytic
understanding of psychosis both clinically and theoretically.
David Rosenfeld's sophisticated approach is based on British
object relations theory. He stresses—correctly, it seems to
me—that the evaluation of the functions of psychotic symptoms
in the transference is more important than the investigation of
their psychogenetic origins. He underlines the importance of
analysing the role that primitive defenses, particularly pathological types of projective identification, splitting, and denial,
play in reducing the patient's very capacity for thinking and for

coming to grips with his intrapsychic reality. Rosenfeld's focus on the central significance of the analyst's functions of containing, diagnosing, and interpretively utilizing his countertransference is illustrated in his moving and convincing clinical data. Overall, the interplay of case material and theoretical formulations makes his book eminently readable and stimulating.

The vicissitudes of the intrapsychic organization of internalized object relations emerge as the basic frame that differentiates various types of defensive organization and clinical developments in the treatment of psychotic patients. At one extreme we find a dismantling of internalized object relations under conditions of primitive terror—and, I would add, a primary disorganization of either the basic affective structures or the capability for sensorial integration in the form of 'pictograms' (Piera Aulagnier's term). Only slightly less severe is the autistic encapsulation of early object relations under conditions of extreme trauma. Towards the middle of the spectrum of severity of psychosis we find the dominance of symbiotic, fused, or undifferentiated relations between self and object, with the patient unable to distinguish his own psychic operations from those of the therapist. Here, in order to avoid pervasive confusional states, the patient may set up secondary defenses in the form of violent acting out. At the less pathological pole of psychosis, we find that differentiation proceeds, and more sophisticated splits between idealized and persecutory relationships are played out in the context of improved reality testing. Dr Rosenfeld covers the entire spectrum of psychotic conditions, describing transference and countertransference developments and the technical management of each.

Of particular interest is his original description of the 'primitive psychotic body image' characteristic of psychotic patients wherein the development of a 'skin' surrounding the body image and a related concept of a differentiated self fails (usually in response to inordinately traumatic early interactions with the primary caretaker). He describes the fantasy of a liquid body content contained within the equivalent of a 'sack' constituted by blood vessels, clinically expressed in the patient's fears of emptying the content of the body or wishes for filling up the content of the body as a prerequisite for remaining alive. This imagery, reflecting a decidely primitive pathological symbiotic state, may not only be expressed in psychotic transferences, it may also underlie certain drug addictions centring around concerns over injecting oneself with liquids.

In fact, Dr Rosenfeld's clinical material not only illustrates this hypothesis of the primitive psychotic body image but also shows how this common core of primitive fantasies may be expressed in drug addictions and psychosomatic illness, as well as in psychosis. He traces the relationship between delusional hypochondriacal concerns and the transformation of these concerns in acting out in the course of treatment. Further, he shows how the transference developments in patients with drug addictions reflect changes in the patients' internalized object relations. In analysing the treatment of patients with drug addictions, Dr Rosenfeld illustrates how each of these stages corresponds to transformations in the system of the corresponding internalized object relations: he documents the progression in the transference of drug addicts from confusional states to splitting of idealized from persecutory object relations, to gradual differentiation of self, and to eventual sublimatory shifts from drug abuse to deepening of regressive involvements in the transference.

Based on the literature currently available regarding the psychoanalytic exploration of psychosis, the clinical experience of colleagues from various psychoanalytic centres, and the experiences of my co-workers and myself, it would seem that we have not yet arrived at an integrated psychoanalytic conception of the psychopathology of psychosis in general, and of schizophrenia in particular. Tentatively, I would hypothesize that the most pathological psychic structure, commensurate with very regressed cases of chronic schizophrenia, consists in the total dismantling or unavailability of any differentiated internalized object relations, with a corresponding fragmentation of affects, of self and object representations, and chaotic fusions of the self and object representations, conditions originally described by Edith Jacobson.

At a second level of pathology, I would include the states of 'secondary autism' (on the basis of the work of Daniel Stern and other infant researchers, I no longer believe it is reasonable to maintain the concept of a normal, 'primary' autism). Here, the unavailability or autistic encapsulation of internalized object relations may coincide with the establishment of a 'skin' of a sort, in the sense of ego boundaries separating self from object representations and guaranteeing a capacity for reality testing at the cost of a complete fragmentation or unavailability of emotional investment.

A third level of pathological development would be represented by the typical 'symbiotic psychosis' first described by Margaret Mahler and beautifully illustrated by much of the clinical material offered in the present volume. Confusional states frequently characterize the early treatment stages of schizophrenic patients at this level of development, although the most primitive confusional states are also frequent in the more severe type of psychopathology mentioned first, and at relatively advanced stages of treatment in the therapeutic resolution of 'secondary autism'.

At a still less regressed level of pathology, we find patients in whom psychotic functioning characterized by fused self and object representations and loss of reality testing in areas of intense emotional involvement goes hand in hand with the capacity for reality testing and the development of more advanced, 'neurotic' conflicts and defensive operations in other areas—the typical disorders in which psychotic and non-psychotic parts of the personality function in parallel. Here, however, we enter into the semantic problem of what we call 'psychotic', and whether we are using this terminology in clinical, descriptive ways, to designate a certain level of development of object relations or the dominance of a certain constellation of primitive defensive operations.

Finally, outside the area of clinical psychosis but still characterized by primitive distortions of internalized object relations, we find the borderline conditions, primitive types of sexual perversions, and psychosomatic disorders. Psychosomatic disorders, however, present the paradoxical combination of surface maintenance of reality testing and a capacity for relatively impoverished but at least seemingly not frankly 'psychotic' relations with others, while, at the same time, the unconscious meanings of their symptoms and the profound weakening of their capacity for intrapsychic and interpersonal communication of affects evinces dramatic similarities with more severe levels of psychotic functioning.

This general developmental frame of the pathology of internalized object relations in psychosis has relevance for the psychoanalytic approach to dealing with these conditions. Patients with deep disorganization of affective patterns and of thought processes in the context of generalized withdrawal from object relations—suggesting extreme pathology of internalized object relations—are practically beyond the reach of a psychoanalytic approach. In contrast, patients with a fixation at a pathological symbiosis, a predominance of the classical fused self-object representations, with loss of reality testing and an inability to differentiate between self and therapist may be approached with the psychoanalytic techniques developed in recent decades. The treatment of these patients is also beautifully illustrated in the clinical material presented in this book.

Here, the focus on the differences between the patient's and the therapist's perceptions of reality, the therapist's tolerance of 'incompatible realities' in the patient's and his own experiences without denying the existence of such incompatibilities, and the transforming of confusional states into more organized states with primitive splitting into idealized and persecutory object relations are central aspects of the technical approach. The focus on and clarification of the immediate reality in the sessions, a simple and clear language on the part of the therapist, the consistent use of countertransference analysis, and the analysis of the present functions of symptoms and defenses rather than their genetic origins are key aspects of the psychotherapeutic technique.

Finally, patients who are reaching the point of differentiation, with a more acute sense of loss of self (precisely because of their growing capacity for a differentiated experience of self) require a focus on the threats to this developing identity. Again, Dr Rosenfeld's formulations in this area are an important contribution to our understanding of this stage of psychotic development. Because of their improved social functioning, these patients may often be treated with psychoanalytic psychotherapy, and their therapists have to deal with the complex interaction of the psychotic and nonpsychotic aspects of the patient's personality.

The Psychotic: Aspects of the Personality commands particular respect because its author maintains an open-ended attitude towards the many still unresolved questions regarding psychosis. He concentrates his efforts on the clinical aspects of psychotic patients that are approachable by the psychoanalytic method; on illuminating continuities of different types of psychopathology where one would not a priori have suspected them; on illustrating the functions of primitive defensive operations in the transference and countertransference; and on conveying a live and in-depth narrative of his technical approach. For all these reasons, his book should be most helpful to the clinician, challenging and stimulating to the psychoanalytic researcher and theoretician, and a significant contribution to a very contemporary aspect of psychoanalytic exploration.

PREFACE

O, let my books be then the eloquence
And dumb presagers of my speaking breast;

O, learn to read what silent love hath writ:
To hear with eyes belongs to love's fine wit.

[Shakespeare, *Sonnet 23*]

I n this book I have tried to present the results of many years of experience as an analyst working with deeply disturbed or psychotic patients, as well as some conceptualizations of both clinical and theoretical aspects that allow for a more fruitful approach, not only to these patients but also to less disturbed ones. The clinical material is not presented merely as a number of vignettes; rather, it attempts to show the continuous dialogue between patient and analyst, a point I elaborate on in this book.

Part one deals with the theory and clinical treatment of the psychotic aspects of the personality. Beginning with a review of the literature, it describes my technical approach to psychotic patients and includes rich clinical material.

The concept of encapsulated autistic nuclei allows me to use new diagnostic and technical approaches. In connection with this concept, I describe a psychotic moment in patients who are survivors of concentration camps. An original point about this definition of encapsulated autistic nucleus in adult patients is that it is also something that it is useful to preserve—a theoretical contribution that is currently accepted and used by outstanding authors like Francis Tustin (1986). Some psychotic aspects of the personality, and the concomitant theoretical developments, are also discussed in chapter one and in chapter three, concerning a patient who received a heart transplant while in analysis.

As, in my view, one of the key tools for the future of research in psychoanalysis may well be the accurate detection and use of countertransference, a detailed account of my own countertransference experience—and the corresponding technical implications—is included.

In chapter five, on child analysis, I stress the importance of supervision and of the supervisor's supportive role so that the analyst, confronted with very severe cases, may keep thinking in psychoanalytic terms, without being flooded by hopelessness.

In part two I develop my notion of the primitive psychotic body image (PPBI).

This model has proved useful to me and other colleagues working with deeply disturbed patients—for instance, those with psychosomatic and somatic delusions, and drug-addicts—in order to understand and prevent suicidal attempts.

ACKNOWLEDGEMENTS

I would like to thank those who helped in the editing of this book: Ricardo Avenburg and Guillermo Brudny, who have discussed with me each of these chapters; Manuel Galvez, Perla B. de Segal, B. Luna de Minuchin, Amalia T. de Zirlinger and Gloria Hanoni, who worked so long for the creation of this volume.

Alfred Painceira and Natalio and Jeanette Cvik, who were always ready for editing and for helping. Benito López, always present in the most important moment in my life.

My family, who for days and nights were always by my side, stimulating me, suggesting ideas, encouraging me, and working with me in the final editing, translation, and correcting of this book: my wife Estela, and my children, Debora, Daniel, and Karin.

The translators, Rosemblatt, Seiguer, Alvarez de Toledo, and Hecht, who have been so professional as well as affectionate.

My everyday helpers Berardi and Mosquera—thanks for their constant and intelligent efforts.

And a very special thanks to Klara King for her wonderful and difficult task.

I would also like to thank my publisher, C. Sacerdoti, who seems to love books since the beginning of time.

I wish to express here my gratitude to all those who have been my teachers and advisors. I feel that it is a great honour for me that they have provided such valuable comments on this book.

Very special thanks are due to Dr. Otto Kernberg for his teachings and Foreword.

As also for their encouragement and scientific generosity to: F. Tustin, B. Boyer, S. Leibovici, A. Green, J. McDougall, A. Marie Sandler, Dinora Pines, and E. and M. Laufer. Finally, I want to thank my parents, and, as an old poem that is centuries old says: I want to thank them for the good deeds and the good intentions.

David Rosenfeld

PART ONE

PSYCHOSIS
AND PSYCHOTIC PART

CHAPTER ONE

Psychosis
and psychotic part:
a clinical approach

O, throw away the worser part of it and live the purer
with the other half.

[Shakespeare, *Hamlet,* Act III, Scene 4]

I
n this chapter I present clinical material corresponding to
two patients, Samuel and Pierre, in order to illustrate some
views on the psychoses. As defined by Freud, by psychosis
we understand the denial of reality and non-adjustment to it. It
is a narcissistic disturbance, a damaged psychic apparatus. In
addition, I develop some concepts about the psychotic part, psychosis, transference, transference in the psychosis, projected
insight—expelled and then attacked outside—and the models
and theories that might be used to explain the emergence of
violence in the psychoanalytic treatment of the psychotic patient
(Samuel). I discuss the usefulness of research into psychosis in
order to create new models and hypotheses—for instance, the
primitive psychotic body image model. Pierre's case, likewise,
shows the alternation between a psychotic part and a neurotic
part, even within the same session.

I also describe the countertransference with these psychotic patients and stress its importance when an adequate technical use is made of it and, particularly, its unique intensity. I feel that the study of countertransference (and of psychotic transference) are the *via regia* to future investigations and for progress in the treatment of the psychoses, just as dreams were the royal road to the investigation of the neuroses. The patient makes the therapist experience intense and violent emotions, which he cannot express in words. This is the analyst's paramount task: to be able to tolerate such emotions for days, weeks, months, or years and to decode them and translate them into words, with the appropriate timing.

The psychotic part

It should be noted that Freud did not develop the concept of a psychotic part, even though he suggested it in several works (Freud, 1911c [1910], 1924b, 1926e, 1940e [1938] and, especially, 1940a [1938:).

The definition of psychotic part might be based on the process that Freud referred to as splitting. It should be pointed out that the process of splitting is not a psychosis. Freud (1940e [1938]) regarded splitting as a defensive process, but one that is more precocious than other defenses.

We may then conjecture that the healthy or neurotic part present in every patient may establish, with that part of the ego, some kind of transference relationship. We understand some things about the psychotic patient thanks to the healthier part with which he can verbalize and conceptualize. We do not know the hidden psychotic part directly: it is a model that we must create as we work. Freud (1925d [1924]) suggests that the psychotic patient may be studied with further research and also that the analyst must discover the things that are behind a wall:

> . . . since the analysts have never relaxed their efforts to come to an understanding of the psychosis . . . they have managed now in this phase and now in that, *to get a glimpse beyond the*

wall . . . but the mere *theoretical gain* is not to be despised, and we may be content to wait for its practical application. In the long run *even* the psychiatrists cannot resist the convincing force of their own clinical material. [pp. 60–61]

In agreement with what has been previously stated, Freud (1925 [1924]) says, in connection with the parts that make transference possible in psychotic patients, that, in psychosis,

. . . transference *is not so completely absent,* but that *it can be used to a certain extent,* and analysis has achieved undoubted success with cyclical depressions, light paranoiac modifications and partial schizophrenias.

In another paper, Freud (1926e) says,

I should have thought that it would be recognizable from the phenomena, the symptoms, of which he complains. This is when a fresh complication arises. *It cannot always be recognized, with complete certainty—the patient may exhibit the external picture of a neurosis, and yet it may be something else.* The beginning of an incurable mental disease . . . —the differential diagnosis—*is not always easy and cannot be made immediately in every phase . . . the illness may have an innocent appearance for a considerable time,* till in the end it displays its Evil character . . . [p. 202]

Bion (1967a) contributed some interesting ideas about the clinical and technical fields. For example, in clinical practice it is very important to perceive the functioning of the psychotic personality. Interpretations should make reference to the possibility of recovering expelled mental functions. As Elizabeth Tabak de Bianchedi (1989) suggests, this implies laying the stress on the function rather than on the interpretation of conflicts, emotions, or doubts. The psychotic personality lacks the capacity to ask itself questions; it is not aware of the conflict. It expels its ego and its perceptual functions. The analyst must help the patient to recover what he has got rid of (not only objects and emotions, but also ego functions which the patient has got rid of through projective identification).

Bion (1967a) states:

I do not think, at least, as touches those patients likely to be met with in analytic practice, that the ego is ever wholly withdrawn from reality. I would say that its contact with reality is masked by the dominance in the patient's mind and behaviour of an omnipotent phantasy that is intended to destroy either reality or the awareness of it. Since contact with reality is never entirely lost, the phenomena which we are accustomed to associate with the neuroses are never absent and serve to complicate the analysis, when sufficient progress has been made, by their presence amidst psychotic material. My second modification is that the withdrawal from reality is an illusion, not a fact, and arises from the deployment of projective identification against the mental apparatus listed by Freud . . . the patient acts as if his perceptual apparatus could be split into minute fragments and projected into his objects. . . . [p. 46]

Psychosis, psychotic part, and neurotic part

A thought which, quarter'd, hath but one part wisdom.

[Shakespeare, *Hamlet,* Act IV, Scene 4]

Freud's (1940a [1938]) description of the splitting of the ego in the psychoses into a normal part and another that 'detaches the ego from reality' is of fundamental importance for the understanding of the psychoses.

In the course of treatment, the analyst avails himself of the patient's neurotic part, with its minimum capacity for verbalization, in order to establish a transference relationship. In other words, if on the basis of some of Freud's writings we infer that in every psychotic there is a neurotic part, this part could be the basis for the establishment of a transference relationship in accordance with his own definition. As from 1913, Abraham began to suggest, perceive, and state that there is transference in schizophrenia (Abraham, 1908, 1911, 1916). As Freud (1940a [1938]) points out,

> even in a state so far removed from the reality as the hallucinatory confusion . . . that at one time in some corner of their mind there was a normal person hidden.

He adds that,

> Two psychical attitudes have been formed instead of a single
> one. One, the normal one, which takes account of reality, and
> another which under the influence of the instincts detaches
> the ego from reality. The two exist alongside of each other.
> The issue depends on the relative strength. If the second is, or
> becomes, the stronger, the necessary pre-condition for a psy-
> chosis is present. If the relation is reversed, then there is an
> apparent cure of the delusional disorder.

A healthy part is necessary in order to work with a psychotic
patient. As Shakespeare puts it: 'Nothing can be made out of
nothing' (*King Lear,* Act I, Scene 4).

Transference in Freud:
a methodological approach

According to Freud's definition of transference, it is a process by
which the unconscious wishes are displayed upon an object
within the framework of a special type of relationship established with them and, above all, in the psychoanalytic relationship (Laplanche & Pontalis, 1973). It is a repetition of infantile
prototypes experienced as if they were intensely present.

Freud (1912b) stressed that transference is associated to prototypes or imagos (mainly that of the father, but also the
mother, a sibling, etc.). The physician will become a part of one
of the psychic series already formed by the patient.

Freud gives a definition of transference that includes a libidinal relationship with the part capable of communicating, and,
from the methodological point of view, this also implies a definition. For instance, even though Freud does not specifically speak
of an 'acute psychosis' but of 'acute or hysterical psychosis', we
might infer that as regards the treatment of the psychoses they
amount to the same thing. Freud (1895d) refers to 'hysteria' and
then to 'hysterical psychosis' and adds that '. . . it can be assisted
to an extraordinary degree by our therapeutic intervention'.

This shows that our work with a patient with an acute condition can be useful (Avenburg, 1975).

Although Freud investigated cases in which, theoretically, transference was not assumed to be present, in practice the opposite phenomenon could be observed. Let us consider the case of Schreber, a psychotic patient, and his relationship with Flechsig, his doctor (see Freud, 1912b, pp. 47, 50, 55; see also transference with Flechsig, pp. 18, 19, 38, 39, 40, 69, 72). Why did Freud not state that these transferences had to do with the doctor? This is difficult to understand, but perhaps not so much so if we re-define it from the methodological point of view.

To establish whether the psychoanalytic treatment of psychotic patients is useful today, the first point to be mentioned is that every investigation is useful, provided that it is carried out in the transference. It is for this reason that I will now discuss the concept of transference and of transference in the psychoses. As stated before, I shall use a methodological approach to this subject.

A first step would be to ask ourselves whether the current definition of transference is useful. We think it is, since it has made it possible to centre our attention upon a certain type of phenomenon occurring in the course of a session (Brudny, 1980).

When a classificatory term that includes some phenomena while excluding others is introduced, we must make sure that what we are defining is a 'natural class'.

In the first place, this class should be relevant.

In the second place, it must have typical and constant characteristics and relationships that differentiate it from what has been excluded from the classification.

If we asked ourselves whether Freud's definition of transference directly involves neurosis and psychosis (Freud, 1912b) or whether it is a definition of a situation of a relational nature, *we might answer that this kind of definition does not presuppose that we are speaking of neurosis or of psychosis* (Klimovsky, 1980). The definition of transference describes a phenomenon that may or may not occur—that is, it defines a natural class and is useful (Popper, 1965).

It might be asked whether Freud made a methodological mistake in his general definition of transference. We might answer that it is legitimate to define a new concept stipulatively, provided that the stipulations are not arbitrary.

Freud's definition of transference is not so narrow, since it can be applied to the study both of psychotic and of neurotic patients. An epistemologist would be inclined to think that there are no methodological mistakes in Freud's general definition of transference, since it makes it possible to study patients as well as the conditions and effects of transference and even the use to which this phenomenon can be put. It may very well be that Freud has given us more than a definition—an empirical statement, an empirical generalization (Klimovsky, 1980).

How and why does Freud come to the conclusion that transference is a phenomenon observed in neurotic but not in psychotic patients? The reason could be:

1. the type and number of patients he saw;
2. the time element.

In my view, this is very important, because, in fact, his definition of transference does not seem to imply that it must necessarily be a transient phenomenon, that is, that it should be detected immediately. It would seem that there is here a kind of methodological mistake, not in the general definition of transference, but in the way in which Freud collected his empirical data. Freud thought that if transference in the psychoses did not appear within a short period of time, then it did not exist. (I must point out, however, that at that time the course of an analysis was usually brief.)

Transference in the psychoses

Somewhat contradictorily, in other writings Freud suggests that the treatment of psychotic patients may be useful for the creation of theories: 'Therapeutic attempts initiated in such cases have resulted in valuable discoveries . . .' (1925d), and also that transference is not wholly absent in psychotic patients. For instance, with reference to psychotic patients, he says that:

'Transference is often not so completely absent but that it can be used to a certain extent' (1925d).

Freud's definition is very useful because it provides information, and we may think that the negative, disruptive, or disorganized transference of psychotic patients would also provide us with information. (Even the patient's indifference is information. Freud describes indifference as the way in which 'they reject the doctor . . .' [1916–17].)

This is similar to the study of particles in a cyclotron, where Wilson's chamber, which photographs atomic particles, provides information. What matters is not whether the pictures are in black on white or white on black, but the information. The same applies to the investigation of transference in psychotic patients: whether positive or negative, it provides us with adequate information, given the adequate elements and time.

After defining transference, Freud seems to have come up against epistemological difficulties as regards the observation of the data.

In his autobiographical study (1925d), Freud says that it is in the extreme forms that the material emerges most clearly. The extreme cases teach us the most. For example, Freud says:

> *Am meisten kommt aber in Betracht, dass in den Psychosen so vieles für jedermann sichtbar an die Oberfläche gebracht wird, was man bei den Neurosen in mühsamer Arbeit aus der Tiefe heraufholt [Gesammelte Werke, p. 87]*

> But the chief consideration in this connection is that so many things that in the neuroses have to be laboriously fetched up from the depths are found in the psychosis on the surface, visible to every eye. For that reason the best subjects for the demonstration of many of the assertions of analysis are provided by the psychiatric clinic. [1925d, pp. 60–61]

Perhaps what Freud called transference in the psychoses was a type of transference that did not fit in with his theory of transference and of the neuroses at that moment.

But if we regard as transferences more primitive and undifferentiated ways of communicating and if we place them within the context of other hypotheses or other theoretical conceptions, some events between patient and therapist may be defined as *transferences*.

The display of the transference in a psychotic patient requires some time and such transference may be abrupt and premature [*d'emblée*]; at other times, conversely, it takes months to detect transference material with certainty. (Abraham did describe transference in the psychosis, in 1908, 1911, and 1916.)

Psychotic transference may be observed particularly in the treatment of psychotic patients and is usually described as premature, precipitate, intensely dependent, thin, tenacious (Bion, 1967b) and based on projective identification. Up to a point, it may resemble what Freud (1926e) described (within a different theoretical model): 'Under the influence of the Id, they have assumed forms of expression that are strange to our comprehension.' This usually happens to a historian of the sciences: that is, he finds that an author describes an event quite accurately from a phenomenological point of view but then omits it from his general theory or else states that it does not exist. Perhaps something similar happens with Freud's neat description and conception of the transference of the most regressive and deepest aspects of a human being.

On the other hand, H. Rosenfeld (1987), when speaking of the psychotic transference, describes a special use of projective identification: 'By projecting their confused feelings and anxieties into the analyst, patients not only get rid of them, they also provide (just as they did in infancy with their parents) the opportunity for the analyst to become aware of their feelings.'

I agree with the definitions of psychotic transference proposed by H. Rosenfeld (1987), Segal (1950), Bion (1967b), and Searles (1965). I would like to add to these definitions the element of 'absolute conviction' about what the patient believes the therapist does to him and also that the patient 'acts accordingly'— that is, that there may be a silent or not openly exposed type of delusional or psychotic transference. In these more silent cases the transference is not openly exposed, but certain reactions to what the patient delusionally believes the analyst is saying or doing to him in the session may be observed.

Another interesting point to be discussed in the case of severely disturbed patients is the concept of transference and that of restitution. The conception of the 'end-of-the-world' feeling, in which the thing and object representations are lost, also implies a breakdown of the transference. This is why Freud (1895d, 1915e) stated that there can be no transference in psychotic patients. But there is a struggle, and that is what makes it possible to re-establish it. Psychotic restitution, delusion, and hallucinations are all attempts at the restitution of the bond. But are we to understand this as transference? *Freud is ambiguous in this respect and does not give a clear answer*. This ambiguity concerning transference or restitution may be found in Schreber's case, where Freud sometimes speaks of transference and at other times of restitution (Avenburg, 1975, and personal communication).

Restitution is the re-connection with the world of objects; it is not established through the representation of things—nor is it imaginary or fantasized—but through verbal bridges, which are not supported by the full meaning of the thing representation. They are attempts, but they are not totally successful (Boyer, 1983; Brudny, 1980; Freud, 1937c; Grunberger, 1971; Ríos, 1985).

When we speak of psychotic transference, if we do not include the concept of the period of time necessary to uncover it and the radar and the microscope to detect it, our answer will be that there is no such transference. As in Eddington's example, if a researcher states that the smallest fish in the Red Sea are one centimeter long, what he is actually saying is that the diameter of the holes in his fishing net is one centimeter.

In agreement with other authors, I feel that the investigation of the transference in the psychoses '*is the main road along which the successful psychoanalysis can progress*' (H. Rosenfeld, 1987).

In the psychoses, the therapist must sometimes supply the integrating ego. Through projective identification, the psychotic patient projects parts of his ego into the therapist. The ego parts that do not function in the patient have to be contained by the therapist, who must wait for the right time to interpret them and give the patient back the parts of his projected self. Perhaps the same may be said of insight: the psychotic patient is not always able to express it with words.

Technical handling

From the technical point of view it is convenient to handle the psychotic transference bearing in mind the following:

1. not to interpret hastily: the optimum and adequate context must be created first;

2. to learn how to contain the patient's projective identifications so as not to be overwhelmed by them (this has been particularly stressed by Kernberg, 1988, H. Rosenfeld, 1987, Joseph, 1988, A. Sandler, 1988, and J. Sandler, 1988);

3. to take countertransference feeling into account as regards the delusional transference that is created;

4. according to some authors oedipal or sexual levels should not be interpreted since it could increase the patient's confusion; I think the same thing happens when the analyst interprets projected partial aspects of the self prematurely (for example, I would not interpret: 'This is a crazy part of you projected into your mother or father');

5. to remember that if the patient finds out that there is somebody capable of containing or tolerating unbearable feelings, while before he thought there was no one capable of doing that, this may mean the beginning of a new conception of the bond and of human relations.

Shakespeare's words are highly relevant here: 'O, throw away the worsen part of it and live the purer with the other half' (*Hamlet,* Act III, Scene 4).

Herbert Rosenfeld (1987) suggests that psychotic transference should be interpreted, when he says that 'Even in the very disturbed schizophrenic patient there are remnants of the sane personality with some capacity for normal thinking, which can be strengthened through interpretations'.

Samuel's clinical material (pp. 18–24) reveals the psychotic transference, while Pierre's case (pp. 25–39) shows how a psychotic picture may be useful to create models that can be of use for that patient and also for others. This is the model of the

primitive psychotic body scheme (chapter eight), for instance
(D. Rosenfeld, 1989).

What is observed in the transference of a psychotic patient is
the same as that which can be seen in the dream of a neurotic
one (Brudny, 1980).

The therapist's role

The analyst's role in the treatment of psychotic patients poses a
question that I shall try to answer: Are we still psychoanalysts
when we treat hospitalized psychotic patients (Boyer, 1983;
Racamier, 1959)?

In this respect, I think that whether or not the patient is
lying on the couch is irrelevant. If the analyst works with the
psychoanalytic model and tries to probe into the dynamics of the
unconscious, using transference elements, this is psychoanalysis
with psychotic patients. *The important thing is to think in psychoanalytic terms.*

The new theoretical and technical approaches should be
taken into account. At present, the analyst works with a team
made up of highly qualified professionals—physicians, psychologists, social workers, etc.—who contain the patient when the
analyst is not present. In several of his works, Freud expresses
an optimistic view concerning the possibility of treating the psychoses in the future.

Other roles during the psychotic transference

1. To contain despair and the 'projected or projective insight' is
   of great importance. Instead of 'projective insight', it would be
   better to speak of an 'incipient insight' that is projected, is
   expelled, and then attacks its own perceptual apparatus, but

projected into the therapist, when confronted with a perception about himself. (It is an apparent—but false—negative therapeutic reaction; it may appear, for instance, when a schizophrenic patient begins to perceive the limits of what he can and what he will not be able to do in life.) It is not due to envy of an external object, but to psychic pain—for instance, when Samuel (see below) wants to attack in me—apart from his projected internal object—his projected perceptual apparatus, since he cannot tolerate so much pain.

2. One must take into account the patient's usual belief, in the case of a delusional or psychotic transference, that the therapist will flood the patient with his own crazy things, a mechanism due to the patient's own crazy parts projected into the therapist, and his fear that the therapist may give them back to him (H. Rosenfeld, 1987) or else to the reality of a psychotic father and mother who flooded the patient with maddening paradoxical messages (Samuel's case).

3. It must be remembered that on other occasions these patients are only occupied and preoccupied with discovering how the analyst's mind works (López, 1985).

*　*　*

An area I would like to consider is that of psychosomatic illnesses. Without attempting to modify the definition of psychosis, it would be interesting to assume that many psychosomatic pictures (which are left out of the classical classification, or included only as bodily or organic illnesses) could be better understood by assuming that there is an underlying psychotic structure that may express itself through behaviour or a bodily action (Lagache, 1968) and that it would be interesting to study and observe, as it might help us to understand some severe psychosomatic pictures from a different angle (D. Rosenfeld, 1987a; 1988, pp. 63–77).

The use of countertransference

Hath . . . not eyes? Hath not . . . hands, organs,
dimensions, senses, affections, passions? Fed with the
same food, hurt with the same weapons, subject to the
same diseases, healed by the same means, warmed and
cooled by the same winter and summer . . .? If you prick
us, do we not bleed? if you tickle us, do we not laugh? if
you poison us, do we not die?

[Shakespeare, *Merchant of Venice,* Act III, Scene 1]

The intense emotions that the psychotic patient makes the
therapist feel—whose quality goes beyond the normal empathy
or transference of normal affects—has been conceptualized by
many authors with the term 'countertransference'.

Apart from the therapist's own problems, countertransference, as a signal, should be used to think and not to expel
or interpret. Methodologically, countertransference is a hypothesis that the therapist creates in his field of work. It is not
a certainty, but a working hypothesis that should be used to
think.

Intense feelings are conveyed to us by psychotic patients
through mechanisms about which we know very little as yet
(projection, projective identification, paradoxical messages, phonology or the music of the voice, broken phrases or syntactic and
semantic disturbances, etc.). From the point of view of information, the way in which a psychotic patient speaks is as rich a
source as memories or dreams in a neurotic one (Liberman,
1970–72; Rosenbaum, 1986).

Sometimes the theory does not comprise and explain the richness, the dynamics, and the dialectics of the clinic. For instance,
while Freud was theorizing about countertransference as a problem (perhaps objecting to Ferenczi, who used it inappropri-
ately—he kissed his patients, etc.), at the same time he used
it with his patients and made notes of it; for instance, in the case
of the Rat Man, where he wrote down some notes on his own
countertransference (D. Rosenfeld, 1987a; see also chapter
seven). Others, such as J. Sandler (1988), Begoin-Guignard
(1986), and Kernberg (1988), have studied the relationship
between projective identification and countertransference.

Some will insist that countertransference is disturbing. I would say they are right, but only if the therapist does not perceive what countertransference means, and if he does not know what to do technically or how to use it. Papers on countertransference are usually written once we have already understood almost everything.

If we do not know what these intense emotions a psychotic patient makes us feel are, we will obviously find it disturbing. I insist that it is a message to be decoded.

But countertransference may be a highly useful tool if we try to discover what it is the patient makes us feel that he cannot express with words (words that never existed to express his chaotic infantile world).

Some tools are disturbing at the beginning, precisely because we do not know anything about them. When Freud discovered transference, at first he thought it was a disturbance, a resistance. Similarly, the invention of the microscope was seen as a disturbance until scientists learnt how to use it correctly with the improvement of achromatic lenses.

Despair, I repeat, is one of the countertransferences that are most intense and difficult to tolerate with schizophrenic patients. Sometimes it is their way of projecting and getting rid of unbearable feelings with which they cannot cope, and so they try to see whether the therapist also feels hopeless—that is, to find out whether his mental state is of constant attention, whether he is active and thinking, different from their childhood parents.

Samuel's clinical material shows that the patient manages to convey affect in the first interview. Later on a feeling of despair appears, which overwhelms the medical–psychological team; finally, he tries to make them all frightened with his violence, whether in the form of hitting or threats with a knife.

Pierre's case shows how he conveys the dissolution of his self (to lose a solid ego) and how it is liquidified and 'he is afraid of bleeding', not only through his conception of the body scheme but also by making the therapist feel it through a broken, diluted, confused, scattered, and disorganized way of speaking.

I would like to state that countertransference is to be thought about, decoded, taken into one's own personal analysis—not expelled through a quick and incorrect wild pseudo-interpretation. In this way it may become an important tool for the future of the research into the as yet unknown world of the psychoses.

Clinical examples

Samuel

> But my madness speaks. . . .
>
> [Shakespeare, *Hamlet,* Act III, Scene 4]

Samuel is a 24-year-old patient concerning whose condition I was consulted by his relatives—that is, by an aunt and his grandfather. I was asked to see him in the town where he lived, since they did not know what to do and he could not travel. This was at the end of January 1989.

His relatives reported that when the patient was 18 years old a diagnosis of chronic schizophrenia had been made by two well-known psychiatrists. Samuel is the elder son—his only brother is two years younger—and his parents are alive at present.

The last psychotic episode, when he was 18, coincided with his moving to a flat with his mother. She had told him she wanted him 'to feel better and more comfortable', but the real reason was that she was divorcing Samuel's father. This is usually a typically confusing maternal message. At the time when he was living in that flat, he had threatened his father and his mother verbally; in the course of a violent episode, his father had hit a closet with his fist and broken one of his wrist bones. This, together with the fact that he had recently again threatened his mother with a knife, moved his relatives to consult me. One psychiartist had suggested that Samuel should be put into a psychiatric hospital for chronic patients. During the interviews Samuel slept on the floor—as he had for the past couple of years—drinking great quantities of liquids and continually fastening and unfastening his shoe-laces.

I interviewed Samuel and his family for several hours a day, and I made a diagnosis of the family and of the patient. In spite of his condition, there were moments when Samuel showed considerable affect, which attracted my attention since this is quite unusual in a patient with a diagnosis of chronic schizophrenia. I suggested an immediate change of medication.

Samuel was then taken to Buenos Aires, but, as he did not want to be hospitalized in a clinic, he refused to go out of the house for 17 days. His mother, who was with him, helped to look after him. He was drowsy most of the time, and whenever we tried to comment upon his mental state or convince him to go out for a walk with one of us, or suggest that he should be hospitalized, he refused flatly and then went to the bathroom and masturbated compulsively. At that time, he would also induce vomiting in the morning, which he had done for the previous few years.

I feel that our teamwork was efficient, since we were gradually able to take him out of the house, go for walks together, and finally, in February 1989, convince him to go enter an open clinic, in which he has remained since then. For the first three months Samuel had daily sessions with me; thereafter he had five sessions a week, with my team seeing him for the remaining days. After one year, this was reduced to four sessions a week (Mauer & Resnizky, 1991).

It is in order to illustrate my contention that transference is not absent in psychotic patients—in contrast with what some passages in Freud's work seem to suggest—that I want to present an example of transference with me in the treatment of this patient. As stated before, psychotic transference is uncontrolled; sometimes premature, but not always; it is violent. Love and hatred are forms of the transference. The episode, which involved two incidents, took place about three months after Samuel had been hospitalized: first, in the course of a session with me at the clinic, he threw a punch at me that brushed my face and glasses. He himself brought in the transference by saying that he wanted to hit me because I resembled his father because of my glasses and my moustache—something I had not interpreted previously.

In the second incident he burst into the room in which a staff meeting was being held, with such violence that he almost broke the door. Apart from myself, there were physicians, social workers, psychologists, music therapists, etc. present at the meeting. Irritated, Samuel sat down and said he hated me and he was going to hit me in the face and then kill me because I resembled his father and had the same glasses and moustache.

He said he was going to kill me first, and then everybody else in the room. I told him he wanted to kill a crazy part inside his head and a crazy father inside him, that he projected this and wanted to see it in me, instead of seeing it inside his head. He replied that he was going to kill all the social workers and psychologists. Then I told him that he scattered onto everybody what was going on in his head and that he wanted to get rid of that crazy Samuel by seeing him in me and then in the people there, but that what he wanted to see outside and kill was what was crazy in him.

He replied that he would kill himself afterwards, and I insisted that he wanted to kill his own crazy part and that we wanted to help him to be cured by means of words, that there was no need to kill.

This was an example of analytic work at a moment of intense transference with me: he fragmented and re-projected me into all the clinic's physicians when he implied, for the second time, that he was transferring his father imago onto me. Such violence in a psychotic patient is perhaps an example of his way of repeating or remembering (Freud, 1914g). It is important to point out that this patient had no memories of his first eight years of life, and that acting violently was probably his way of bringing his childhood back, through actions and not through memories.

In this respect, it should be mentioned that Samuel's mother had never touched him, caressed him, or breast-fed him during his first two months of life, because of an alleged hepatitis. When he was older, the patient was violently punished by his mother with a belt. According to her, this started when Samuel was eight years old, but when his grandmother and aunt visited him at the clinic, they told me, as a secret, that both his parents had begun to beat him when he was five. This perhaps explains part of his violence and the leitmotiv of his childhood: the hatred that invaded his mind. It would seem that he chose to become drowsy, psychotic, fragmented, to hate and be violent, in an attempt to deny not only outer reality but also his sad inner reality, in which there was a child beaten and abandoned by his father—who would not talk to him for months after a trivial incident—or by his mother, who, when she lost control of herself, destroyed what he cherished most—his bicycle—and went as far as to cut the tyres with a knife several times a week. This outer reality and his inner world were fragmented, wiped out, as expressed by Samuel himself: 'I have no memories of my childhood before I was eight.'

This hatred was perhaps his way of bringing back his childhood world. But now there was a difference: there was a psychoanalyst and a medical and psychological team who could listen to his hatred, help him to express it verbally and work it through. At least he discovered that there were other people who could contain him, accept him, and tolerate those awful things in his mind, without feeling frightened or beating him (Houzel, 1987; Limentani, 1966; Racamier, 1959; H. Rosenfeld, 1987).

* * *

Now we deal in detail with material corresponding to a period starting in May 1989, in which the patient began to create mental spaces and brought a dream.

After the transference episode in which he associated me with his father (it is worth mentioning that the first two times he said that I resembled his father, and on a third occasion he said that I 'was' his father—a concretization and not an 'as if'), Samuel began to write to those he hated and wanted to kill and to those he loved. He wrote letters in which he expressed his hatred and affection towards some people. This was highly significant, since it showed that Samuel could now write instead of hitting. Later on he asked that his letters and other writings be published as his first book of memoirs; they were compiled and published as a small book in June 1989.

Little by little, he recovered his own history. First he tried to find out the origin of his name, and, while he was writing his book, he rediscovered the relationship between his name and

that of his grandfather—whom he now saw as a significant figure—and a biblical history according to which 'King Samuel
was a friend of King David'—an obvious transference reference
to David, his therapist.

It should be noted that in his ambivalent bond with me,
marked by quick alternations between love and hatred, there
gradually emerged the capacity to write instead of acting and
hitting another patient (a woman with behaviour traits similar
to those of his mother) or threatening his therapist. Apart from
beginning to get rid of his hatred and violence through writing—through the secondary process—he expressed his wish to
draw cubes and triangles in the drawing classes he attended at
the clinic. What is remarkable here is that that very afternoon
he asked the psychologist on duty to teach him to draw cubes
and pyramids, but with a three-dimensional perspective—that
is, with depth—'because he didn't know how to'. On this occasion, the emotional contact with the psychologist was quite
intense. His learning to draw spaces with depth coincides with
the fact that Samuel had a dream that week and brought it to
the session. It is as if a perspective and a mental space capable
of holding a dream had begun to be built in the patient.

I should point out that, even though on two other occasions
the patient spoke of what to him were dreams, we believe that
these were in fact daydreams. In one instance, however, the fact
that he had awoken in the middle of the night and then told his
dream to the doctor and the psychologist on duty allows us to
infer that it was really a dream.

The dream was as follows:

> Samuel was afraid of suffering from an incurable illness, on
> account of which he had little time left. Then he asked two
> doctors for help: one was good and helped him, while the
> other was not so good to him.

As regards being very ill, I had a hypothesis, but did not make
an interpretation; I thought that perhaps he feared that his
mental illness was incurable.

The first thing that struck the patient himself in this dream
was the fact that there was a bad doctor and a good one. My

interpretation and what he thought made him say that perhaps I was the bad doctor while the physician in charge of administering drugs was the good one, something he always remarked. Samuel said: 'Ah, sure, you're the bad one and Dr T. is always the good one. . . .'

Concerning the illness in his dream, I asked him whether he did not think it might have something to do with the fact that on the previous day he had learnt that his grandfather—who paid for the treatment—had had a brain haemorrhage and was very ill. I added that perhaps, because he had not been able to think about it or speak with me about the bad news, he felt he was his grandfather, who had little time to live in the dream (his mother had broken the news to him and then attached no importance to it, which confused him).

Two days later, when we had the negative result of a test carried out because of suspected hepatitis, we were able to understand this dream better. We realized that that part of the dream also represented Samuel's fear of dying from an organic illness.

This clinical material suggests the presence of some encapsulated areas in his mind (encapsulated secondary autism: Tustin, 1986; S. Klein, 1980; see also chapter two).

The clinical material is included here to show the emergence of less psychotic or healthier parts of the mind that have learned to create mental spaces. The alternation between the more psychotic part and the healthier one was frequent.

*   *   *

Samuel's case allows me to propose several alternative hypotheses about the origin of violent reactions in psychotic patients. It may well be that violent and aggressive actions are, in this patient, a means to remember his childhood. These contents, this prevailing idea or affect, may have been all that was preserved in his childhood world, wiping out all other memories.

From the point of view of transference, when Samuel showed intense violence against me, he concretely and directly showed the tremendous hatred preserved in his childhood mind. In addition, Samuel projected the crazy part of his own self and his maddening inner objects into the analyst, in an attempt at killing them in me.

In summary, the following hypotheses may be formulated to account for this patient's violence:

1. It is a way of expressing his infantile world.

2. It is designed to kill in me a projected part of his self.

3. It is an attack on his incipient awareness or insight, but in the analyst's perceptual apparatus. He mistook his head for his therapist's and then attacked what he thought was his perceptual apparatus, but in the therapist—that is, his own perceptual apparatus projected onto me was attacked because it made him perceive how painful his inner world and his madness were. Thus, through projective identification he attacked in me a part of his own mind that was beginning to gain insight.

4. It is used to make the other feel what he felt when he was violently beaten from his fifth year on (and he was certainly successful when he threatened me).

5. When a mother transference emerges, it is the fear of seeing me as a mother who emits maddening messages—for instance, paradoxical messages—by which everything he may do or say will be wrong (D. Anzieu, 1975). (This is also an apparent—but false—negative therapeutic reaction.)

Perhaps Shakespeare explains it more clearly:

They'll have me whipped for speaking true, thoul't have me whipped for lying, and sometimes I am whipped for holding my peace. [*King Lear*, Act I, Scene 4]

Pierre

> No, I'll not weep.
> I have full cause of weeping, but this heart shall break
> into a hundred thousands flaws, or ere I'll weep. O fool, I
> shall go mad!
>
> Shakespeare, *King Lear,* Act II, Scene 4]

I am concerned here with Pierre's return to analysis after a three-year interruption. I will describe the first interviews and a complete session in order to bring out his fantasies and his body scheme conception.

I will then go back to a time, three and a half years ago, when, being in treatment with me, he went through a psychotic episode after a brain operation designed to remove a benign tumour (glioma) on his chiasma opticum.

After the operation and some improvement in the psychotic picture, he had to return to his habitual place of residence, where he owned an estate and worked as a veterinarian. It should be added that his father had died from a bone myeloma before Pierre's operation. Later on I shall describe this post-surgical episode in detail and show how research carried out during a psychotic episode may be useful for the creation of models or theories that may facilitate the theoretical and clinical understanding of the material. Even if we do not attain our objectives in terms of curing, investigating, and creating theories about something so complicated, is useful in itself for an understanding of psychotic patients.

In May 1989 his family decided to bring him back again to Buenos Aires for a consultation with me, to which he agreed.

One of his relatives reported that the patient was violent at times, drank a great deal, carried a gun with him, was often involved in brawls, and his family was afraid that he might lose control. So they decided to hospitalize him at a clinic in Buenos Aires. When he arrived, one of the members of my team was waiting for him and accompanied him to the clinic. I interviewed him that very night and found him drowsy and somewhat confused. He said he had fallen asleep with the radio on and that he was startled when the nurse came in to take it away. First he became frightened and then he reacted violently.

* * *

In the course of the three years after the interruption of his treatment with me, Pierre had formed a family. He had three sons, and the onset of his current disorganization coincided with the birth of his third son a month earlier (it is relevant that Pierre himself is the third son in his own family). He married a woman with whom he had fallen in love as a young man and with whom he had never been able to have sexual intercourse before the wedding. She is quite affectionate with him and is able to contain him.

Another important item during the last period is a convulsion he had while riding, as a result of which he fell from his horse. It should be pointed out that the patient had stopped regularly taking the anticonvulsive medicine (Lotoquis) prescribed to him after the brain operation.

Also relevant is the fact that Pierre was involved in a fight at one of the dances he had attended. He could not remember in any detail what had happened, for he had drunk a great deal of wine. He had said something to a woman who was accompanied by a man, who turned out to be a policeman. A violent fight had ensued, in the course of which he was seriously beaten up. His wife reported that after this episode he began to say he was not feeling well, that his blood pressure was low, and that he felt weak. One day his wife found him drinking a glass of pure alcohol—in order to cheer himself up, as he said, because he felt constantly dizzy and about to fall down. All this material was reconstructed by me on the basis of what the patient and his wife said in the course of an interview.

I will discuss in greater detail some relevant data obtained during the first interviews in May 1989, in which there reappeared some elements that had already been present in the post-surgical psychotic episode.

In the following interview, the first after three years, Pierre spoke about the reason why he was not feeling well. His language was muddled, confused, slow, full of pauses and hesitations. He said he had been aggressive for quite some time and had had a number of arguments with his wife, since she became angry when he went out at night. First she became angry, and then she forgave him. He spoke tenderly of his children, especially the eldest, who has been named after him.

In the course of this interview Pierre's speech was still at times muddled, broken, and marked by unfinished phrases. He repeated that he was frightened because they had taken away the radio he was listening to, that he was dizzy, and that he had been brought to Buenos Aires because sometimes he got into fights with people. He also said he was worried because his memory was getting weak and he could not see well and believed that people lied to him. He was afraid they might do him harm by not telling him the truth. He said several times that his trousers were too big for him and that they kept falling down because he was getting thinner. To prove this to me, he stood up and showed me his stomach. As a matter of fact, what I saw was that his weight seemed quite normal, or that he was possibly a little overweight. When Pierre replied that he was frightened because he was losing weight, I pointed out that he had agreed to see me because he was very frightened and wanted me to help him. Pierre nodded. I added he must be very frightened thinking that the convulsion or dizziness indicated that there was something wrong with his brain again and that a new operation might be necessary. I assured him I would take care of him, and the team of neurologists and surgeons who had operated on him would examine him the following week.

I then asked him why he thought he was getting thinner, and he answered that his bones ached a lot, while he touched his femur, his knee, and his ankle. He insisted that his bones had been aching for a month and that that was why he was getting thinner. He added that he was taking analgesics.

I then decided to ask him to remember some of the things we had spoken about three years earlier, after the operation. I added that he still seemed to think that he had a myeloma and that was why he thought he was getting thinner and his bones ached.

PIERRE: It must be psychological, right?

In the next interview, his wife said that in the course of the previous month Pierre had gone to various places to get blood transfusions, in the belief that he was suffering from anaemia, or else that he had very little blood (see sessions three years earlier described below).

It seemed that a delusional body image (primitive psychotic body scheme) was again present, in identification with the father with a myeloma or cancer and about to die. Pierre said then that he had very few red cells, very little blood.

At some point during the interview I asked him whether he did not think that this was like being mixed up with his father—that is, when he thought that everybody was deceiving him and that I was lying about his diagnosis, and that he felt he was being eaten up by a myeloma and about to die. Then, for the first time in that interview, Pierre spoke more clearly than usual and said:

PIERRE: Then this is the way to have him near, right? What I think is that my father will come back and will insult me today . . . that's what I fear . . . because I stopped taking my medicine and I drank wine and I went out a lot with women and then I had a convulsion a year ago [when he fell from the horse].

Then he spoke about the son born a month earier and repeated once again that he was worried about losing his memory. He repeated then that he was also losing weight. In the course of the same interview I asked him whether the birth of his youngest son might have had some influence on something, some relationship with his current crisis.

PIERRE: I don't know. . . . It might. . . .

D.R.:   Perhaps having a large family with three sons, just like your father, makes you believe that you're already your father with many sons. Perhaps that's why you feel like your father, and you think you are an old father, with a myeloma, about to die. (*Pierre thinks for a while.*) Perhaps this is the idea you have. . . .

PIERRE (*at that moment, amidst a confused babbling, he suddenly speaks more clearly*):   Then, doctor, this is a psychological idea . . . this is psychological. . . . And this is what you are going to cure?

At another moment he said that when he was in the country, he carried a gun with him, but that it was something quite normal, so he did not understand why people became so frightened about it. I told him that it was natural for the family to be worried because he might shoot somebody if he happened to lose control of himself.

In the same interview he referred to his wife, and I asked him how he got along with her. He replied he was afraid of having sexual intercourse, and then, after some unintelligible phrases, he whispered in my ear, in a man-to-man style:

PIERRE: The thing is, I can die during coitus, I can die while having sexual intercourse. . . . Then, when I fear that, I take a lot of anticonvulsive drugs.

I answered that he mistook coitus and orgasm for a convulsion.

At another point, there was the following dialogue:

D.R.:   Notice that you feel you're getting thinner, that you have very little blood. Apparently, you got mixed up again with your father, and, besides, you think they are lying to you about the diagnosis. Do you think that's why you wanted to come back to Buenos Aires and see me?

PIERRE: This question of coming back to Buenos Aires made me remember that I accompanied my father to Buenos Aires and they already had that cancer diagnosis, the bone myeloma, and I told him: 'There's nothing wrong with you, Father, nothing wrong. . . .' So I was lying to him.

D.R.: (*Pierre stares at me*):   Then, because you came to Buenos Aires you think you're as ill as your father, and I'm lying to you.

The following day, in another session, Pierre said in his broken and confused way of speaking that he had visited a typical place for tourists in Buenos Aires ('Caminito', the name of a famous tango) and had visited some relatives who lived nearby. According to Pierre, they were not very friendly, and then he added that he thought his wife did not love him very much because the sexual intercourse he had with her that afternoon was not very good. Here he made an association with his mother and added:

PIERRE: And I was looking around and buying clothes, doctor . . . and this fashion of wearing colourful clothes . . . it's not manly to wear those colours. Pullovers . . . they look like a woman's pullover. You know what I mean, don't you? You know. . . . Besides, today I didn't have a good sexual relationship.

D.R.:   Notice that you associate the fact that you didn't have a good sexual relationship with wearing colourful clothes. It seems that you're worried because if you don't have a good sexual intercourse, you're afraid you're not much of a man.

In response to this interpretation, Pierre remembered that his father used to beat him and tell him not to shout. He then said he did not feel 'very strong' and complained that his brothers, who were healthier than he, made fun of him. These remarks were punctuated by insults.

The end of this session is quite remarkable. I told him that his crisis had started with the arrival of his youngest son. Pierre spoke again of his aching bones, the knees, the transfusions, and he stated once again that his brothers were taking his money away; he suspected they were cheating him and robbing him of his money. This fantasy was then displaced onto the transference, and the patient began to think that I took too much money from him. It is an example, a subtle, microscopic hint of the beginning of a delusional transference in which the analyst takes out his blood and his money. With this patient, this material is a sign of future difficulties as regards payments.

In another session, the idea that his father would return to insult him reappeared. The material seems to suggest that in Pierre there was a hated father who persecuted him, attacked him, and made him ache all over, from the inside, and a father projected on to the outside who made fun of him, insulted him, and wanted to rob him of his possessions.

* * *

The session I now transcribe—it took place 10 days after he entered the clinic—clearly shows his paranoid condition and the conception of his body scheme. At the end of it he expressed with words something close to an insight or understanding of his relationship with his father:

> PIERRE: I had a kind of dream. . . . I was in the country pre-paring some barbecue and eating . . . and I dreamt . . . there was a horse race, there was a big party, and I screwed a maid, and with that maid I had sexual intercourse when we went out of a house . . . and then I went to a festival in the town. It was a party in the town's main square, one of those typical small-town festivities, do you know about that? . . . I felt all right when I woke up. (*He answers a question put by the analyst.*) No, I wasn't anxious. But what bothers me . . . d'you know what? . . . this . . . being here.
>
> D.R.: Being in the clinic?
>
> PIERRE: Yes, er . . . being . . . that's it . . . they do things to me on purpose and getting in my way, like that girl who step-ped on my foot in the street and hurt me with the heel of her shoe, that was on purpose . . . the girl at whom I shouted 'big ass' . . . and it's also on purpose that they laugh at me . . . that people here at the clinic play jokes on me and I'm the centre of attention for everybody (*the analyst thinks here of a self-reference delusion*), or they make fun of me (*some unin-telligible phrases*), they hide my radio's earphones . . . or they put biscuits in my bag on purpose . . . people here at the clinic . . . well, I take the biscuits out afterwards.
>
> D.R.: Do you think it's on purpose?
>
> PIERRE: Yes, yes, on purpose. . . . Perhaps another patient or somebody puts them there and then he didn't remember where he had put them (*the biscuits*). . . . (*Silence.*) And today they gave me biscuits because there was no bread . . . bakers were on strike. (*Silence.*) I'm afraid of social gatherings, of being with people . . . or a group to talk. . . . I'm afraid of an older person or a stronger one.

D.R.: (*here the therapist thinks of the transference, wonders whether Pierre is afraid of him, of a father, as he had said in the first interview, or of an older person who might harm him; following this hypothesis, he asks*):   Are you afraid that somebody might hurt you, someone older? Who can he be? Could it be your father, or myself?

PIERRE: Yes, the two things would be like Father and being hurt. I'm afraid of speaking with the girls. . . . I get frightened. (*He says something unintelligible, but the therapist does not want to interrupt him.*) I'm a bit frightened. (*Again unintelligible.*) I get very angry when they reject me. . . . It's a pretty maid who told me: 'Don't touch me when there's people around', and I was touching her arm . . . and that was in the dining-room. (*Here the narration becomes highly confused, time and place indicators are missing, so that it is impossible to know what he is talking about.*) It's that maid, she's OK, she's very pretty, I feel like screwing her, I gave her a piece of candy, and she said: 'You've got to respect me, I'm on the clinic staff. The patients are here, don't touch me before so many people, you're a patient', Maria said. I said: 'I'm normal, but you're very pretty, you're very beautiful, why should you worry?'

This shows that the patient is trying to have a sexual relationship in the clinic, just as he did after the operation three and a half years before (see session after the operation).

Then Pierre began to talk about his sight problems—his difficulty in seeing what is in front of him. Although he has improved a great deal since the removal of the tumour that was pressing the optical nerve, he finds it difficult to see letters and numbers directly in front of him, so he looks sideways, as if his lateral vision were better. These remarks led to very interesting material, which I will transcribe literally:

PIERRE: I want to speak to you about my vision, my sight, because my wife kept telling me: 'Look at that house, look at that in the paper', and I didn't feel like reading, I read, but, you do know what happens? The light in my eyes bothers me. . . .

D.R.:   Like this table lamp here?

PIERRE: When the lamp is like that or the sun is in front of my eyes, it bothers me, I can't read. That's normal, isn't it?

D.R.:   With the light in your eyes, yes. But perhaps you're worried about something else.

PIERRE: But my eyes were worse before I was operated on, right?

D.R.:   Yes, but how are they now?

PIERRE: Well, now they're a bit better, but d'you know what happens? Another doctor told my wife I'm a psychotic, right? I think it was my sister . . . what does psychotic mean? And my wife caresses me as if I were a little boy and she laughs . . . but do you know what happens? I think she makes fun of me. She's laughing at me, right?

D.R.:   Why?

PIERRE: I don't know why. . . . It must be her revenge because I told her that I had no sexual pleasure with her when we made love yesterday when we went out . . . or that I am not a man. (*These are obvious persecutory or delusional fantasies: when he is caressed, laughed at, or made fun of, and if he has no sexual pleasure, he believes he is being accused of not being a man, of being a homosexual.*) And I get angry at this phobia I have, as if I were, do you know what, doctor? An imitation of my father, right?

With admiration and surprise, I asked him about this linguistic creation of his own.

D.R.:   What's that about an imitation of your father?

PIERRE: Well, the imitation of the father is all that about my bones aching. . . . Besides, my father was always angry.

D.R.:   Like you.

PIERRE: That's right. He swore and shouted at me, he beat me and on top of that he told me not to shout, he told me

'Don't shout, you moron', and you know what, doctor, I . . . I am the imitation, as if what I wanted were to imitate. . . . Then I'm suspicious, I am suspicious when I look . . . and that must be the problem with my eyes, right?

D.R.: What's that about being suspicious in your way of looking? Is it because you don't see well what's in front of you?

PIERRE: It's that not seeing well makes me suspicious, and that frightens me.

It is obvious that his vision problems created for him an area that is not visible or not clearly delimited, and so outside his control, and this makes him feel persecuted. Then Pierre went on with his remarkable description.

PIERRE: Doctor, I imitate my father's shouting, because he also shouted and swore all day long . . . and I also imitate him by not allowing myself to see well . . . not to see things well. And I am imitating him in everything . . . even in being a peasant like my father and in not seeing well, same as my father. My father looked straight ahead, he could see well, but when somebody talked to him he looked sideways.

D.R.: Why? Did he wear glasses?

PIERRE: No, because he was suspicious . . . he looked sideways and turned around like this, sideways. He always had an angry face and that frightened people. D'you know what, doctor? It was his defense against fear.

D.R.: That's right.

PIERRE: Well, then that's why he shouted at me and beat me, right? (*Silence.*) And I feel guilty of leaving that behind . . . of getting out of it.

And then, accompanying his incipient insight, I told him:

D.R.: You must feel very guilty of leaving your father, of not being like him any more. To say good-bye to him makes you feel very guilty, because there's a boy, Pierre, who hates him, who is very angry because he beat him, another boy who feels guilty because he didn't save his father from the myeloma, and a third boy who also feels guilty because he lied to him. It's a mixture of a lot of guilt and a lot of hatred, that's why you cling to him. Apart from hating him, your only way of having him is to get mixed up with him. And that's why you're only now discovering that perhaps your tendency to look sideways has no organic cause, that it may be a way of resembling him, as you have just discovered by yourself. Your father was constantly angry, looking sideways. Notice that you show me your pain, your knee and your foot, and you think you have a myeloma, just like your father. You believe you're getting thinner, just like your father when he was ill.

PIERRE: And I would like to confront him, right?

D.R.:   But can or can't you? What d'you think?

PIERRE: Hatred made me feel guilty, right, doctor? That must be why I imitate, right? Letting go of him . . . er . . . er . . . it might also be not to see better, right?

D.R.:   Yes, it may be.

PIERRE: And even so, and besides, that I couldn't see well because of the pressure on the chiasma opticum, right? That is, apart from the chiasma opticum, I imitate him, don't I? Now I can remember things better.

D.R.:   Yes, you're thinking, you're thinking by yourself, and you're beginning to realize that you imitate your father. I think you're thinking correctly, better than in other years.

PIERRE: Besides, my father forced me, he forced me to be a veterinarian, to live in the country, he put me there. I didn't want to go to the country. I wanted to go to the city, the business was shit. (Silence.) Well, perhaps I wanted to be near my father, right? I was begging for love, to be near him.

D.R.:   You had many brothers, and you were the youngest, always late for everything. . . .

PIERRE: I was always very badly treated as a child, doctor. I want to make my personality grow. . . .

D.R.:   To have a new baby born.

My last interpretation was based on the fact that in the previous interview his wife had mentioned that Pierre had wanted to have sexual intercourse during that week in order to have another baby.

Body image

The concept of the primitive psychotic body image is a theoretical conceptualization of the body image, based on clinical work with psychotic patients going through acute crises.

Another new concept is the notion of liquids as the nucleus of the primitive psychotic body image and their possible transformation into solid or semi-solid substances as an indication of a change in connection with the body image, that is, a more integrated ego nucleus which shows a different type of structuralization of the self and the body image.

DEFINITION: By *primitive psychotic body image* I mean the most primitive notion of the body image to be observed in certain patients whose work begins while they are already regressed or who regress during their treatment. In my view, the extreme notion of what can be conceived of as primitive psychotic body image is the thought that the body contains only liquid or vital liquid, one or another derivative of blood, and sometimes it is coated by an arterial or venous wall or walls (not always). There is only a vague notion of a wall that contains blood or vital liquids.

In turn, as can be seen mainly in crises associated with acute psychosis, this membrane containing the blood may be perceived to have broken or to have been otherwise damaged and to result in a loss of bodily contents, leaving the body empty, without either internal or external containment and/or support. (*Pink*

Floyd—The Wall, the film directed by Alan Parker, expressed these feelings in an outstanding visual language.) Sometimes, the experience of becoming empty is linguistically expressed through a sudden and incessant verbal flow: the patient cannot stop talking and his voice and the therapist's overlap.

Clinical material

The following fragments of clinical material pertain to Pierre, at a time three years earlier than the preceding material. In it, one is able to observe the way in which I intervene and interpret the transference in a post-operatory psychosis rooted mainly in fantasies about the primitive psychotic body image. It is worth pointing out that the tumour for which he was operated turned out to be encapsulated and benign—a glioma—and it was entirely removed.

It is my intention to show the analyst's role in the transference, and also to highlight a rich and clear material on the fantasies that the patient Pierre reveals to us regarding the image and fantasies about his body, especially those referring to his bodily fluids to which we refer as the primitive body scheme or psychotic body image.

The first unexpected incident, which startled neurologists, surgeons, and myself, was a post-surgical psychotic episode—a delirium in which the patient affirmed with conviction that liquids were being extracted from his body. These included the encephalic/spinal liquid, blood, semen, and urine as vital fluids. The third night after the operation, Pierre sought to verify that he had not been completely drained of liquids; for this purpose, he had sexual intercourse with his girlfriend, who was with him at the time. His intention, according to his own words, was 'to see if any liquid came out. . . .' One can imagine the expression on the faces of doctors and nurses when the patient, with the bandage on his head awry, said what he had done.

An example of his primitive psychotic body image during his delusional episode after the removal of the (benign) brain tumour is shown in this fragment:

PIERRE: I'm afraid of having leukemia. . . . I have begun to despair . . . to worry because of the destruction of the red cells by the tumour. As if I were afraid of becoming empty . . . emptied of blood . . . as if I were soft all over. . . .

I then asked him:

D.R.:   Soft?

PIERRE: Yes, everything soft . . . like a sack full of blood . . . I'm afraid of having a hemorrhage, and that everything . . . will come out. . . .

The accuracy with which he expressed his fantasies concerning his body image is remarkable. The conception of the body as a sack full of vital fluids or blood (primitive psychotic body image) is clearly formulated here by the patient on a verbal level.

I will now reproduce parts of the material corresponding to the first weeks after the operation. These fragments underscore fantasies regarding Pierre's bodily image or body scheme and show the way in which I intervene in connection with the delusional or psychotic transference (for example, when he identified himself psychotically with his dead father).

PIERRE: (*in muddled language and stuttering*):   . . . yes . . . I'm afraid to urinate, I'm afraid to bleed . . . to have blood come out, you know?. . . . That when urinating blood might rush out and I could bleed to death.. . . . I'm afraid that the tumour is lodged in the bladder, prostate gland, testicles. . . . I think I have bone marrow metastasis.

In this material it becomes increasingly clear that the patient is convinced of the following: (1) that the tumour was not removed; (2) that he has malign metastases; (3) that he is his father with bone-marrow cancer; (4) that I am deceiving him, as his father was deceived.

D.R.:   And what did you think?

PIERRE: Well, I thought I could bleed or something like that.

D.R.: You thought lots of blood could come out?

PIERRE: Well, yes. . . . I think like an external haemorrhage. I made Mum look at what came out.

I began here to intervene in the transference. I must make clear that the transference with me increased every time that encephalic/spinal liquid was extracted from him for studies. I became someone who hurt him or took his vital fluids—a vampire.

In the following fragment, which corresponds to the third week after the operation, we can appreciate my interpretation of the transference related to the psychotic identification where the patient believes he is the father with bone-marrow cancer.

During the session, while he talked about his meals, Pierre said,

PIERRE: It's as if this were . . . eh . . . the desire to gain weight, don't you think?

D.R.: Are you afraid of losing weight?

PIERRE: It would appear so. Dad lost weight when he had the myeloma.

D.R.: Do you realize the panic you are in is because you think you are your father?

PIERRE: It seems as though I were Dad with all the same symptoms, right? That I might limp, that the medication were destroying me as dialysis seemed to destroy him, right? And it seems I'm afraid I might have to undergo dialysis, right? It's as if I had the tumour . . . and the tumour had invaded all of me, that the operation was too late, you know? That you had lied in the diagnosis, when you read me . . . how do you call it?

D.R.: The anatopathological?

Models and theories

In psychoanalytic practice one may sometimes find examples like those I present, and that is why the primitive psychotic body scheme is a useful explanatory model for a variety of clinical cases. There may be different explanatory models, but for the time being I find the primitive psychotic body scheme the most useful and comprehensive, in so far as it is perfectly suited to many of the clinical phenomena I observe. It helps me to incorporate into a single model developmental generic and transference concepts, both with schizophrenic and with psychosomatic patients. When we construct a model, we find it useful first for one particular patient but then often for other patients as well. To this we might add, provided it is consistent, a developmental-genetic theory of infantile bonds that must be empirically demonstrated in the transference with the therapist.

The primitive psychotic body scheme is a non-observable entity, but when we construct the model it becomes powerful from the explanatory point of view. This does not mean that the model represents the ultimate truth, as is the case with theology, but only that it is a useful model for the time being.

Atomic physicists see the effects of atoms, not the atoms themselves; in the case of psychoanalysis and the primitive psychotic body scheme, we can observe the effects of the model on various types of patients. Science is the capacity to discover facts beyond observation (for example, atomic theory). The power of science (Klimovsky, 1980) lies in the theoretical models of what is beyond observation, and how those models may be observed in the empirical basis. And of the atom, I say that *it is something that cannot be observed directly and about which we know a number of things through indirect inference. These are models of non-observable entities but of great explanatory power as regards what is being observed.*

The specific explanation of what happens in each case is legitimate and undeniable: each phenomenon seeks its explanation, so that it is not surprising that this chapter should have precisely that methodological quality.

CHAPTER TWO

Identification
and its vicissitudes
in relation to
the Nazi phenomenon

Introduction

W e can write about identification from different points of view: theoretical, developmental, genetic, or clinical. But when we attempt to write about identification disturbances in connection with Nazism, things become complicated. What am I supposed to do as the author of a paper of this kind? Methodologically, the approach includes two poles to be developed: Nazism, on the one hand, and identification, on the other. So I ask myself: Is it possible to describe the Nazi phenomenon? Is it possible to remain within the boundaries of cold scientificism? Is it possible to bring together and develop the two poles of this proposal?

In connection with the first question, I considered making a study of inanimate or non-human bonds of Nazism and its psychosocial effects, and defending man's dignity and human rights. Also, I thought of describing some of the patients and others who had fled from an extermination camp.

Thus, after brooding for several months over the subject of this chapter, I concluded that there are certain phenomena of Nazism where the mere fact of putting them into words would seem to minimize their horror.

As Mrs S told me in the course of an interview: 'How is it possible to express in words the inhuman organization devoted to the extermination of babies and children?' This woman described to me the mathematical, coldly planned organization designed to nip identities in the bud, which forced her to cremate and incinerate hundreds of babies brought to the concentration camp in trucks. She said to me: 'Doctor, if I tell you that there were hundreds of babies and children per week killed, or if this figure is written in numbers—1,000,000, one million—Jewish children thus exterminated, do you think, Doctor, that these words describe what happened?'

In connection with this I wondered whether it would not be more appropriate to write that the most serious phenomenon caused by Nazism as regards identification disturbances is the smoke and ashes of millions of Jewish children and youngsters, millions of young free-thinkers, political dissenters, intellectuals, gypsies, anti-fascists, religious dissenters, massacred in extermination camps and gas chambers. This is the most serious disturbance resulting from Nazism in connection with the identification processes.

In connection with the other questions, although it is inadmissible not to include an intense emotional response to the description, we thought that we should try to study—despite the limitations imposed by language—persecution situations during Nazism and the disturbances they cause in identification processes, using the instruments of psychoanalytical science (Klimovsky, 1971).

The scientific description of facts does not negate their ethical implication (Nagel, 1958).

When language refers to something, it does not reproduce it in all its magnitude, as stated by Bertrand Russell in *The Problems of Philosophy*; one can refer to things in two ways: by 'acquaintance' [*familiaritié,* in French], which is the direct contact, the personal knowledge, or by 'description' [*signalement* or *definition* in French], where things are referred to through language although we are not in direct contact with them. Nazism cannot be described by acquaintance or by words evoking direct experiences, but it can be done by description, and that is what I shall attempt.

After these considerations, which show the great emotional difficulty and complexity of the subject, I think it is possible to make a scientific approach to it by discussing some very interesting and paradigmatic (although not entirely general) clinical cases, and from them to derive certain theoretical conclusions. These theoretical models can be applied to other similar ones but must take into account that it is *not* an exhaustive mechanism to be applied in all cases.

The clinical material I selected shows identity and identification disturbances as related to analytical transference and Nazism; even though they are not the ultimate or final situations of extermination camps, they are clear enough examples to show the identification disturbances.

Finally, I selected material behind which Nazism lurks as a horrifying background but which seems to me adequate for the circumscribed and specific objective of discussing the vicissitudes of identification.

* * *

One of the patients who suffered severe identification disturbances as a consequence of the Nazi phenomenon is Pablo, a case that is presented in some detail in chapter seven on somatic delusion, hypochondria, and body scheme.

Pablo had escaped from Germany with his mother when the Nazi persecution started (Berenstein, 1981; Bettelheim, 1967, 1990; Dimsdale, 1979; Kijak & Pelento, 1982; McDougall, 1985, 1986, 1989).

When he began treatment with me, his desperate effort to

work through his losses and mourning over his mother led him to try to preserve his earliest identifications, achieved through highly regressive and primitive mechanisms characterized by confusion with his mother's female body. He thus tried to recover his lost identifications and bonds. Among Pablo's most vivid memories is the persecution and punishment his mother and brother suffered at the hands of the Nazis. Another memory concerns an episode that includes a very special pattern of object relationship: white biscuits, which were lost in the snow while he was running away and which, because they were white, could not be seen and found again. This shows how difficult it was for Pablo to preserve anything and also how he lost the things he managed to take. This is a pattern of bonds and identifications that are lost. It is my belief that massive, total, pervasive persecution makes it very difficult to preserve identifications: *identifications formed under the power of terror are hard to preserve.*

In the course of a session he spoke about a dream in which he saw a fellow called Davis, who 'was nothing special, not too good and not in the least intelligent, whom I met in the Army'. Pablo his children and Davis, who was the driver, were in a lorry that caught fire and fell into a ravine.

This dream was dealt with in several sessions within the transference, by linking it to what we had seen at the beginning of his treatment: his fear of surrendering to somebody who cannot 'drive' him well and may destroy and set fire to his male and female infantile parts (symbolized by his son and his daughter in the dream). The dream obviously reveals that he distrusts my ability to 'drive' the analysis–lorry and also associates Davis with David, my name. At that time, he saw the therapist as a father who could abandon him or as a madman who might lead him away from safety. In later sessions we understood that the dream also represented his infantile history and his fear or a sign of an impending breakdown.

The patient developed a somatic delusion and was convinced that people thought he had female lips and cheeks. Hiding his face behind a beard and hair, he used to run along the streets to my consulting room.

His efforts to recover his lost bonds and identifications consisted of more regressive, more fragmented defensive systems, with ego dissociations and projections of varying severity but more serious than those observed in the two cases I shall now present (Bleichmar, 1982; Brudny, 1980; Erikson, 1968; Grunberger, 1971; Laplanche, 1979; López, 1983; Searles, 1979; Sibony, 1988).

Mario

The patient, who was over 40 years old, looked younger; he was tall, dark-haired, athletic-looking, in spite of which his fear, anxiety, and withdrawal were obvious. In the first interview he spoke about his problem: a stomach pain had returned, his physician had diagnosed gastric ulcer and advised him to start psychoanalytic treatment, which Mario did. When he was 32, he had married a woman with whom he did not seem to have any problems; they had two daughters, 7 and 8 years old at the time of the first interview, and a boy of 4. He had still been engaged when his father died, and he had not been able to make up his mind to get married because he had not wanted to leave his mother alone. He was an only child.

In the course of the first interview the atmosphere was harmonious: everything seemed to be all right, except that Mario seemed too formal and over-adjusted. He described his mother as a generous, hypochondriacal woman, less educated than his father and himself. He was a typical representative of the Jewish-Spanish Sephardic community of the Bulgarian city in which they were born—Roustchouk, on the Lower Danube. It was a wonderful city for a child: people of very different origins lived there together and spoke seven or eight different languages. Apart from the Bulgarians, there were many Turks, and in a neighbourhood close to theirs there were Greeks, Albanians, and the Sephardim who still spoke as they did when they were expelled from Spain in 1492 and on the whole had strong ties with their community. There were also Armenians, Roumanian gypsies who came from the other side of the Danube, and a few Russians. They spoke Italian when they were visited by their Italian relatives.

The patient said that his relationship with his eldest daughter was quite tense; he was impatient with her—for instance, he slapped her once because she did not want to take part in a swimming competition. On the other hand, he adored his son. But he soon returned to the question of his stomach. That was what really worried him. When asked about his father, he said he was a gentle, affectionate man whom everybody loved and who used to play a lot with him. He remembered that his father used to make fun of him when he could not pronounce certain words correctly.

His first memories concerning fear dated back to his eighth year of life, at which time the Germans had bombed Roustchouk: blood, mutilated bodies, death, and terror. They fled to an aunt's house and then hid in a mosque. He felt very anxious when he spoke about this, as if he were re-living and re-experiencing this episode with the therapist.

When they returned home, the Nazis had already occupied the country. They were forbidden to listen to the London broadcasting station, but he told other children that his father had listened to it. Enraged, his father ran after him with a knife until an aunt of the patient's managed to calm him down. When the Nazis started looking for his father, they left the city disguised as Moslems and reached the Dalmatian coast. His father was arrested there, but luckily he fell into the hands of the Italian army and was set free. The Italians and Italy had since then become an admired symbol. They ran away to Trieste, where the 'men in black' tied them with chains and took them to the city of Turin, where they were released and then lodged. After that he lived alone in an orphanage. These months were long years for him. Full of resentment, he thought that his parents had got rid of him. He remembered with fear the air raids of that period. It was only after several years of analysis that 'he rediscovered that that was less dangerous than being found to be a Jewish boy'. Afterwards, once the family was reunited in a small town, they managed to survive by making shoes. When the Germans got near the town, they ran away to the top of a mountain, where they became acquainted with a group of anti-fascist guerillas. A miraculous safe-conduct saved them from a 'razzia', and they arrived in Rome hidden in rice boxes. Fortunately, there they found their uncle in his house.

When Mario was about 11, the Americans liberated Rome. From that period he remembers having masturbated against hard surfaces—a wall or a wardrobe. When the therapist asked him about it, the patient said that his parents had made a secret of sexuality, as if it were something bad. Only when he was 20 did his uncle explain to him all about sexual intercourse with women. Some time later he arrived in Buenos Aires. A relative got him a job in a small factory. In the meantime, he learnt that his grandparents and two of his mother's brothers had been killed in Bulgaria. He started secondary school and became the best student. He was over 30 years old when he had his first sexual relationship.

Beginning of treatment

This patient was in treatment with an analyst who was supervised by me for two years. He was treated four times a week during this period of the analysis. The patient's behaviour was formal, with a narrative–obsessive language or style. His fear of treatment was not manifest, since it was dissociated. His therapist, a Catholic, remembers having seen him really frightened only once, and that was when they were talking about the persecutions between Christians and Jews. Then the therapist said: 'I am a Christian, and you are a Jew. Do you think I am a threat because of that?' The patient was on his feet at once. Deeper feelings now appeared in the dreams he brought to his sessions. This is the first dream:

> He was walking towards the consulting-room, near which there was a car dealer who sold Italian cars, 'Fiat', which was true in real life. He saw four men with the typical appearance of secret agents or paramilitaries (who haunted Buenos Aires

between 1977 and 1978) in their well-known green cars. 'In the armpit of one of them I saw a gun; I tried to take it away from him while I shouted: "It's a misunderstanding, don't shoot, don't shoot." However, they started shooting with a gun with a shortened barrel. I woke up frightened.'

The associations to the dream led the therapist to stress that all this took place a few yards from the consulting-room, almost at the door of consulting-room. But the patient's associations were very poor; he almost paralysed his associations. His terror of the therapist and his distrust of treatment were obvious. Even so, there was one element that stood for safety: Italy, the Fiat from Turin. (It should be remembered that the patient and his family found shelter near Turin.)

This is another dream of his first year of analysis.

'What a strange dream. *There was a ploughed field, and a man dressed in a dinner jacket appeared; he had a hose from which blood was coming out, and he watered the field with blood.*'

The patient felt a strong anxiety, which he evidently transmitted to the therapist, who started worrying about the patient's health. The dream was seen as a situation expressing a notion of his body scheme: to surrender affectively or to participate in a sexual encounter (hose–penis) was experienced as becoming empty, as bleeding out. Besides, this dream helped to formulate hypotheses concerning his feelings about sexual intercourse and bonds based on a primitive conception of his body scheme (Rosenfeld, 1982a, 1982b, 1985). These hypotheses helped him to understand some inhibitions as regards sexual intercourse.

The Yom Kippur or Atonement Day session

During his three years of analysis, the patient preserved his apparent formal adjustment, his pseudo-identity, and his narrative-obsessive linguistic style to describe real facts and speak about his commitment to his job. He would hardly show any fear in the transference, except when the therapist told him: 'I am a Christian.'

He would always find a rational explanation for his tendency to miss sessions: the factory, having to work late hours, etc. The patient seemed to be dissociated. At this point, something happened in the supervision. The therapist, a highly sensitive, good container and an affectionate person, brought material corresponding to a session in which we could detect the dissociation and the existence of an area that was out of contact.

We attempted various hypotheses on technical approaches, in order to get in touch with the encapsulated or supposedly dissociated areas; one of them was to suggest that, since one of the following sessions coincided with the most important Jewish religious festivity, Atonement Day or Yom Kippur, the therapist should make it clear that if the patient did not want to come to his session, he did not have to—that is, that his therapist would respect his being a Jew and that he did not have to hide in the mountains again. Three sessions later, something completely new happened: the material brought by the patient showed how important his Jewish identity was for him.

This had not become manifest before; it seemed to have been encapsulated and kept away, preserved by the patient, as well as he could, within his self. In this session he remembered the time when he used to ride on his grandfather's shoulders and was filled by the peculiar smell of his hair. He went as far as to say: 'I seem to smell it in the session.' Then he told the therapist he had watched *Holocaust* on television and described an episode in which the father of the family in the film met a brother, and they both walked together along the railway tracks. At that moment, the patient stopped. His mind seemed to go blank, he remained silent, he skipped the following scene and then started speaking about another part of the film. The therapist, who had seen *Holocaust* that very night, pointed out his mistake to him, saying that he had also stopped, remained silent, and then gone on talking after skipping a whole scene in which the father walked with a man called Moses. The patient's tone of voice suffered an abrupt change and, deeply impressed, he said: 'Doctor, you're right. I've just remembered my name is Moses.' The patient had lived in Argentina for more than 30 years, during which time that name had never reached his consciousness, nor had he ever spoken about it or mentioned it at home. He was 14 when he arrived, and it was as if, ever since then, part of his identity had remained encapsulated; now, after that long hibernation, it had emerged again, well preserved, in the course of a session. Deeply moved, his therapist asked, trying to overcome his own surprise: 'But then, your name isn't Mario but Moses?' 'Doctor, I have just remembered they used to call me Misha, as a diminutive of Moshe.' Very seldom have I seen a therapist so deeply moved in the course of a supervision hour.

In another session the patient reported that he had attended an important event in the Jewish tradition: the 13-year-old celebration, known as Bar-Mitzvah, of his partner's son. Obviously moved, the patient said he had found himself crying at the Synagogue. He added that he had felt frightened and that, like his dreams, he was suddenly filled with emotions and memories: Roustchouk, voices calling him Misha, his own image on his grandfather's shoulders, the strong smell of his hair.

Then he told the therapist: 'I will never recover that name, because the Registrar's Office where it is written down, my true name, was destroyed and burned down by a bomb.' And the patient remained overwhelmed by deep emotion for the rest of the session. In the linguistic construction we observed that he was referring rather to his own name, to his own lost self (Liberman, 1970–72; D. Rosenfeld, 1976).

Obviously, after this session, this was not the same patient who for weeks on end had spoken endlessly about his work and his manager or had offered logical explanations to justify his tendency to miss sessions. The initial rigid structure had given way, and another communication style had emerged. Later on, other areas of his personality could be dealt with more easily: his relationship with his wife, his children, his partner, and the possibility of having another child, which used to frighten him. Likewise, there emerged for the first time a memory of his third year of life: bound by a white sheet, he was being taken to have his tonsils removed. In utter darkness, he was illuminated by the light beam coming from the doctor's mirror, which had a hole in the middle. A nun told him not to cry, that his mother would not come because she had died. The material suggests castration in this patient's material.

Childhood feelings and memories connected with his father, previous to the Nazi persecution, also began to emerge, which made it possible to deal with the mourning over his father's death from another perspective. For instance, the memory of some mischief. When he was a child, he had drawn away the chair on which his father was about to sit down so that he would fall. The 1982 war between Argentina and Great Britain over the Falkland Islands aroused feelings of exacerbated terror in Mario–Moshe. Although in the course of the session he said: 'This is too much for a child', it is our belief that he now had new and better resources to face this war as well as the kidnapping and abduction of people in the streets of Buenos Aires, which always reminded him of the day his father was taken away and sent to jail. Very early childhood memories cropped up, suddenly and in a disorderly way. The patient himself realized that there was a 'hole', a gap in his earliest childhood. And one day he asked his mother what had happened in his early years in the town of Roustchouk. The mother told him facts, anecdotes; among others, one in which a neighbour gave him a present. The patient, in a deeply regressed state during the session, unwittingly spoke in Italian. In this way he expressed, in a very concrete manner, the linguistic regression he allowed himself. And, as the poet says:

Il est parvenu maintenant au terme de sa route, il se dévoilé et éclairé les vingt années de mutisme écoulées dans son ombre. Il ne pourrait pas autant révéler s'il ne s'était tu si longtemps. . . .
[Elias Canetti, *Territoire de l'homme*]

He has now reached the end of his journey, he takes off his veils and clarifies the twenty years of silence elapsed under his own shadow. He could not have revealed so much if he had not remained silent for so long. . . .

Inge

... as 'twere with a defeated joy,
With an auspicious and a dropping eye,
With mirth in funeral and with dirge in marriage,
In Equal scale weighing delight and dole. . . .

[Shakespeare, *Hamlet,* Act I, Scene 2]

Inge came for treatment when she was about 46 years old. She was a teacher who made a living teaching mathematics at a primary school, a task whose limitations she found difficult to overcome due to her inhibitions. She was pleasant-looking, fair-haired, and spoke very fast, with a marked manic tinge. She had come for treatment because she lived in a constant state of anxiety, which prevented her from concentrating and working. Her relationship with her 15- and 16-year-old daughters and her 20-year-old son was good, although not without ups and downs in the case of her son because he had decided to study abroad. She described her busband as a polite man but too formal, distant, and even cold. After a trivial accident he had a medical check-up, and his physician diagnosed a neurological injury of systemic origin, static for the time being. All this, added to her mother's old age, resulted in Inge's decision to start treatment. I supervised this patient's analysis over a period of six years. The patient was treated four times week.

As a relevant item, she referred to her father's death, when she was 19. She said that after that loss she had engaged in a manic hyperactivity and started working in a travel agency so as to be able to travel and go away. Her mother's parents were of Jewish origin: her grandmother was German and her grandfather was Czech, like Inge's own husband. Her father, a Jew, was born in Germany; in his youth he had an accident, resulting in a neurological injury to one of his feet. Inge described her mother as a very beautiful woman, coquettish, highly seductive, who would leave her alone to go skiing or out with friends. But Inge also stressed that her mother would starve herself to death, if necessary, to give Inge whatever food there was, at the time when they were running away. She was an only child. They had fled from Germany when Inge was 5 years old and the Nazis started persecuting the Jews. Her most pleasant memories had to do with going out with her father and, above all, with the constant show of affection in her relationship with her maternal grandparents: the beloved granddaughter, pampered by grandparents who were perhaps stronger than, and not so unstable as, her own parents. Her grandparents were deeply attached to their first granddaughter, and at times their role overlapped with that of her parents, since it was the grandparents who actually supported the whole family with their business.

Languages and flags

Perhaps the material corresponding to her first year in analysis shows more clearly her double (or triple) identification with languages, countries, flags, and, of course, her own identity.

The patient said:

'In a dream I felt they hadn't left anything for me to eat. Mother and father had eaten everything up. Food must have been something very important in my life. My mother looked after that, she didn't neglect me. But the other day I saw a lot of things in my mother's refrigerator, but none of good quality. The biscuits were stale. All this about food comes from my childhood, when we were running away from Germany to hide in Switzerland. My father was sometimes absent. Mother didn't eat her apples, in order to give them to me. In 1930 they left Germany and went to Italy for a time, and I was born there. I remember that when I was a child, it was the rule to go skiing, and my nanny always rescued me from the cold showers my mother forced me to take. Mother always made me eat what I didn't like. We were always moving from one place to another, changing schools, it was terrible. I can't believe that at the time when we were running away from Nazism and lived in hiding, father travelled while mother and I had not enough to eat. And then the question of religion. I was baptized by our maid, who loved me a lot and

was afraid something might happen to me. Afterwards we
were all baptized. We were all converted Jews who went to
Mass on Sundays. Then we managed to get on a ship. The
voyage, the panic. The trip was terrible because several
people were sent back. It was a luxury ship, with dancing
every night. There I was, full of anxiety about the trip, and
they with their tuxedos, their evening gowns, dancing, while
I was throwing up and running a temperature all the time.'

I chose this material because, in the course of the supervision,
I found it quite representative of the patient's mixture of
religions and countries (Germany/Switzerland/Italy) and of her
ambivalent relationship with her mother and the maternal food.
I want to make it clear that her therapist interpreted this very
fragment as a dream reflecting scarcity of sessions and the belief
that the therapist was like her parents—that is, that she kept
all the food to herself and gave Inge nothing. It also shows a
6-year-old little girl overcome by the anxiety aroused by their
flight and her terror over the death of her grandparents who had
remained in Germany. And, while she was forced to mourn for
the abandoned grandparents, her own parents, in a kind of
manic show, kept dancing all night. In another session of that
same year there was another indication of the mixture of flags
and languages. The patient said:

'I have realized that I don't know how to write in Spanish.
Where does all this originate? In my school copybooks. I
didn't know Spanish, and at school I had to draw the Argentine flag, and it was an unbearable duality of religions and
countries. *I used to wear the Argentine emblem and the Italian
one under it. As far as I can remember, I was always looking
for the same thing.* Religion and patriotism: the time of the
war when I kept my fingers crossed while I sang the national
anthem. I kept as a relic a book by D'Amicis in which a boy
travels across different countries. *When my parents went out I
used to hold Mass and take out my Hebrew Bible as well. It
was a very confused period.* They sent me to a Catholic school.

Whenever I walked past a church, I made the sign of the cross. My mother insisted I should do so. When we were running away, mother always insisted that we had to look like Catholics. That was about the time when I learnt of my grandparents' death.'

The origins and the bonds, as well as the gradual building up of her peculiar inner world, can be clearly seen here: an infantile self linked to Germany and to her German-speaking grandparents, and another, more superficial self, that of the Spanish language and the Argentine flag, which, in fact, hides another part of her self: the Italian language and flag. These seem to be three concentric circles: German/Italian/Spanish. It is a time of confusion: she said she had a Mass book and, under it, a Hebrew Bible: a double inscription of her identity. A double identification; her grandparents, that is, the Hebrew Bible, what she knew of her infantle world until she was 5, and the German language; and, over-printed, what was unknown to her: another language, Mass. By resorting to very peculiar defensive mechanisms, Inge turns what is known into something unknown and the unknown into something known. Perhaps this is the core of her self, of her identity: a beloved place where her grandparents are, but also a very sinsister place, because her grandparents were in Auschwitz and she still seems to be inside them.

When, in a later session, she brought the material in which her mother went skiing and met her lover in Inge's presence, it was in our opinion not a coincidence but another manifestation of the same associative chain: it is the origin of her infantile guilt at the oedipal level; to have become her mother's accomplice in the destruction and mocking of her father's role, simply because she happened to be present then and had never spoken about her mother's unfaithfulness (apart from her own oedipal motivations). This oedipal guilt later on adds to and strengthens her guilt over the grandparents killed in Auschwitz, since she knows her parents chose to save her and run away on the ship, but at the expense of having to leave her grandparents behind (Freud, 1914c, 1917e; Laplanche & Pontalis, 1973; Pines, 1986).

The ink

We shall now consider material corresponding to the following session, which includes a dream—that of the ink—and an explanation of the way in which her defensive mechanisms cover up the infantile writing and write over it new and superficial identities. The patient said:

> 'I had a dream. I was sitting with somebody at a table, in a coffee-shop, waiting for something. They kept bringing things to drink and I protested. This is not for me, I said. A man appeared and I was writing on a few sheets torn out from a magazine. The ink poured over the paper, I was writing over the illustrations. I was writing to my family in Canada, because they were celebrating an anniversay. We were all there. My paternal grandparents too [they were 85 years old and lived in Canada]. *I thought I had to write a copy in case somebody should ask for it. I was happy, on the one hand, but as I wrote, the pen kept blotting, and I kept writing over what was already written. I was looking for a kind of re-encounter that had to do with my family in Canada. I was going to surprise them, but I had the feeling I was . . . what a crazy feeling. . . . I was writing over what was written, denying what was under it.'*

I think that this dream reveals Inge's true history, which is the one that is written: when it becomes blurred, she tries to write over another history, another language, another flag, and another identity. But the ink keeps blotting, over-spilling, and she cannot preserve her original history or childhood writing. Her primary identifications are disturbed, and the new writings darken or cover up the early ones. The earliest introjections are thus hidden by the ink, which spills over, and the new writing, which is superimposed and thus hides the previous inscriptions.

We had to ask ourselves repeatedly whether she was really hiding or preserving it, or whether she encapsulated it or erased it forever.

The old writing seems to be the true history, the childhood world, the grandparents, the Hebrew Bible: over it, she had to draw the new writing, the new language, Spanish, the Catholic

Mass—with which she tries to cover up the previous one. The inscriptions are superimposed and show the disturbances in her identification and also how hard it was for her personality to become integrated—a double identity, a double writing. We shall now see how this cover-up is rectified in the following dream.

The Xerox dream

Four years after this session, the patient said:

'I was dreaming I was playing with the buttons of a machine: one of them was light blue and when I touched it some lights went on. A button like the ones in the Xerox I used in Canada. It works with coins. The button was square, with green stripes. It fascinated me. But in the dream the button was light blue; it was striking. I was in a room and the walls were light. The system of the Xerox I used there was really fantastic. I was astonished: I could do anything I wanted and photocopy anything. I felt fascinated. It had to do with who resembles whom. Sometimes I feel I resemble my depressed mother. But in the dream it was the other way round, the smile came out. I remember the family had a lot of fun when father came, and his parents who live in Canada are funny grandparents.'

Then her associations centred on her grandmother in Canada, her marriage, and her father's injury, and she said: 'It must have been very important for father that such a pretty woman should show interest in him.'

The interpretation was that she can recover young parents by forming a couple and that she was able to retain interpretations in her trip to Canada instead of losing them. It is our belief that this dream marks some changes in her mental apparatus. It is the opposite of the ink that pours down and rubs out. The Xerox does not rub out: it takes elements and copies them. It records them, it does not lose them. The ink sticks instead of getting lost. Everything remains printed. And that is her current change: this new model of mental apparatus allows her to keep and print. It is a rectification of the model of identification, since she can introject part of the object in order to preserve it and keep it, rather than cover it up, neither crossing it out nor hiding it.

A hypothesis that proved useful and was reaffirmed was the fact that the blue colour of the button had to do with the blue eyes of the therapist, whose watchful and protective look made her feel she was in Canada.

And the same may be said of the following episode concerning some photographs, in two sessions between which four years elapsed. In the course of the second year of treatment, after returning from Europe, the patient said:

> 'I still haven't managed to have the photos developed. I'm afraid I'll never be able to; the thing is that if I don't have them developed and I don't see them, it is as if I hadn't been to Europe.'

This clearly shows her introjection mechanism: a person who receives and has received things that get covered up and lost if she is not helped to develop those photos of her inner world. That was exactly what her therapist interpreted. It must have been an accurate interpretation, since four years later she brought to a session photos to be developed. The therapist and the patient became a processing lab of her infantile inner world. For the first time in her treatment, she brought a photo that showed her, as a child, with a doll, her parents, and the grandparents killed in Auschwitz. Only it took more than two hours to develop this picture: it took four years of good analysis to develop her childhood world in a session.

The German language and Auschwitz

When her mother died—during the fifth year of treatment—there was an outpouring of direct material connected with Auschwitz and her grandparents, the German language, and music. Now she started again to listen to music and songs in German, by Mahler. She said: 'German fascinates me.' She remembered that before she was 5 she only spoke German. 'I didn't like German opera as much as today', she added. 'I've forgotten Italian. Music comes from my father; he was a very good piano player. At home, music and German were listened to together.' Then she added: 'Now I find more pleasure in music than ever before in my life' (Guiard, 1977).

Two weeks after her mother's death, the patient said:

'I felt I needed to speak about mother's death many times. . . . My daughter thought I was very happy when I returned from the session. . . . And, of course, I was: the spell was over. Mother has projected guilt on to me. . . . I know grandfather died in the gas chamber. . . . We don't know more than that, but about my grandmother, we do know she had to dig her own grave. The letter they got from the Red Cross after the war telling them about this must have been a terrible shock. Yes, I'm going to look for it and find it. Yesterday it was mother's birthday. I thought it was important for me to go to the cemetery and take some flowers to father. I've never cared to go to the cemetery. I told my husband I'm not going to throw their ashes into the river, as mother asked me to do. I'm going to keep them where they are. It's like having roots somewhere. I thought how terrible it must be for father and mother not to have a grave to see their parents; it must have been terrible. While I was going to the cemetery I thought all this, because, if I wanted to solve my problems I would have to do what my mother couldn't do. Perhaps I could find another solution. I asked them to send the urn with the ashes. Then I went to mother's flat. I need to feel all this intensely.'

These sessions after her mother's death mark the beginnings of the working through of a mourning process that includes, at the same time, her father and the grandparents killed in Auschwitz. Only now can she rectify not only her mourning, but the mourning her mother could not experience over her own parents' death, something she would try not to repeat; she would try not to lose, not to scatter the ashes; she would try to have roots where she could bury her dead. That is what could not be done with the grandparents in Auschwitz. She almost seemed to be burying, for the first time, her mother, her father, and her grandparents, something which, up to that moment, no one had been able to do. It should be noticed that she used the verb in the present tense when she said: 'It must be terrible for father and mother not to have a grave to see. . . .'

Only by burying them did Inge stop being with her grandparents in Auschwitz. There was a lot that was loving and a lot that was uncanny; a mixture of life and death. Being mingled with the dead had a lot to do with her intellectual inhibitions and her frigidity.

And she did not only bury the dead, but also recovered what was more alive and vital in her childhood world, and this she showed when she brought a photo album she had found in her mother's flat. In the album there were photos of the patient herself when she was a child, next to her young and smiling mother; with the grandparents and her father. With her silence, she almost seemed to say: What a pity I don't have a place where they can all be together! But, obviously, she had found the place where she could keep what was most valuable of all of them: herself. And this was confirmed by the material she brought the following month.

The patient brought up the subject of the ashes again and again, as something which worried her a lot. She said: '. . . I'm going to put the ashes next to father's. . . . I envy my friends. They are grandmothers and my feeling is that . . . now I feel I'm ready to be a grandmother, I'm ready for grandchildren.'

That is how she buried the dead with the dead and recovered from her grandparents killed in Auschwitz what was more vital about them: her wish and her capacity to be a grandmother (D. Anzieu, 1980; Avenburg, 1976; Liberman, 1970–72, 1978; see also chapters seven and ten).

Theoretical conclusions

Carrying out an in-depth study of the subject, we would find two systems, one that we might define as the detachment–withdrawal model (loss) and the other as the model of autistic encapsulation. Part of the material seems to point to the former.

In the encapsulation model, there is a shielding of early identifications that are later found fairly well preserved (Inge's language and grandparents, the name of Moshe, Judaism).

As an explanatory model, I would suggest that there is a dialectic interplay between two systems: one aiming at encapsulating (which does not mean integration but preservation) and thus shielding identifications, and another which, in spite of everything, loses valuable identifications as a consequence of terror. The inner drama develops between these two mechanisms. Technically it is advisable to bear both mechanisms in mind.

I think that massive and socially pervasive traumas, like Nazism, disturb identifications, even the most primitive ones. All the patients affected by these traumas constantly lose identifications and valuable elements of their self. One patient loses the cookies in the snow; the other loses blood through the hose and his name, Moshe, when the Registry was bombed; Inge's pen blots easily, she is left without food in the dream, and she loses a language. The loss of a language or one's name is almost like losing a structuring universe.

Technically it is useful for the analyst to pay attention to the elements of loss, in order to avoid mourning. It is likely that loss, disarticulation, or dismembering of identifications is the consequence of a logical-pragmatic paradox created by massive terror: the danger implicit in preserving identifications that, at the same time, imply or include threat and death. Besides, to become identified with the beloved object may mean to share its fate. It is for this reason that I believe that some patients get rid of certain basic identifications (Watzlawick et al., 1967), as for example, the first patient, for whom identifying himself with his father, a man, an adult, and a Jew was equivalent to sharing the fate, the persecution, or the death of his father.

The paradox is as follows: to be like me you must go away and not be like me; to be like your father you must not be like your father. This paradox, like those developed by the theory of communication in psychosis, is difficult to solve (Liberman, 1970–72; Watzlawick et al., 1967).

In the cases of the material corresponding to Mario and Inge, I suggest the use of an explanatory model which makes it possible to put together elements revealed by the material; in this respect, I find the concept of autistic encapsulation quite useful (Tustin, 1972, 1981, 1984). This explanatory model allowed me to understand how, in certain patients, the childhood identifications were preserved as if within a capsule. I am describing here a mechanism that, I believe, was used by the last two patients; and I do not use the concept as a clinical diagnosis. In both instances, the possibility of using this encapsulation mechanism derived both from the personality structure itself and from the fact that the whole family group had not been totally lost—not a usual case during the Nazi persecution. This does not apply to Pablo, a patient marked by very painful and early losses and different ego defence mechanisms.

Autistic encapsulation, which preserves the most valuable elements of the self in the face of a terrifying outer world, may sometimes preserve many of the introjections and identifications and avoid total loss. It would be as well to remember that looking for memories and recollections at a sexual hysterical level is not the same as looking for autistic encapsulations in which the structure of the infantile self is preserved.

Tustin (1981) describes encapsulated autism developing with traumatic separation processes experienced by highly sensitive children; encapsulation is a way of shutting out and protecting oneself against the external world, against the unknown, the non-ego. These are children whose internal wounds are always open and painful. One of its aims is to preserve the precocious integration of a personality which has been integrated hastily.

On the basis of experience, it may be concluded that in many neurotic children the processes of secondary encapsulated autism have become isolated in a 'pocket' of functioning, so that the developmental process seems to continue normally. This is our hypothesis transferred to adult patients.

The concept of autism is taken as a normal developmental stage which sometimes may last longer than it should but may also become rigidified and chronic (Bergman, 1968; S. Klein, 1980; Mahler, 1968, 1971; Meltzer et al., 1975).

This encapsulation enables me to differentiate it from other mechanisms used by survivors of Nazism. As already stated, in other patients a severe ego splitting led to a fragmentation of the ego structure.

Disturbances of identity and pseudo-identity are clearly shown in the last two clinical cases, in spite of which they require a more thorough theoretical discussion. The same may be said of the complex question of the disturbances in the previous identifications and the resulting final identity.

CHAPTER THREE

Psychosis
and cardiac transplant

with Natalio Cvik

HAMLET: Angels and ministers of grace defend us! Be
thou a spirit of health or goblin damned, bring with thee
airs from heaven or blasts from hell, be thy intents
wicked or charitable, thou com'st in such a questionable
shape that I will speak to thee. I'll call thee Hamlet,
King, father; royal Dane, O answer me! Let me not burst
in ignorance, but tell why thy canoniz'd bones, hearsed
in death, have burst their cerements; why the sepulchre,
wherein we saw thee quietly inurned, hath op'd his
ponderous and marble jaws, to cast thee up again. What
may this mean, that thou, dead cor'se, again in complete
steel revisits thus the glimpses of the moon, making
night hideous, and we fools of nature so horridly to shake
our disposition with thoughts beyond the reaches of our
souls? Say, why is this? Wherefore?

[Shakespeare, *Hamlet,* Act I, Scene 5]

Introduction

We would like to establish clearly two aspects that are
evident in the following clinical case: the transference
psychosis and the delusions (expressed in the trans-

63

ference–countertransference interplay), and the role of the father in the evolution of this patient. These two elements, within the framework of the sessions, allow the therapist to detect the rejection of the transplanted organ.

In the clinical material we will see how the patient sometimes becomes his own father; he imitates his voice, his accent, and his father's sayings. At other times he becomes his own son, who died at the age of 19. He believes that he is resurrecting him, as he carries inside him the transplanted heart of a young man of the same age. At one point during the treatment he plays the father taking care of his son, and it is then that he best takes care of the heart of a young man he fantasizes to be his own son, for whom he is caring.

Clinical example

Let us take a look at some of the facts of this case:

The patient, whom we shall call Hamlet, is 51 years of age. The early death of Hamlet's mother and the bond that he established with his father enable us to study the development of a pragmatic paradox that coincides with the later appearance of a serious disease. We believe that the existence of this paradox, which the patient could not escape, resulted in the patient's disease.

Before surgery

Hamlet had sought psychoanalytic treatment after being told that he had to undergo cardiac surgery, with an indication for a heart transplant. He was in a state of extreme anxiety and despair, and in this condition he began treatment. He appeared to be an intelligent, tuned-in, thinking person, with sensitive feelings. He had divorced and re-married, and he had a 10-year-old daughter.

One of Hamlet's sons had died a few years earlier, at the age of 19; before that, Hamlet's father had died as well. His mother had died when he was two. She had been very ill for a year after the birth of his younger brother.

Hamlet's father had been a poor immigrant who, after the death of his wife, had remained with his two sons: Hamlet (who was two years old at the time) and a younger child.

The most salient feature of the father—which appeared early in the transference—is that he had been excessively demanding, something that was translated in the need for his elder son to be constantly active.

The father's history allows us to infer that he did not contain his son during his mourning over the death of his mother, and that he demanded an adult behaviour, which inhibited the patient's normal development. I believe that this resulted in an overadjustment as a response to the father's demands. This was expressed during the session by Hamlet's behaviour. He entered the consulting room imitating his father and repeating the following words in a monotonous sing-song: 'Run, don't stop. Work, don't play. Work, earn money. You're only worth as much as you've got.' This demand involved a paradox: no effort is sufficient to fulfil the father's wishes, as they are experienced as something that cannot be satisfied, as if the father were always asking for more.

On the basis of these elements and Hamlet's history, we believe that the seriousness of the picture is the result of the fact that his verbal orders ride on the early maternal superego.

We believe that by not stopping and by moving in a manic way Hamlet felt that he was not dead like his mother, and, at the same time, he fulfilled his father's demands. This hyper-motility was expressed within the session by the speed at which he talked and, according to him, at which he thought, and by the way in which he constantly moved his legs, feet, or hands. As regards his work and everyday life, the patient's acts were dominated by this hypomaniac pace (the way he worked, his quick business trips, the compulsive practice of sports, bizarre acts 'so as not to waste any time'). Only in this way did he feel alive, by perpetuating the denial of his mother's death.

We believe that repetition of his father's sayings as if they were his own could be a way of keeping the father alive inside him. If Hamlet ceased to be the demanding father (as he was with his family and employees), he would be doing something equivalent to killing his father. On the other hand, if he ceased to be what his father demanded of him, he would be disobeying and losing him. The patient was an orphan child who needed the containment of a father who could tolerate and transform his pain. However, from within and from outside, he found himself with a father who did not allow him to be a child and suffer the loss of his mother. In addition, he needed this cruel father, who was father and mother at the same time, so that his need to fulfil the wish was ever greater. *The paradox of his childhood was that his father's demands that he should live and grow killed the child in him and hampered his growth.* This contradiction is clearly expressed by the disease that he developed later in life, as an adult.

After being operated on, Hamlet wanted to stay alive but felt that he could not contradict the father (the paternal superego), which demanded that he should be hyperactive and submissive to his wishes. *Taking care of himself implied not running, 'wasting time' and being calm, something he could attain through an identification with the therapist who contained and looked after him.* By taking care of himself he contradicted the paternal message: 'Run, work, don't play.' If he does not run, he lives, but contradicts the superego; if he does not contradict it, his hypermania leads him to death. (Our idea is that the patient is dominated by a primitive superego shaped and strengthened by his mother's early death. This creates a cruel and sadistic core of the self. This infantile superego rides on the father's superego. The structure of the patient's inner world is based on the wishes of the superego, which can only be understood from the conception of the primitive superego. The patient's inner world can only survive if he fulfils the wishes of this superego.)

A few sessions into analysis with Dr Cvik, Hamlet and his therapist began to discover (and this was pointed out to him) a dissociation between an adult aspect of himself, capable of communicating problems and situations within a real framework, and another aspect, which denied everything and took refuge in magical solutions and fantastic problems that had nothing to do with his current health condition (infarction, heart failure). He responded to this interpretation in this way: 'That omnipotent person is me: I call him [Pepito].' He also said: 'I have always achieved what I wanted in life, with my own effort. I have worked, and I completed University when I was 23.'

The progress summarized here took weeks. Every project that was not adequate for his reality and his current condition of heart failure was interpreted to make Hamlet see that omnipotent part of himself that he had created, to which he adjusted his behaviour and which had currently turned him into a victim of the omnipotent self that dominated his mind.

Session on the days prior to the transplant

A few days before the date for surgery was fixed, Hamlet lay on the couch, curled up, trembling, and crying like a frightened baby. It is worth mentioning that generally he did not accept either the couch or a fixed setting; neither did he accept the end of the session: he would remain in the office longer and pay only as he wished. However, he was always on time and would never miss a session. (At the end of sessions, painful farewells—that is, mourning—were possibly reenacted in the transference: the patient believed that saying good-bye meant dying. As supervisor of this case, I always suggested that the analyst should pay attention to the ends of the sessions in order to interpret them.) At that time, Hamlet authentically showed himself as a two-year-old crying over his mother's death, or perhaps perceiving that a part of him—his heart—would die, or that he himself could die.

At this time Hamlet told the therapist about his decision to travel to the United States to consult a famous specialist, who had told him about the need for a transplant. He expressed the fantasy that, on this trip, he would find the magic drug to save him from the transplant.

The therapist insistently pointed out that, due to his critical physical condition, by making a trip, with the accompanying stress, he would be risking his life. The magic fantasy of recovery was related to his wish of magically saving his mother when he was two. Nothing could stop him, but he consented to be accompanied by one of his sons. The consultant physician sent him back to Buenos Aires, after confirming the indication for transplant, as only one sixth of his cardiac muscle was functional, the rest being completely destroyed.

He related, with humiliation, that on the flights to and from the United States he had felt ill and had to be pushed in a wheelchair.

Countertransference

At the beginning of treatment the analyst perceived intense countertransferential sensations that even led him to feel pain in the precordial region. This made him think that the countertransferential feelings and sensations had to be considered as messages to be decoded, in which Hamlet would be expressing, without words, the pain over the deaths of his mother and son. The analyst believed that such intense sensations corresponded to moments of transference psychosis.

By means of the analysis of his countertransference, the analyst ceased to feel physical pain and then interpreted Hamlet's messages in connection with the feelings of mourning he had not worked through. While he was thus containing the patient's anxieties, the therapist quoted the verses of poet Antonio Machado, who wrote: 'Caminante no hay camino, se hace camino al andar' ['Oh traveller, there is no path, but you shall make your way as you tread along']. After reflecting upon these verses, the analyst interpreted the patient's panic at not knowing what the world—his world—would be like after the transplant, and how knowing that he had to make his own way in this new life filled him with anguish and terror (Boyer, 1983; Guiard, 1977; Racker, 1960; Resnik, 1987; D. Rosenfeld, 1988; Searles, 1979).

Transplant surgery
(fifth month of treatment)

Hamlet was prepared for cardiac surgery; he was waiting for the moment when a donor heart was obtained for transplant. The donor turned out to be a young athlete who had died in a car accident.

Hamlet had sessions with the analyst until one hour before he went for surgery. He only resumed analysis when he was authorized to leave the special care unit.

Post-operative period:
the dream about the vampire
and the dream about the hunter

During a session held in hospital, after the surgery, the patient said that, for the first time, he could feel the 'old ticker' (his heart) working well. He added that he had had a bath and had dried himself and that he was doing exercises with his legs. Then he mentioned a problem he had had since childhood: he bit his nails, and he could not stop doing it. He was very worried that this might cause an infection, since he also scratched his nose. He added: 'I can't stand long nails.'

He immediately associated nails with claws and, with both hands, made a gesture as if his hands were two claws tearing at something. Then he remembered a dream he had had the day before: he dreamed of a vampire sucking his blood and emptying him. (My experience has shown that fantasies about vampires sucking blood are very usual in patients who have undergone cardiovascular surgery. They appear in dreams, nightmares, or daydreams. In one patient, I have theoretically conceptualized this as a conception of the primitive psychotic body image or of the core of the self, which is emptied out. At other times it represents an early superego or breast that drains and empties, instead of feeding—see chapter eight.) The therapist interpreted that this image corresponded to the patient's fear of being emptied of his new heart. He associated the vampire with the claws that tear away the heart. He continued to associate, now with his father: 'My father always bit his nails, but he criticized me for doing the same thing.'

During the same week he mentioned that he had dreamed again, and he handed the therapist a paper napkin on which he had scribbled some notes, so that he would not forget the dream.

In it, Hamlet saw himself dressed as a hunter, with a 'large shotgun, a very large one'. His first wife appeared in the dream, and he believed that his younger son was also in it, but in fact he was not. He mentioned that the action took place in a run-down hotel. No other relative appeared in the dream.

The run-down hotel *represents* the hospital, a very luxurious establishment. The denigration expressed by the phrase 'run-down hotel' refers, in fact, to the perception of his own deteriorated body as an inadequate container to lodge his new guest: the heart of the young athlete.

The therapist pointed out that the shotgun could be interpreted in many ways: it could correspond to feelings of guilt over his intense death wishes towards someone else (to go hunting) that would provide him with the new heart that would save him from imminent death, or else it could be related to his fear of being hunted by the young donor, in a retaliation.

The delusion of the intruder
(fifth month of treatment)

> HAMLET: What may this mean, that thou, dead cor'se,
> again in complete steel, revisits thus the glimpses of the
> moon, making night hideous, and we fools of nature so
> horridly to shake our disposition with thoughts beyond
> the reaches of our souls? Say, why is this? Wherefore?
>
> [Shakespeare, *Hamlet*, Act I, Scene 6]

The patient greeted the analyst in his hospital room, shouting: 'Out, you intruder! I want no intruders, you're invading me!' During this episode the patient was in a state of delusion in which the analyst was one of the intruders who invaded him.

Let it be clear that this delusion did not appear on the day following the transplant, nor immediately upon leaving the intensive care unit, but, rather, when he was about to be discharged from hospital.

The analyst had been seeing Hamlet every day, and, when he was near his recovery and discharge, the patient suddenly and surprisingly received him in this state of delusion, which enhanced the impact on the therapist. (The therapist made a note after the session to the effect that he believed that this delusion might indicate a rejection of the therapist in the transference, and that he feared that it might presage—or indicate—his rejection of the graft—see chapter four.)

I believe that the patient *was projecting* to the external space—to the hospital room or the consulting room—and to the transference the unfolding of his inner world: something that in a persecutory or delusional way got into his body. The room seemed to represent his body, in which the alien heart or the analyst were intruders (Searles, 1960). It is in this space that we suppose he rejects the therapist. Could it be possible that he is also rejecting the introjection of the primitive protecting figures of his childhood—possibly his mother—the breast, and his father? Is it the spectre, the ghost? Who comes in as an intruder? The ghost of his mother? That of his son? Is it Hamlet's ghost that is reappearing?

In addition, we believe that he is reacting to this very special situation in the same way as he experienced his childhood bonds or introjections (Diatkine, 1972; Lebovici, 1987).

The following day a routine heart biopsy showed signs of rejection, and the cardiologist asked the therapist to prepare the patient psychologically to receive the news of the rejection, which implied that his discharge would be delayed. (We are not stating here that psychoanalysis can always detect transplant rejections: We are only presenting an experience where we can find some signs, which were considered and interpreted as a hypothesis that the patient was rejecting a part of himself, of his new identity, or something coming from outside, which is very dangerous and is invading him.)

The following session began like this:

The patient said that in the hospital, with the doctors and the nurses, he felt that he is being taken care of, they come rushing as soon as he calls. Using the same words as the analyst, he added that the prospect of going home made him feel helpless, unprotected, and in danger.

The therapist interpreted that the prospect of going home also meant that he was well and getting better, that he would rejoin his family environment, and, above all, that he would be reunited with his small daughter, whom he missed very much.

In another part of the session he interpreted that the small daughter represented the infantile part of the patient, which had been left unprotected.

The patient went on to say that 'the intruder was inside him and that he had to perform mental immobilization exercises and send messages from his mind to his sick heart, in order to attain harmony between his mind and his heart'. (The similarities with some phrases of the Schreber case are remarkable.) The therapist told him that the intruding heart was the healthy heart.

After a period of recovery, the patient was discharged; from October onward he was now able to go out, walk, and attend the consulting room. The insomnia that had afflicted him became less serious.

Sometimes he came: (1) with the more adult part of his self; (2) as a trembling (2-year-old) child, as he had come during the beginning of his treatment; (3) as another part of the patient with his omnipotent self; (4) with his adolescent part; (5) confused with his adolescent son, whom he brought back to life and resurrected inside himself, as he carried inside him the heart of a young man whom he believed to be his son, or the heart of his son; (6) looking like his father, when he imitated his voice, his accent, and his sayings; (7) as the mother, in the transferential dynamics, projected in the therapist, who thus assumed the role of the mother (or of the grandmother, who had lovingly taken care of him as a child). It is at this time that the material about his feminine aspects, which he mistook for homosexuality, became clearer: this was a total or narcissistic early identification with his mother, which became more intense two years later, when she died. We could see that, for him, searching for and being with his mother was in fact like becoming and being the mother–feminine–woman.

In moments of regression, this was the way in which he could find his mother, though at the expense of feeling tied up and confused with a woman. His defence before this consisted in: (1) promiscuous sexual escapades (particularly some years before) to prove to himself that he had a penis and that he was a man for many women; and (2) appearing as a child with an omnipotent self, trying to prove that he needed nothing from anyone (the breast, the mother, or the therapist). All this was mixed up with an intense homosexual panic.

The overdressed session
(eighth month of treatment)

On the day of this session the patient rang the bell, came in, and sat in the waiting room. When the analyst saw him, he thought: 'I see a strange person. It's not that I don't know him, but in fact he doesn't look the same.' The first thing that attracted the therapist's attention were the clothes Hamlet was wearing. Later he wrote: 'There is something weird about him. His clothes are very weird. He seems to have an arrogant, penetrating look that attracts my attention, and he is decidedly overdressed for the occasion, the time, the day, and his usual way of dressing. It is as if I were looking at another person, someone bizarre, dressed in a jacket, shirt, and tie, all in weird colours. Almost as if he had disguised himself.'

We may now suppose that Hamlet succeeded in making the therapist feel what was wrong with him: that he did not recognize his own identity and felt he was someone else. He was telling the therapist at the non-verbal level that he felt as if he had disguised himself, not only with strange clothes, but, rather, with another person's heart. The following is an excerpt of that session:

> The patient gets up, goes in, looks around and starts an uncheckable discourse in which he curses, insults, and denigrates his son and the two managers who are running the company during his absence due to the heart surgery. He shouts: 'That'll show the bloody bastards! I'll beat the hell out of them! They'll see who I am, how I am going to run the company! They destroy it, they don't know how to run it, and they steal what I created and gave life to.'

(The name of his factory is an apocope for the name 'The House of God', which could be the magical mother—God—created by him and to whom he gives life. There may be a likeness or resemblance to the God-father of the Schreber case. In another moment of the supervision we believed that the factory—which is very large and has a great production output—was imagined by the patient as an inexhaustible breast that he had created out of nothing and that perhaps was his way of recreating and giving new life to his mother.)

In addition to the shock produced by the clothes, the therapist was surprised by the disruptive violence, by the intrusive nature of the outburst and the insults, and he had to analyse his countertransference in order to be able to start thinking and interpreting.

The therapist interpreted that Hamlet rejected the situation or the reality in which he was living and the fact that he had just been subjected to a heart transplant. He told Hamlet that he would like to be the one he used to be, the struggling youth who was going to show everybody that he was omnipotent and healthy.

* * *

The patient's rejection and abusive violence when referring to the ineptitude of his managers and his son in running the factory during his absence were the expression of the abuse to which the more omnipotent aspects of himself subjected the heart that had replaced his own heart—a heart that had managed everything wonderfully and maniacally until the transplant. The analyst interpreted this attitude as a rejection of his new heart and thought that it might be the expression of an organic rejection (see chapter four). This was later confirmed by a routine heart biopsy, which confirmed a rejection of such magnitude that it was necessary to admit the patient to hospital again and treat him with special anti-rejection medication from the United States and France.

In the session we are referring to we can observe the delusion and the unfolding of his psychotic transference.

Now we can state that, countertransferentially (see chapter four), the patient made the therapist feel what he himself felt: that he was a transplanted patient, and that this was humiliating. The analyst believed that, in others (his son, the manager), Hamlet attacked his weakest and most infantile parts, which he could not stand. Perhaps this is the way in which he had managed to survive since childhood: from the age of two (when his mother had died), he attacked anyone who saw him as a two-year-old child, trembling and crying. This is a different way of understanding the patient's apparent 'evil'. In fact, it was a massive projective identification, in which he attacked externally his own infantile aspects, which he saw in other young people.

Another possible level of analysis is that he attacked the others in the same way in which he felt he was attacked by being deprived of his mother and/or his heart.

Briefly, *we believe that the patient did not recognize himself. He had lost his identity with the heart grafted in his body.*

He may have been depersonalized: the heart was not his own, it was like a mismatched garment, something that did not integrate into his body image, and he acted this out with the clothes in which 'he looked overdressed'.

In this way he unfolded in external space what occurred inside his body and his mind, such as the strange clothes and another person's heart.

Session
(following the overdressed session)

In the following sessions we can see a transferential unfolding of some of the patient's aspects or parts: (1) the adolescent; (2) the healthy part who loves his wife and his daughter; (3) the psychotic part; (4) the omnipotent self.

The patient entered the session, saying: 'What's the hurry? Why are you running?' (imitating his father's voice). (He had turned his father's habitual sayings into something less maniacal. His father used to tell him: 'Run and don't stop, run and work.')

Then Hamlet said that he wanted to learn to detect the organic rejection psychologically. He mentioned that he had visited another patient with a transplant, an engineer who had been operated on three years earlier. This man had a cough and a temperature, and he detected these symptoms when it was too late (he was unable to detect the symptoms of the rejection). Hamlet had, on the contrary, with the help of the therapist, been able to detect them somewhat in advance.

Later on he added that during the previous weekend he had attended the wedding anniversary of a relative. He was sitting at a table with his wife and his brothers-in-law. As he was bored, he stood up and went to the table where the young people were sitting. There he said: 'Make room for another teenager.' He sat down there, producing an outbreak of merriment.

In our opinion, this anecdote shows that, by becoming his adolescent son, Hamlet was trying to resurrect him. Never before had the patient acted out so clearly the way in which he had become his own son, believing he was resurrecting him and keeping him alive through his adolescent behaviour or by taking care of the heart of a young man who had died at the same age as his son.

Session
(after the overdressed session)

Hamlet mentioned that his relationship with his wife was better during the weekend; they were alone with their daughter, and they could talk about their problems. Then he referred to the company. He talked hurriedly, he skipped words, his phrases were incomplete and he was unable to complete them. At one point he related an episode about the managers, but instead of saying 'gerentes' [managers] he said 'gerontes' [old people].

The therapist told him that, as a patient with a transplant, he felt sad, he felt as if he is becoming an old executive.

Once again Hamlet worked himself up: 'If I want to dismiss the whole lot of them, I will!' Then he calmed down and said: 'I can't now. I don't put people to the sword. I don't come in for the kill, it's all over now (beginning to stutter). I'm no longer the drill sergeant. I'm no longer one of those who climb, kill, and attack.' He looked at the therapist fixedly, without taking his eyes off him and without speaking.

In the session the patient was aggressive, although he acknowledged that he was no longer the same. There were moments of silence and perception of his illness.

Delusion: he speaks Polish
(fourteenth month of treatment)

Hamlet was admitted to hospital because of another rejection episode. In the session the patient held the therapist's hand and told him: 'You are the only contact I have with reality. Everybody tells me it's nothing at all, but I am seriously ill, and you are the only one who tells me this.' He began to speak in Polish. At the end of the session, the therapist asked him: 'What did you tell me in Polish?' 'I don't speak Polish, my Mum and my Dad spoke Polish', Hamlet answered.

He looked like a child between his Mum and Dad, or he played Mum and Dad talking in Polish. He became Mum and Dad talking inside him, who were thus accompanying him during the last days of his life. In this way he regained the infantile bonds and the dialogue between Mum and Dad.

Despite certain moments of negative transference, during this period the patient countertransferentially aroused a deep affection in the therapist.

When he held the therapist's hand, Hamlet felt looked after, like a child. This is the moment at which he let himself be looked after by the maternal aspects of the therapist. Another moment in which he let himself be taken care of like a child by his mother was the moment previous to the surgery, when he trembled in the session. These are two moments of maternal transference, in which he permitted himself to be a child. However, during the rest of the treatment we can observe the patient's defence (the fit, the violence)—that is, the omnipotent narcissistic self. He is a child who, instead of crying because he lost his mother and the breast, works it through in a delusional way, believing he has been deprived of them on purpose.

* * *

The patient died shortly afterwards from a complication that had arisen in response to the immunodepressive drugs he was taking.

This patient reminded us of Shakespeare:

HAMLET: I am dead, Horatio. Wretched Queen, adieu! You that look pale and tremble at this chance, that are but mutes or audience to this act, had I but time—as this fell sergeant, Death, is strict in this arrest—O, I could tell you—but let it be. Horatio, I am dead; thou liv'st. Report me and my cause aright to the unsatisfied. [Shakespeare, *Hamlet*, Act V, Scene 2]

CHAPTER FOUR

Countertransference and the psychotic part of the personality

Definition of resistances

From the standpoint of the field of analytical transference, resistances should not be defined as facts attributed only to the patient. The definition of the term 'resistance' depends on a detection and a definition made by the therapist. Resistances only exist once the therapist has defined them as such. They are therefore dependent on the therapist, who alone can perceive them and define their sphere (Lagache, 1968).

But the therapist may be led to believe that the therapeutic process is satisfactory because the patient responds in a way the therapist considers 'good' or 'well adapted' to his interpretations.

It may happen that the patient's semantic sense of his psychoanalytical cure is reversed. He will then ascribe to it a distorted meaning. Occasionally, the patient gives grossly formal responses, which mask an additional disguised way of manipulating the therapist. Sometimes we suspect that something is wrong with the treatment when we start getting consistently 'good' answers, which are obviously stereotyped and simulated (Liberman, 1970–72).

I would also like to point out that *overcoming resistances should not be equated with forcing the patient to recollect his memories, or to speak, because some patients* (especially obsessive or melancholic subjects) *will probably think we are imparting them orders that they must obey or giving them a task to accomplish;* they might also feel compelled to contribute material in order to appease their persecutor, or to repeat the game to be forced once more, even intrusively.

* * *

At another level, Freud did not realize (1917c) that *when we establish the fundamental technical rule,* it immediately becomes the target of resistance. Freud also showed us how obsessive patients render useless the fundamental rule, while patients who suffer form anxiety hysteria carry the rule to absurdity. 'Sometimes we feel the objective of confounding (confusing, perplexing) the therapist, of making him feel powerless and to triumph over him, is stronger in the patient than his sounder and more logical wish to get well'. Freud asks himself whether there may be some neuroses where associations fail for other reasons: here we include countertransference.

To 'confound' (confuse, perplex) the therapist, to 'make him feel powerless', to 'triumph over him': thus we enter the vast sphere of emotions that the therapist feels in the analytical field; we shall refer to them as we develop the theme of countertransference.

Among other reasons, my interest in countertransference relates to its technical and clinical use. It is important to point out that there are often differences between a theoretical concept and its practical application. For instance, Freud's theoretical proposal concerning countertransference has, among other objectives, the aim to define his position, his neutrality, vis-à-vis acting-out episodes. Furthermore, although in theory Freud approached countertransference as a perturbing factor, in practice he used it adequately. In the course of treatments, he took advantage of the emotions his patients aroused in him as precious guides for his reflection.

In the notes Freud took during the sessions with the Rat Man (1909d), we find a superlative and remarkable example of his methodology. In chapter seven I develop this idea thoroughly by using Freud's notes to show how he worked with countertransference and countertransferential aspects.

We might add here that when the patient tells him about the death of his three-year-old brother, Freud's understanding and handling of the transference are notoriously perturbed because this history evokes in Freud the memory of his own brother, who had also died at the age of three. In my opinion, the coincidence in the two histories causes a blind spot, which generates an obstacle to countertransference.

The above comments indicate that clinical psychoanalysis is much more mobile, more variable, and more dialectical than its theory. While the theory has remained rigid and stereotyped, Freud's notes went far beyond it in scope. Therefore, I think the clinical dialectic is much richer and encompasses much more than its theoretical concept. Theory by itself does not always explain the clinical complexity. The clinical use of countertransference was much richer than the general theory at the time.

From the scientific and methodological perspective, the concept of countertransference is a definition open to theorizing, once the analyst has become aware of certain affects and certain feelings, which, even when nebulous, may perturb his emotional life. This phenomenon pertains to the patient, and the analyst can detect it in the analytic field as a logical and conscious phenomenon. It resembles a fan with two ends: at one end, we find the personal resonances elicited in the analyst by material coming from the patient (serious, gross neuroses are to be excluded). These are feelings (sensations, affects); since we have all gone through similar stages during our development, we have the ability to share similar feelings.

At times, countertransference can become a perturbing element. This refers, of course, to those moments when the countertransference is not detected as such but is felt as a feeling (sensation) that cannot be decodified.

At the other end, we can detect countertransference as a useful signal, enriching our perception of the analytic field. At that other dialectic instant, it serves as an indicator for our work, our thinking, and our interpretation.

I specially want to stress this fundamental aspect. Countertransference is not an element that should be hastily projected. On the contrary—the analyst should use it as an indicator for his work. This series of diffuse affects and often confused sensations that constitute the countertransferential aspect of psychoanalysis must be meticulously and precisely elucidated. Only then can countertransference become a useful element for our reflection, since it enlarges and enriches our perception of the analytic field.

Failure to detect feelings and sentiments linked to countertransference may hinder the thought process of the analyst. The consequences of this obstacle may vary from a deficient use of transference to destructive or sexual acting out with the patient.

There is one central concept I would like to emphasize: unless we detect the countertransference, we will not be able to see in perspective the perturbations it has caused. Countertransference may be disturbing, but the analyst should be able to overcome this effect through his reflection (thinking, reasoning) capacity. In my opinion, an accurate perception of countertransference is mostly the result of a good psychoanalytic treatment of the therapist himself, associated with a responsible supervision of his work.

One can only write on the subject of countertransference once one has used it as a warning signal. It must be decoded and then used technically. If countertransference is not understood and decoded, it is very difficult to write on the subject.

D. W. Winnicott (1965a, 1965b, 1971.) tells us that he had to learn to examine his own technique each time difficulties arose in a phase of resistance; he found their cause was always a countertransference phenomenon, which required a deeper self-analysis on the part of the analyst.

Countertransference

The term 'countertransference' originates in clinical psycho-analysis, beginning with Freud's writings and subsequently expanded on by numerous authors; among them, we may cite Baranger and Avenburg (1975), Baranger (1969), Boyer (1983, 1987), Brudny (1980), Grinberg (1956), Guiard (1977), Heimann (1990), Kernberg (1984), López (1985), Racker (1957, 1960), Ríos (1985), and Searles (1979).

The term 'countertransference' has had, and may still have if not adequately clarified, different connotations, according to its various possible definitions. This term remains very general and may encompass many facets. When Freud mentions counter-transference, he seems to refer to an obstacle, a resistance.

In the present chapter, we use it in the sense of certain feel-ings, certain affects the therapist experiences when confronting facts that are specific to the transference field and to his emo-tional relationship with the patient. It is therefore a signal—just a signal—that needs to be decoded, reflected upon, and finally evaluated by the therapist to be better understood, and not pro-jected. The therapist must try to translate into words the feel-ings evoked in him by the patient through his pre-verbal language, or through the phonology or music of his voice. Above all, he must differentiate these feelings from his personal neur-otic problems (Aryan, 1985b; Bleger, 1967; Gálvez, 1980; Guiard, 1978, 1980; Krakov, 1987; Liberman, 1970–72; Lutenberg, 1983; Rubinstein, 1982; Tustin, 1981, 1986).

Countertransference is a phenomenon that can shed light on certain elements of clinical psychoanalysis, if it is kept in mind during all investigations. In my opinion, it is an indispensable tool, especially for very perturbed or psychotic patients.

Occasionally, it may fail to express itself overtly as a fact or a phenomenon, and stem from an a priori methodological defini-tion of our objectives. If we take black-and-white photographs, we will end up with black-and-white pictures, and we might say that colour does not exist; but, of course, colour pictures also exist. The same happens with the greater richness provided by the proper use of countertransference.

If we are clinical analysts, we can say, 'it is always hypothetical' to affirm that a given fact is truly related to the patient. And any hypothesis can be either accepted or rejected. Therefore, assigning a countertransferential nature to a given material is, up to a certain point, a hypothesis. There is what we might term the *'pertinence'* of a feeling, an emotion, or an experience that we are aware of concerning the material in the history of our patients. We will call it the pertinence relationship. Each time we suggest one hypothesis, certain variables are ruled out, others are maintained. In this sense, pertinence is always a modifiable hypothesis, which depends on the experience and the psychoanalytic practice the therapist postulates in the field of his work. There is also such a thing as pathological countertransferences. The pathological nature of these reactions has been examined, among others, by Racker (1957; see also Etchegoyen, 1978, 1991; Resnik, 1987; H. Rosenfeld, 1965, 1987) and by León Grinberg (1956) who created and defined the term 'projective counteridentification':

> projective counteridentification is induced by an excessive use of the projective identification in the patient, which in turn causes specific reactions in the therapist, who is unconsciously driven to play the roles or the functions imposed on him by the patient. [Grinberg, 1956]

Clinical examples

The rubella (or German measles) case

A patient was in treatment with me originally for 7 years (4 times a week for the first year, and 3 times a week thereafter). The following rather unusual episode occurred in the fifth year of analysis, while the woman was three months pregnant: I caught measles and had to stop working for a while.

Once the diagnosis was confirmed—I remember it was on a Sunday—I called the patient and told her: 'I won't be able to see you for about two weeks.' The patient asked, 'Is anything wrong, Doctor?' She told me she was concerned about my health. I answered: 'I must tell you the truth, I have caught measles. Have you had the disease?'

PATIENT: I think my mother told me I had.

THERAPIST: I would like you to make sure. Could you please confirm it?

In the meanwhile, I collected information on available diagnostic methods, both locally and abroad. The following day, the patient confirmed that her mother had told her she had actually had measles during her childhood.

We agreed that she should have an antibody dosage (titration) performed. The findings of the test showed *NO* antibodies to the disease. We were both devastated by this information; the laboratory test clearly indicated she had *NEVER* had measles, thus contradicting what her mother had said. My patient went to see her childhood paediatrician, who told her that some eruptive diseases are not always accurately identified and may be erroneously diagnosed as German measles. This is probably why her mother had thought that she had had them, while the laboratory test was the real proof that she had not.

I recall that the patient had the antigen brought from the United States.

In one of our telephone conversations the patient referred again to something we had analysed many times at the beginning of her pregnancy: she had become pregnant despite an intrauterine device being in place—that is to say, she had run the risk of a spontaneous abortion due to this contraceptive device. The patient remarked: 'How hair-raising, I became pregnant with the device in place and ran the risk of aborting, how frightening now with the measles.'

I felt many things in the countertransference, but perhaps they are better expressed by a dream—actually a nightmare— which recalled my residency at a hospital years earlier. A patient had died, supposedly as result of being incorrectly diagnosed by the chief resident. I woke up feeling upset and as I recalled that death, the first thing I thought of was, 'like the dream Freud had of Irma's injection'—'the things one digs up after so many years'.

According to my dream, it seems I felt more than a little responsible for—virtually guilty of—something that had happened and that might happen should the patient catch German measles: the death of a pregnancy.

Subsequently, I saw the patient once again after nearly a month's interruption. The patient brought a dream about dragons (or an animal with big teeth attacking her from behind). I remember it was connected with a dream she had had during her first session seven years earlier, since countertransferentially I thought, 'how interesting, this is the first dream she brought, but this time it is turned around, the relationship to the attacking teeth is inverted'.

In that first dream, she was sitting at a table with food on it and then lying on the couch. I (the therapist) was sitting in my usual armchair, my bookcase full of books behind me. Some oral elements appeared: among these, some grains of rice, which flew off a plate (of rice) that she had on the table and was about to eat; they became encrusted on and passed through my books, reaching the wall behind the bookcase behind me.

The associations were useful, but it was only some time later that I was in a position to understand more clearly and to interpret that all her associations had led one to understand those multiple grains of rice as her teeth, and how she wished to get inside me orally—to know and possess my bookcase—literally to eat up my books, my professional knowledge, in order to know all I knew (the books inside my mind). Her hunger–greed and intrusive curiosity were such that the ordinary container was not enough; she ran through everything. She wished to penetrate and go through, like a hungry and intellectually curious girl.

I remember this was taken up again several times during her treatment. In this dream we often saw her hunger, her greed, her remarkable intellectual curiosity, but, above all, something she herself later said (in a particularly warm tone of voice): 'Above all, I wanted to know what happened, and what happened to me when Daddy died.'

This was evidently true. Apart from her first childhood years, her father's death at the beginning of her adolescence had a great deal to do with her quest for scientific knowledge. She also sought this in the psychoanalytic treatment: she wished to know the secret of her affections, pains, sorrows, wealth, and goodness.

Postpartum period

When her daughter, Ingrid, was born, the patient had her third Caesarean operation with general anaesthesia. I remember she said: 'I was dazed when I woke up; I heard the doctor say, "It's a beautiful girl". I caught the "beautiful girl" and understood "pretty" to equal "healthy" and immediately went to sleep.'

When the baby was two months old, the patient came down with such a virulent attack of German measles that she had to consult two specialists. My countertransference and my preoccupation led me to consult other specialists once again.

Countertransferentially I thought the same thing as the patient, in practically the same words: 'Do you realize, Doctor? I held off the German measles until after the birth. In this way I protected Ingrid.'

It was not now as dangerous for the baby.

Once again I had to take stock of myself and review my countertransferential feelings, which fluctuated around feeling confused about how the patient's present German measles had started and reliving the somewhat guilty feelings.

Forgetfulness and countertransference

'Who is it that can tell me who I am?'
'I am a fool, thou art nothing.'

[Shakespeare, *King Lear*, Act I, Scene 4]

The patient loses her identity and becomes depersonalized; she makes the therapist feel this through projection

Mrs U asked me for an interview. I received her with a certain curiosity, feeling slightly mystified: her face and voice seemed familiar. She disconcerted me at first by greeting me as though we had never met. Her hair, though dyed another colour, her face, her speech, all reminded me of an ex-patient of mine who was very like the person now before me. But she carried on speaking of her current problem, which centred around her adolescent children. Her speech was fluent, with manic characteristics, jumping from one subject to another: how she got on with her daughter, her husband, her son.

She then began to talk of her troubles with her couple which, as I was gradually able to discriminate, were her problems with her lover friend.

My thoughts went to and fro, listening to the difficulties that led her to see me and her manic behaviours, at times disorganized and confused; on the other side of the desk, I hesitated and doubted, asking myself whether or not this was the same patient I had seen about seven years ago and who had abandoned her treatment before the year was up. Quite obviously, it was she.

During the first interview my uncertainty was due to two facts: she gave me both her maiden and married names, and she had changed the colour of her hair. Some order was brought into my thoughts as the facts I had about her—her brother and her sister-in-law—began to coincide. Moreover, when later I compared the telephone number she had just given me with that in an old appointment book, it was the same one as before. Although I had initially suffered from a certain confusion, through these ways I was able to get over the impact that one experiences when something familiar becomes unfamiliar [*unheimlich*].

The following material corresponds to a subsequent occasion, when I had recovered from the impact and corroborated the patient's identity. The material is illuminating after that first encounter—or, rather, re-encounter.

The patient had been in treatment with me seven years before because she felt she could not contain her children, and also due to her anxiety and fragile self. She had problems with her husband and an extramarital relationship. For me, her return meant picking up the links with an ex-patient; for her, it was seeing an unknown 'psychotherapist' for the first time.

The patient's mental state displayed, at that time, marked manic traits and characteristics of depersonalization. I shall attempt to show the mental state of the patient and her transferential relationship after this re-commencement of the treatment.

The session began with a misunderstanding or distortion. The patient related in detail that she was taking amphetamines—in order to lose weight, according to her. In my opinion—and so I told her, in clear, simple language—she used amphetamines to produce manic states in an attempt to get over moments of depression. But the patient carried on talking about the need to take amphetamines to get 'several kilos off her'. *I pointed out that perhaps it was to get rid of an excessive weight she had on her mind, in her head—the weight of worries, anxieties, confusions, disorganization, or things that frightened her. Without understanding me, distorting* my words, the patient replied that I was angry with her because she was taking amphetamines; because of this, she was going to abandon the treatment.

The speed with which she exchanged amphetamines for treatment made me point out to her the fact that she had distorted what I had said to her.

In the second interview I asked her: 'Do you not recall being in treatment with me? In this office, with this window, with this balcony?' She answered: 'No, no, no.'

The subject of the slimming pills then reappeared, and she repeated the semantic distortion, and again, in her answer, I observed that a battle was going on inside her: amphetamine pills versus treatment, drugs versus Rosenfeld, dependence versus omnipotence. She turned around and distorted the meaning of my interpretations. She only understood what she believed and not what I said.

My curiosity: the patient intrigues me

During my interviews I attempted to reflect upon my perplexity, on my curiosity, my wish to know how it is she has again come to see me as a therapist (has reelected me), apparently denying, splitting off, or repressing to the extent of not recalling having been in treatment with me before. While thinking about this, I asked her how she came to choose me as a therapist at the present time. She answered: 'Because somebody else sent me.' I then pointed out that it was important she herself should decide to come to me, and not only because somebody else had sent her. I insisted on what I had already said: 'To try to place what consulting room she found herself in, in what space, in what mental space, or whether or not she knew where she was.' I also asked her: 'Where are you? Are you here, or is someone else's head here' (the person who sent her), 'who had come here to treatment?'

She clearly became anxious, continued to talk about the amphetamines, and repeated that I was angry with her because she took amphetamines and this made her consider abandoning the treatment. Again I pointed out that she assumed things that were going on in my head. 'When I point out what is happening to you, you change the subject', I said to her.

It is interesting to note in this vignette how whenever I interpreted something that was going on in her mind, she quickly changed the place, the space, and began to assume something that was happening in another mind, Rosenfeld's mind.

Here I would ask: *may this, which linguistically is expressed and explained in a few phrases, be illustrating what happened to the treatment seven years ago? I believed I was working in the patient's mind and she lived and investigated another mental space, another mind, and thus, the patient's mind was not on the couch being analysed. If this hypothesis were correct, we should have to suppose that the patient's mind was never inside her. She inhabited the other's mind. Perhaps this would explain one of the reasons she does not remember: if her mind was projected elsewhere, in another person, there is evidently some truth in the fact she—her mind—was never under treatment in my office, never treated by me.*

During the course of the following session, I showed her how she came and idealized me, she was hopeful and sure I was going to help her, and then, suddenly, she wanted to abandon the treatment. Thus I underlined her abrupt changes of mind, the way she alternated between idealization and flight.

Later on I investigated most carefully whether she remembered having been in treatment before: and the patient, referring to a supposed therapist (not me) said:

PATIENT: No, they were interviews; it wasn't a treatment because that person was treating my brother and I *did not think* it would be correct for him to treat us both.

This reply made me reflect the following: (1) either she was referring to some other therapist, (2) or her indifferentiation with her brother was so intense that she was ignorant of who had been in treatment before.

I wonder whether from this phrase one might assume that while taking part in the previous treatment she was confused with her brother. If this were so, it has certain internal logic in terms of psychotic thinking: she came confused with her brother. It would be exactly the same whether it was herself or her brother in treatment.

The enigmatic previous therapist: who was he?

Let us now return to the material. I carried on my investigation into the 'enigmatic' previous therapist. One must bear in mind what *a mysterious countertransferential feeling it is to be trying to find out who one was for the patient and, ultimately, who one really is*. It was not so much a question of to be or not to be, as Shakespeare says, but rather whether I had or had not been an existent being for this patient. Why was it that at the end of this session a scene out of *King Lear* came into my mind, and I found myself reciting, 'Who can tell me who I am?'—I am able to affirm that being the object of someone else's negative hallucination is an unimaginable, extremely odd experience.

I cautiously asked her who this previous therapist had been. She did not remember; she did not know his surname. I asked her if she had seen some other therapist, and the patient replied she had not.

During another part of the session, she corroborated in a way what I had pointed out, saying that, for her, psychoanalysis consisted in another person directing her and telling her what to do, giving her advice. It was at that point that I indicated that I would not be the person directing her as she proposed. She had organized her mind and her life depending on someone else to direct her, as though she did not think, as though she did not exist.

The previous fragment is most illuminating, since it permits us to construct the following hypothesis: *Very probably she projects her mental apparatus and, in consequence, the other thinks for her, directing her mental activity as a result of taking on her projection.*

The patient is perhaps explaining what she did in the previous treatment, seven years ago.

This hypothesis occurs to me: that in that treatment with me, she took my interpretations as commands or instructions to be carried out. Subsequently, she left the treatment owing to an anxiety crisis and due to her husband's health: her husband had had to undergo cardiac surgery at that time. In addition, she also said she had financial difficulties.

Now I believe that *she deposited her mental apparatus in me on the occasion. But her mind was in another space, in another time, in another person. The space belonging to the treatment did not lie between us. Perhaps she was projected emptied inside me.* From the above we may assume that she was not analysed by Dr Rosenfeld, but living inside Dr Rosenfeld, the latter thinking for her.

The patient's narrative

A fact that it is important to note is that, during her puberty, the patient escaped from the war in Europe. Consequently, *it is possible to surmise that she deposited in me nearly all the self of a girl fleeing in terror from the horrors of war and extermination. She had no mental space in her own mind, in which to split off or repress. Thus, once all her self was placed in another mind, in another space, the patient placed light years' distance between herself and that part of her self; as a result, she found it impossible, seven years later, to meet up again with what she had deposited in me. She found it impossible to tolerate the horrors of war and persecution in her mind and learned to live and survive in this way, 'losing large chunks of her mind along life's long road'.*

Within her logic, she deposited in me her thinking apparatus. Later she went away, and when she returned, she said: 'I was never here.'

Here I pose four hypotheses, with different theoretical and technical implications: (1) whether she *lost* parts of her mind, placing them at a considerable distance; (2) whether she projected onto another her identity problems (troubles): she did not recognize her self in this other and through countertransference made me feel it, which is why I ended up saying 'who am I?' (3) whether she sought a depository in me or, (4) *whether she autistically encapsulated a portion of her mind at the time she was under treatment with me.* In this case she would be in the same situation as those patients who autistically encapsulated their childhood together with the horrors of the Nazi persecutions. Her case would be similar to those described in chapter two, in which only after forty years and within the session was one of the patients able to remember his name for the first time since his childhood, and another able to remember the language and songs he thought he had lost when he was a child.

Discussion of the material

Let us now return to the material of that session. The patient tries to draw me into the role of deciding for her. She then tells me of a peculiar exchange of paradoxes in her communication with her lover–friend: first she obliges him to decide to leave her; secondly, he does not come to a decision; and lastly, she leaves him. I asked her why the decision to break off the relationship occurred precisely at this moment. This was when the interplay of paradoxes appeared more clearly explained: she decided to break off with him because he did not fulfil the role proposed by her of 'obliging the other to direct and decide for her'.

It is easy to see that this friend did not fulfil the role of deciding the future of the relationship and of managing it: *I pointed out to her that what she did outside was related to the transference. Her capacity to decide and to think was placed in another, and she wanted me to decide for her: right through from thinking for her up to deciding to undergo treatment. This, which occurred with me, is what she did outside with her lover.* On this occasion, the session ended with my expressing the following: 'Where are you? If you put yourself inside someone else, you must end up feeling completely empty'.

I suspect her return to the treatment came about because she plunged into a state of confusion and disorganization when she failed to find someone else to decide for her and to direct her. *This can be seen microscopically in the transference. In her logic, if the others do NOT tell her what she must do, she thinks the others are objects persecuting and harming her:* because it is the others who do not think and do not direct her. This patient's fantasy of cure and of well-being entails that everybody should direct her: but as I did not do this, nor did her friend, we were people who attacked her, or at least we frustrated and harmed her, therefore she left us. It was very dangerous for her to use her own mind.

It is illustrative to mention that, in the course of the following two weeks, the patient moved several times, from the house she lived in with her husband to the one she lived in with her lover–friend. She would decide to live with one, then with the other, and thus seemed to make 'decisions'. The connection with the transference and the difficulty she experienced in establishing herself (moving into) my consulting room is obvious. '*Where shall I deposit my mind?*' the patient seems to be asking herself. She is as yet unable to say, like Fool in the scene of the hovel in Shakespeare's *King Lear*: 'He that has a house to put's head in has a good head-piece' (Act III, Scene 2).

Her husband occupied a tolerant, 'accepting' role and spoke seriously about her changes of domicile, unperturbed by the situation. Meanwhile, the patient *took quick, sudden decisions to escape from her confusion.*

In another session, after more than two weeks of 're-analysis', the patient said that two things had occurred to her. One was that she had made a mistake over the floor my office was on and on entering thought she was *in another building*. This happened after a long week-end in which she had not seen me for four days. For this reason I told her *she was extremely sensitive to the lack of sessions: the sessions and the time-table organized her, and when this order was missing, she got lost and became confused; perhaps she did not know who I was when in that mental state.*

During the same session she related a nightmare she had had recently. 'Someone held on to my hands and was forcing me. I was on the bed and they were forcing me. . . . My hands were held by the other person and I could not defend myself, and when I was finally able to free myself, there was something, a wall or a place that divided things. There was a girl underneath and I was on top wanting to shout for help, but I could not speak, I could not shout, I felt so distressed I woke up.'

It is of interest that in the dream she could neither speak nor shout; this dream seems to indicate a split-off self: above/below or perhaps mania/depression.

The subsequent associations led me to believe and to interpret that in the dream she could not come to speak or shout all the terrors contained in her mind and expressed the fear that I would not listen to her. In other words: owing to the holiday, I did not listen to her during those four days without a session, her voice shouting, overcome and dominated by her fears. One must add her hatred and vengeance as well as her attacks against me and, perhaps, her desire to possess me completely.

From this nightmare on, I found confirmation that she was anxious during those days without sessions. There was no one to listen to what happened to her. My absence was transformed into immobility, terror, and persecution: for this patient, the object's absence is bad and harms her, immobilizes her, and floods her with panic. Another, *split-off, part of her self observes from below*.

At the end of this same session, the patient started to speak in a confused, disorganized manner, which was extremely difficult for me to understand and to transcribe. Now, several years later, re-reading my notes, I suspect she entered a confusional state, the result, perhaps, *of the restoration and reintrojection of the dream inside her* through my interpretations. At the same time, I was only able to take note of a large number of *charac-*

ters she mentioned, some *pursuing* her, others *approving* of her, and others *criticizing* her. I wrote then:

'It seems that by means of this language she is expressing the fear she felt in her dream, but through a confusional type of speech, here and now with me in the present. At only one point does she try to organize herself around an object that pursues her: at one moment it is her mother. At others, she hates someone else. But she quickly becomes disorganized, and those who criticized or pursued her in her previous sentence now approve of her. Subsequently she says she does not hate, the others are the bad ones who hate.'

We again observe the sudden changes from idealization to persecution, from persecution to goodness, from mania to disorganization and depression, and from formal logic to psychotic logic.

I would like to add something for the better comprehension of the dream. I said at the time that the patient tied up in the dream was terrified due to my absence. I must add something that is possibly connected with the latter.

At some point during the first and second week of analysis, she said she felt reproved, scolded. It is possible that this imagined reprimand was transformed by her into torture, and it is also possible that she experienced the analysis and the analyst as someone who wished to possess her mind diabolically. It is clear that for her, to surrender or to submit to an infantile dependency becomes transformed into something terrifying: she distorts this experience and believes that the hands, instead of caring for her, will attack her. This is the infantile world she imagines and lives in; and this helps to explain much about her repeatedly moving house and her flight from analysis.

She is unable to trust anyone absolutely and flees from one analyst to another, from her husband to her lover, and from one flat to another. The dream shows her terror of giving herself up on a couch.

Referring, once again, to the large number of persons who are mentioned in the last part of the session, the fact that they are numerous indicates, as I said before, the disintegration of the self, where she becomes fragmented and fragments me in a multitude of characters who criticize her or approve of her: she is immersed in each of the characters, and each of them in turn represents a part of the therapist who was fragmented in small pieces and placed outside.

Next I shall add something from subsequent sessions. Let us recall that on one occasion the patient confused the building and the floor that my office was on.

Regarding the dream she related several days previously, the patient said something that surprised me a great deal. It seems that she did not have complete sexual intercourse with her lover–friend; only on one occasion did they attempt to have intercourse, but he did not achieve an erection. To this friend she used to say something that is interesting to consider from a linguistic point of view. She would say: 'Don't stay, don't go away', and then, 'yes I shall go, yes, I shall stay'. These were linguistic ways of expressing the rapid shift or fluctuation from going away to staying, in a flat or in the treatment.

In this same session the patient added one more thing that is also interesting on a linguistic plane: 'There's such a plague going on, not only in my head but in everybody else, all the situation is absurd. But for me it isn't so absurd because I am used to living in the midst of madness. Therefore at this moment I simply feel badly, but I don't feel it so tragically as a spectator would, that is, looking at it from outside it must be pretty dramatic.'

In the following session she said she was going to cry. I asked whether she was crying. She said: 'I don't know what is the matter with me, the thing is I am wound down, I have relaxed, I feel relieved.' She added that on the days she did not have sessions she did not leave her house.

Here I interpreted: 'See what a coincidence this is, you were immobilized in your house till the time you came to see me. . . . this is connected with the dream you had. In the dream, too, you were immobilized, tied up, or a prisoner, and you have been doing something similar these days, you are immobilized in your house without going out, something like being trapped and a prisoner.'

She answered: 'No, I don't go out, I don't do anything, I am waiting for my session, but when the time comes for my session I would like to go, but then not to go.'

I then again took up the previous interpretation: 'In the dream you were immobilized, you were trapped. That is to say, what happened in the dream is what you did during those four days; you had no sessions, you were immobilized and trapped on the bed.'

The patient answered: 'Then I want to be analysed. . . . (*silence*) . . . (*silence*) . . . my mother. . . .'

The important thing is that it is a more healthy part of her that said, 'I want to be analysed.' I asked her why she mentioned her mother at the end of the sentence. She then answered that she always found some excuse not to see her and added: 'Basically it is fear, fear that my mother will censure me, fear that my mother won't approve of me.'

Unlike the previous occasion where there were manifold characters who criticized, pursued, and approved of her, she now explained this on a more organized level and much more clearly. Here I was able to interpret that 'perhaps she confuses me with, and thinks I am, her mother who criticizes her.'

In another session in which she spoke once again of the weight she had put on, the patient said in a more neurotic language: 'Of course, when I want to be in treatment with you I know I'm very unwell, that I am ill, that separated I don't feel well. I don't feel well when I'm married, I'm not well with my children, I have no relationship as a couple.' 'But apart from not feeling well, there are many more things, I'm worried about my reactions, I'm worried because my sexual relations have always been bad, I'm worried because I am being very aggressive at present, I answer back disagreeably, I worry because I'm putting on weight, I worry. . . . I worry about not being able to stop myself.'

Here one perceives a description in a much more neurotic language. It is on a different level from descriptions in previous sessions.

In this session she also said: 'I know that if I were well I would not eat so much. I realize amphetamine is a drug, I must be balanced, I must be well; moreover my character changes completely with the amphetamine and for the worse, it makes me very depressed but it takes my hunger away.' She tried to explain the problem, saying: 'We are all fat at home, my mother, my brother. We were in the habit of taking amphetamine, my mother, my brother, and I, that is to say we never led a normal life, carried on a balanced diet or had normal family meals.'

In this session there are two indications that a good contact has been made. One is when she describes her family life and the disturbed oral links that prevailed; and the other is when she says she must learn to eat (be balanced).

The patient explained here what she meant by eating well and organizing herself. It is precisely through food that she sought some sort of order, and she expressed it thus: 'Ever since I can remember the diet was a regimen (regime) for me, regimen, organization and what do I do. I am very unpunctual, completely haywire, totally disorganized.'

Here I interpreted that she was afraid of becoming disorganized mentally, and that was the reason she came to treatment, so that I would organize her. But obviously it will not be through food.

Near the end of the session the patient said: 'However much I diet, however much I go through treatment, I shall never be thin, I shall always be like my mother.' Here one can see clearly the effort she was making to be different from her mother, that is, to 'un-identify', to 'un-confuse' herself from her mother. I interpreted something along these lines, and she said: 'I cannot connect it. I am afraid to be found incurable, of not being able to be thin, that is why I am not in psychoanalysis, I am not in therapy, I am not in any regimen.'

This is very important because in the middle of the session she spoke of becoming cured, and suddenly, as though it were a psychotic part of her, perhaps confused with her mother, she said that *she was not* in treatment, that *she was not* in analysis. Therefore, suddenly she was not in treatment with me.

Perhaps some clue towards an explanation of her being and not being in treatment with me has now been outlined. Here her identity disturbance becomes more manifest: she does not know who she is—whether she is her mother or herself—whether she is or not in treatment. The loss of her identity allows me to suppose that she does not recognize herself, and this is precisely what she projected onto me. She does not recognize herself, does not know who she is and transforms this, projecting it in the fact that it is Dr Rosenfeld she does not recognize, she does not know who he is, nor who he was before. This is why I referred to King Lear asking himself, 'who am I?' just like the patient, who does not kow who she is. But she projects this and, like King Lear, ends up by saying to me: 'you are nothing. . . . I do not recognize you, Dr Rosenfeld.'

I shall conclude by stating that the patient decided to abandon the treatment after the third week, when I told her she had been in treatment with me before, in the very same consulting room. And I specified the date for her, at the time of her husband's operation, and also told her the problems she had had at the time.

Evidently she was not able to tolerate the reintrojection of all her infantile world, the parts of her that were ill, and she needed to maintain split off. (E. and M. Laufer suggested that she also wanted to maintain a delusion of the negation of reality, and if the therapist were to become involved (in this denial of the reality that she had never been in treatment before), she could get worse (Laufer, 1991).

Currently, with more knowledge about encapsulated autism, I would have waited a good deal longer. Working with survivors of concentration camps, I have learnt that many of them need not three weeks but 40 years to be able to put up with, tolerate, and recover the world of their childhood and their memories, which have become encapsulated and defended against in this way, outside the lineal passing of time.

Perhaps my greater theoretical knowledge about autism and suspended time (time which does not pass) would have led me to be more cautious over the timing of my interpretations and not to have spoken so soon about her previous treatment with me.

I repeat, today, knowing more about these phenomena, I would have waited till she was able to face her anxiety and what she had kept encapsulated. There are patients, survivors of Nazi concentrations camps, who keep within the autistic capsule their mother tongue (which they believed lost or inexistent) as well as past memories. In two cases described by me (see chapter two) it was not till after 40 years had elapsed that, during a session, one of them was able to speak his mother tongue, while the other patient remembered the songs her father had sung to her when she was a child. She recovered not only the songs, but also the bonds with her childhood.

CHAPTER FIVE

Child analysis: technique and psychotic aspects of the personality

with Alicia D. de Lisondo

Fillet of a fenny snake,
In the cauldron boil and bake;
Eye of newt, and toe of frog,
Wool of bat, and tongue of dog,
Adder's fork and blind-worm's sting,
Lizard's leg and howlet's wing,

. . .

Scale of dragon, tooth of wolf,
Witches' mummy, maw and gulf
Of the ravin'd salt-sea shark . . .

[Shakespeare, *Macbeth*, Act IV, Scene 1]

A dragon, a monster, teeth, hands,
a skeleton, monsters, spears, arrows,
heads. . . .

[A drawing by the patient, Aty]

This study seeks to highlight the importance of supervision in clinical work. In support of our argument, we discuss material from the case of a patient whose behaviour suggested a psychotic condition. There were, however,

101

certain areas where he preserved parts of his 'self', and we refer to these as 'encapsulated nodes'. The patient's childhood was unusual in the extreme, rooted in events that read like a true adventure story. An infant from an Indian tribe was about to be sacrificed when he was rescued in the nick of time by two anthropologists. They were able to get him away and eventually found a couple willing to adopt him. And so the story began.

First of all we comment on certain items of significance that emerged from interviews with the parents and sessions with the child. We then move on to some of the suggestions regarding technique made during supervision, since these led to important changes in the direction of treatment. Included are several of the patient's drawings, which reveal a remarkable facility for plastic forms of expression. This adolescent boy—Aty by name—used pictures as a means of communication, which prompted the supervisor, Dr Rosenfeld, to suggest to the therapist, Dr Alicia Lisondo, that she use a similar mode of expression in her communications with Aty.

We conclude by examining some of the more important material uncovered by both treatment and supervision. Treatment began in January 1988; the supervision sessions referred to took place in October and December 1988.

The child's background

Aty was 15 when his adoptive parents brought him to consult the therapist. They explained the role of the anthropologists in the adoption and said that he was a few months old when he came into their care. He had malaria and was running a high temperature; he was also anaemic and undernourished and appeared to have rickets. Helped also by the anthropologists who had rescued Aty, the therapist managed to piece together the story of how this child, born of Indian parents, came into the care of this couple.

It all began in a Brazilian tribe, living in virtual isolation. A group of anthropologists had, nevertheless, been able to establish enough contact to be allowed to live with the tribe for a time and study its customs. During their stay, a woman died while giving birth to a son. According to the tribe's mythical rites and practices, a baby born under such circumstances is deemed guilty of having caused its mother's death; consequently, he has to be ritually sacrificed.

The child, with his head and eyebrows shaved, was about to be killed as custom dictated, when he was saved by the anthropologists, who fled through the forest and managed to leave him with an enemy tribe. He was placed in the charge of an Indian woman, who had no milk and therefore could not breastfeed him. The baby thus depended for nourishment on milk purchased at the nearest river port, several kilometres away. There can be little doubt that the child went without food for several days.

Meanwhile, the anthropologists knew of a couple who for some time had been seeking to adopt a child; they 'wished to offer another human being the wonderful opportunities' they had had. The rescuers therefore approached these future adoptive parents. The mother was a very warm person, with a great capacity for making good where things had gone wrong. She had worked in an orphanage and wanted to 'play her part' by helping another child. She already had one child by her husband, a high-ranking professional man.

It took months to piece together what information was available, and gaps still remained in the pattern of dates and events.

It appeared that the child was born in November. One-and-a-half months later the couple was approached by the anthropologists, and they agreed to adopt the baby. He arrived in April, four months later, at which point the adoptive mother had just become pregnant again. Her second natural child was thus conceived after the decision to adopt Aty, but before she had actually seen him. The patient's exact date of birth could not be established, since the new parents had no real way of finding out.

The child weighed 4.7 kg on arrival and was suffering from severe malnourishment and malaria. His survival was in the balance, and the new parents knew nothing about him or his tribe. It should be kept in mind that Aty might have died.

Why the name Aty? The parents felt that he should be given a name connecting him with his origins and the community into which he was born. They subsequently regretted their choice, however, the name being difficult to pronounce (A-ou-i-ty, but everyone said A-t-y).

Some details of Aty's first months of life

During his first months, Aty loved to bite on things and treated his bottle as little more than a dummy. He never used his lips to suck when being fed milk, but instead gulped the liquid straight down. His parents told of how strange it was to watch him swallow, using neither lips nor tongue, simply propelling the milk down into his gullet.

After a month of unremitting care and concern as to his survival, Aty's parents discovered that his eyebrows and hair had been shaven. Until then they had not quite appreciated how awful he looked. 'You'd have thought he'd been in a concentration camp . . . he was all skin and bone', were their very words when describing his appearance. During that period, the baby would cry abundantly every time he saw anyone, and the parents spent their first months with him feeling quite desperate, not knowing what to do or how to calm him down. If they tried to clean his ears with a soft sponge, for example, he bit into it so viciously that it ripped in two. They sensed that he was in a state of constant terror, as if caught in a time-warp of absolute panic.

Another important fact is that, between the age of six and seven months, the child fell seriously ill and had to be given several blood transfusions. It was then that rickets was diagnosed. Aty also suffered frequent bouts of diarrhoea, brought on in part by vitamin deficiency.

The therapist learnt that the attacks of diarrhoea, which were by no means minor, persisted until he was three years old, compounded by the malaria mentioned earlier. This information is essential for a proper grasp of the psychoanalytic supervision sessions. Children afflicted in this way feel that they are being drained, squirting forth liquids and semi-solids, all of which fosters a primal somatic psychotic image.

One aspect upon which Aty's parents placed particular stress during the interview was his fear of nails, needles, and loud voices. These possibly seemed to him like sudden intrusions, as if someting were being driven into him from outside. He dreaded close skin contact with others and possibly felt laid bare in the face of external stimuli, as if he had been skinned alive (D. Anzieu, 1987; Bick, 1968; Geissman & Geissman, 1988; Houzel, 1987; D. Rosenfeld, 1989; Tustin, 1986).

Another interesting dimension came to light when the parents voiced their misgivings over having left on a European trip lasting several weeks when Aty was just one-and-a-half years old. Being left behind like that was a decisive factor, deemed by us in the supervision sessions as paramount, coming as it did on top of all the losses Aty had already sustained. Nor should it be overlooked that, upon her return, the mother was again with child, which was a major blow for Aty.

Let us now consider how the child responded when his parents arrived back. There were no signs of any strong reaction, and he did not appear sad at having been left behind. If anything, he was aloof and detached, although his behaviour was as normal. His parents, however, found it hard to look him in the eye, and he avoided looking at them, keeping himself to himself and often hiding in some remote corner of the house. The child had clearly undergone a profound transformation and occasionally would even break into fits of rage for no apparent reason.

The patient's condition at the outset of treatment

Aty's behaviour around the time of the initial interviews was a source of some concern to his parents. If they asked, for example, 'How are things?' he would close in on himself and act as if such a question constituted too great an invasion of his space. This response led us to think further about the patient's general apprehension of anything coming from outside. One possible conclusion was that all external input hurt him in some way, being perceived as an intrusion or invasion and, hence, a threat.

In general conversation Aty held back, not liking to discuss his affairs with others. Yet he displayed an astounding ability to communicate and express himself via the plastic medium of his drawings; according to his parents, he had drawn beautifully ever since he was four. Some examples of drawings produced during treatment are included in this chapter.

Another relevant factor brought out by his parents was his tendency to cut himself off. They imagined this to be his way of preserving and protecting his innermost self. Yet, equally, he was capable at other times of turning into a boisterous teenager, liable to burst all of a sudden into fits of violence.

In reply to a question from the therapist, the parents confirmed that they had told Aty about his background; he himself had, moreover, maintained some contact with the anthropologists who had saved his life and arranged for his adoption. Aty nonetheless wished to hear nothing from his past, displaying no curiosity whatsoever as to where he had come from, despite his parents' endeavours to interest him in his origins and the customs of his tribe.

Furthermore, the therapist was informed by the parents that they knew nothing of Aty's real father, whose role in the saga thus remained marginal. Rumours had reached them that he might be dead, but the patient himself had never shown any desire to find out about him.

On another occasion, during one of the many interviews with them, Aty's parents described him in the following terms to the therapist: 'He can be quite bright, but has severe difficulties relating with other people.' They, as parents, 'had not always been able to understand him'. His mother at one point asked the therapist whether she thought Aty might one day become an artist, as she and her husband had noticed that his drawings were the sole outlet for his expressive needs. The child's facility in this respect should be kept in mind in view of the large part it subsequently played during treatment and in transference.

Let us now look at Aty's development as he grew up. Physically, he was quite different from his parents. At fifteen, he seemed big for his age, with indigenous Indian features. His intellectual abilities were well below the level expected in his adoptive family, where much emphasis was placed on intelligence. At one stage his father, who is of Japanese descent, stated that, with his 'slit eyes', the child somewhat resembled him.

When the therapist enquired about Aty's behaviour over recent years, his father replied immediately that the child 'always looked suspicious'. His eating habits seemed to retain indigenous traits; if someone passed him a slice of bread, he would place it in the palm of his hand and, for certain meals, would eat without a plate. Throughout his life he had continued to swallow his food in the strange manner described earlier, as if he were an Indian living in the jungle.

Pursuing the question of the parents' response to the child, the therapist found that the father spoke up first, saying that Aty was a source of constant frustration to him; he really no longer knew what to do. The mother then intervened to say that Aty shrank from any physical contact—for example, if she tried to stroke his hair. In her view, the boy felt a strong need to keep other people at a distance. (During supervision, Dr Rosenfeld described that information as a valuable pointer, to be borne in mind in the transference situation. The therapist, too should keep her distance vis-à-vis the child, assessing where the optimum position was and remembering that the notion of distance applied as much to interpretation and words as to physical approaches—A. Anzieu, 1986.)

Another source of parental concern was Aty's isolation. He would often remain apart and remote, not integrating into family life at all; two months might elapse without his speaking to any member of the family. It was left to the parents to attempt to incorporate the boy into the family group, the paradox being that, if they got too close, Aty felt invaded and closed in upon himself again.

The father was also somewhat concerned by the fact that, in the village where they lived, people had coined nicknames for

Aty, referring to him as 'the Indian' or 'the well-known doctor's son', robbing the boy of his own identity. His mother made the following point: 'It is Aty who is most like his father', alluding to his slit eyes.

Some fragments of the analysis: points arising during supervision and their impact on treatment

We start with some extracts from the therapist's initial interview with the boy. We then propose to comment on certain parts of the subsequent treatment, focusing in particular on what we view as the 'keystone' session, since our working through of it during supervision led to substantial changes in the course of the therapy. Included also are some of the supervisor's comments and suggestions.

The patient was accompanied to the first session by his father, and the analyst was struck by the boy's likeness to the picture painted by his parents. On entering the consulting room, he looked the therapist in the eye and asked where to sit.

The supervisor detected signs of a positive relationship between patient and therapist, especially during that first encounter. As witnessed, at that time Aty was good at establishing eye contact, and further indications of a sound relationship emerged as the session progressed.

After he had sat down, Aty placed a large box between himself and the therapist, which she perceived as a kind of wall or boundary. He then proceeded to draw compulsively.

He announced that he was going to use a black pencil and, with a few brief strokes, sketched in the outlines—which he subsequently went over again—of a composition of eyes alongside sharp, spiky teeth. He coloured these in and then went on to draw a strange, grotesque-looking figure, resembling some character from mythology. When he had finished, there was a moment of silence before he handed the sheet of paper to the therapist with the words: 'I've got a lot of friends. . . .'

During supervision, the therapist said that her counter-transference reaction was one of pleasure at seeing the patient draw. Dr Rosenfeld pointed out that the patient's words signalled a potential for establishing a positive relationship. The transference suggested the beginnings of a strong bond, with Aty intimating to the therapist, via countertransference, that she might become his friend. Sometimes the patient enjoyed a relationship of trust with his parents, viewing them as true friends, and the therapist, in her turn, felt very warmly towards Aty and experienced a powerful and moving countertransference reaction. It was agreed that the signs pointed to the development of positive transference.

Later, the patient said: 'Daddy told me that I could come on my own once or twice . . .', then paused before adding that he would not come in that case, since he would rather stay at home and ride his bike. There followed a short period of silence, after which he picked up a piece of paper and began to draw various disjointed figures. They looked to the therapist like dead people, and she started to wonder what existential dilemmas were buried deep inside Aty.

As he drew, he provided a running commentary, explaining that the picture represented a skating track similar to the one he was building at home. '. . . I've got a skating track as big as the door of your consulting room . . .', he said. He also commented on the person in the drawing (FIGURE 1).

According to him, the person in the picture was 'coming and going', and he declared immediately: 'Tomorrow I shall come all on my own, all on my own; maybe I'll be a bit late because I already have another appointment.' The therapist happened to know that he had an appointment with the educational psychologist. The supervisor put it to the therapist that, via the picture and commentaries, the patient was juxtaposing two separate locations: home and the consulting room. This demonstrated an ability to make connections, since through his drawings and associations he had forged a link between two different people and two different places. Moreover, the skating track possibly revealed his need for support and orientation in finding his way in life. Talking it through, we realized that a change had taken place within the patient during that first interview. Initially he

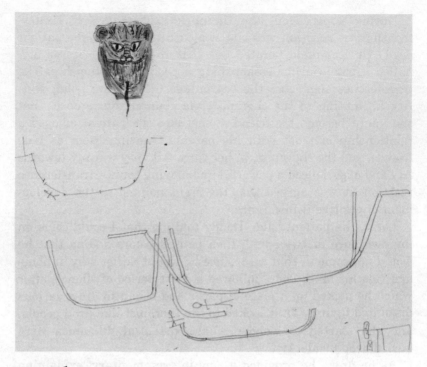

FIGURE 1

maintained that he would rather stay at home and ride his bike; yet later he was drawing a person 'coming and going' and announcing his intention to come on his own the next day—one more sign of a sound relationship with the therapist and a positive feeling towards her 'space', that is, her consulting room.

At the end of the session, Aty reiterated his determination to come on his own next time. This took his father completely by surprise, for he and his wife saw their adopted son as a sick child, totally unable to go places alone. Yet taxis were apparently no problem for Aty; he claimed he knew how to phone for them or hail one in the street. The therapist experienced a strong countertransference response during that session and told the father that she would see his son four times a week. She wrote down the address on a piece of paper and handed it to Aty, bidding the pair farewell until the following day.

Next day, the boy arrived for his appointment half an hour early; he was on his own. When the therapist opened the door, he looked at her and said: 'Hello.' He then went in and got ready to draw. He drew throughout the session and while thus involved did not look up at the therapist. At countertransference level, she herself felt gratified to see that Aty was using coloured crayons and, at one point, asked him what he was drawing. 'This is a skating rink and those are people . . .', was his reply (FIGURE 2).

It has been suggested that the boy was trying to establish connections. One hypothesis is that he sought to recreate images

FIGURE 2

of the therapist, using the paper upon which he drew as an intermediary through which to communicate with her without having to look her in the face. It has not yet been possible to establish whether looking someone in the eye brought with it the risk of emptying/giving himself, or the fear of harming/killing the other person. We have speculated that Aty was afraid to confront and take in the world outside simply because he saw it as too dangerous.

The therapist, with her sensitivity and perspicacity, believed that entering into contact with her had enabled Aty to organize the contents both of his mind and of his drawings that much better.

The pictures illustrated children inside an enclosed space. These children were as if encapsulated within separate zones of communication, with connecting lines linking the various capsules or rectangles. We did not deem this to be a case of absolute autism because of the patient's capacity to arouse empathy and countertransference reactions in others (see 'encapsulated autism', Tustin, 1986; S. Klein, 1980; see also chapter two).

The following point of detail was interesting to observe. The boy set his watch alarm to go off five minutes before the end of the session and, when it was time to leave, asked the therapist: 'When am I coming again?' This question in itself signalled a positive relationship, and the patient's efforts to construct for himself the notion of time are also worthy of note.

It should be pointed out that, during the sessions preceding supervision, Aty had done quite a lot of acting out, either leaving before the time was up or hurling objects at the therapist. At such moments, she herself felt paralysed (Begoin-Guignard, 1986).

We give an account below of part of a session, bringing together the actual material, the comments made by the supervisor, and the subsequent changes in therapeutic technique.

Session

The therapist had spoken to Aty's parents as he had frequently been missing appointments. They explained that the boy had, at a certain stage, stated his wish to stop analysis. One day he said: 'It would be better if I died because I am causing you too many worries.' His mother was very anxious and frightened in the face of this suicide fantasy.

Having heard that information, the supervisor proposed a working hypothesis. When the boy skipped sessions, he thought he was destroying the therapist, abusing not only her but also his mother; hence the punishment fantasy. Maybe he even confused himself with the therapist under attack, a possibility for investigation during subsequent sessions. The supervisor stressed, however, that such a hypothesis should not be put forward as an interpretation, the idea being to wait for the actual material to confirm or refute it.

If premature attempts were made—without heed of proper timing—to interpret things such as the patient's aggression and sadism, his drawings of arrows and porcupines, his absence from sessions or need to hurl objects, he would simply view it all as punishment for causing his mother's death and, he believed, destroying his analyst.

When he missed appointments, he fantasized that he was attacking the therapist with nails, knives, or arrows (which he drew). He believed she would die and needed to know whether he would survive. His suicide fantasy was thus intimately linked to another fantasy in which his only contribution was, he believed, destruction.

Aty probably always thought that he was killing or harming someone; hence his need for auto-punishment and the fantasies of his own death.

The therapist later provided a very plausible explanation of Aty's failure to attend sessions: by staying away, he sought to make her actually feel the pain of being lost and abandoned. This was his way of communicating his own childhood experiences of object loss.

Session preceding the nail and eraser 'keystone' session

This session took place in about October 1988, the patient having begun analysis in January.

Aty would normally hide in the waiting room before the session, so that the therapist had to ask: 'Where can the patient be?'

Eventually, he edged into the room, trying to keep a distance from the analyst and avoid touching her. He then sat down, placed the file containing his drawings on a table, and proceeded to draw, keeping half an eye all the while on what was going on.

THERAPIST: You want to see me again and you are afraid to see me again.

ATY (*peeps over the top of the cupboard.*)

THERAPIST: Aty still wishes to know who I am.

ATY (*pushes the sheet of paper to one side so that it hangs over the edge.*)

THERAPIST: Aty, why don't you show me your drawing?

ATY (*shields the paper with his hand and sets about erasing part of it.*)

He then dropped everything and ran out twenty minutes before the session was due to end. The drawing illustrated two hearts, one inside the other; beneath them lay a strange and phantasmagorical tangle of cobras and serpents (FIGURE 3).

When working on this material during the October supervision session, we established something that would henceforward govern the actual technique of analysis. If the patient chose to communicate in fairy-tale mode, then the analyst would have to adjust accordingly and use plastic forms of expression herself to put across her interpretations. In other words, since Aty externalized his inner world via drawings, the therapist would need to do likewise, offering him her interpretations in the shape of drawings and visual images. The supervisor had another suggestion in conjunction with this, namely that the therapist should show her appreciation of the the drawings by reproducing the patient's images in larger format in a separate picture of her own. After all, Aty compressed into his drawings all his emotion and affects; through them, he expressed his inner being.

By way of illustration, if the patient drew two hearts surrounded by cobras, serpents, and other frightening things, the

FIGURE 3

therapist, rather than replying in words, should herself draw two big hearts on a separate sheet of paper and say to him: 'Aty, that is Alicia and this is what is happening between us.'

The supervisor's advice led to a major shift of emphasis in analytic technique. By following the patient's lead and communicating in his preferred fashion, while at the same time 'enlarging' images expressing normal and transference emotions, the therapist could rescue and enhance those parts of his 'self' capable of positive emotional investment.

'Keystone' nail and eraser session

The therapist was pleased to see Aty. On his back was a rucksack, which he did not remove, giving the impression that he might leave at any time. After hiding in the waiting room, he went into the consulting room and immediately turned his back on the therapist, refusing to look at anything. Making sure to avoid coming into contact with the therapist, he then sped off behind a cupboard—which he used as a defensive wall between himself and her—and started to draw.

Next, he put his portfolio down on the table, peering up from behind just enough to be seen and casting a sideways glance as if checking up on the analyst.

THERAPIST: What I want to do is save hearts. I've been waiting for you these last few days, Aty.

ATY (*flings his portfolio over the top of the cupboard. He is in a state, but continues to draw and then shows the result to the therapist, watching her all the while out of the corner of his eye. His glance is piercing and harsh; his eyes eventually meet hers.*)

The supervisor's advice regarding technique was for the therapist to take the boy's drawings and give him hers in exchange, passing them over the top of the table and sustaining his gaze. Since Aty spoke through his drawings and they constituted his language, she should reply in kind.

Coming to grips with this session in supervision provided a vital key for the future conduct of treatment.

ATY (*hurls a nail he had removed from the cupboard— although his action is a controlled one.*)

THERAPIST: You throw at me everything that is bad in you. Yet Aty, too, has a heart.

ATY (*perches on the edge of his chair as if about to flee.*)

THERAPIST: Do you want to leave me on my own? Then I'll be left on my own, too, just like *you were left on your own* those many times. I, Alicia, however, intend to keep this heart.

ATY (*does not react. He casts a piercing, threatening and fear-inspiring look to his left. Then he throws a rubber eraser at the therapist's face.*)

THERAPIST: Aty wants to get inside me with all his destructiveness, but I will not allow Aty to hurt or wound me. (*She speaks firmly and, at the same time, picks up the eraser and puts it on the table.*) Yesterday, whilst I was waiting for you, I saw that last drawing of my heart. Now I also see that Aty feels the need to throw erasers at me. The heart is deformed, in need of a place to hide, and you come to me with this tangle of confused emotions. The Aty who drew the heart is the same Aty who hurled all those things today.

The supervisor pointed out that the therapist's counter-transference had, on this occasion, led her to speak a great deal; perhaps she experienced a need to get out what the patient had tried to put into her.

ATY (*looks at the drawing for the first time. He then flings down the cheque in payment of the session onto the desk.*)

THERAPIST: You are giving me something, you are paying me; together we have made a heart today.

ATY (*completes his drawing*) [FIGURE 4].

At the end of the supervision session, the therapist said: 'All I know is that it makes me shiver even to think that Aty, with all his wealth of expressive energy, might now be gone.'

FIGURE 4

FIGURE 5

The supervisor maintained that the patient was not destructive per se; he rather needed to force a way into her head and, in a projection identification, to get the eraser inside her head.

Once the eraser had been driven into her head, he could try to undo the harm he had done inside her. In this process, her head became confused with his own, and, since his drawings were his form of communication, the act of erasing signified his desire to make the monsters and knives hurting the therapist disappear.

Such attempts to prize a way into the therapist's head in order to erase and undo harm could easily be taken as a straightforward attack. Yet the patient believed that the drawings he produced (of monsters and knives) could inflict direct harm and therefore sought to erase the images he had inserted into the therapist's head—which, in turn, became synonymous with his own head. He threw the eraser at her to wipe out the drawings he himself had put into her. For him, erasing meant wiping out what he had drawn, since that was his mode of communication. It was not a matter of attack, the supervisor stressed, but rather of the patient's own particular way of making repair.

Aty made no distinction between a sheet of paper and the analyst's head, which explains why throwing a rubber eraser at

FIGURE 6

her head signified rubbing out the monsters and knives previously put in there. He seemed to be saying to her: 'I wish to
erase the harm I have done you with those drawings of monsters, serpents, and knives' (FIGURE 3).

The fact that Aty's own head and that of the analyst became
conflated in his mind is illustrated by the drawing of the linked
heads (FIGURE 7). Understanding this helped re-focus the
therapeutic response towards Aty's special code for making
amends (FIGURE 8).

We should now like to dwell briefly on the apparent negative
therapeutic reaction manifest in this case. In the analytic situation, it is vital to distinguish between the kind of thing witnessed here, with the boy's seemingly violent approach to
making amends and the violent way in which other patients
attempt to get inside the analyst. In this instance, Aty's violent
behaviour did not stem from a negative therapeutic reaction,
but from a desire to repair. Frequently, analysts of psychotic
patients mistake the latter type of response for invasive aggression, rooted in desire, whereas it is in fact the patient's way of
making good the damage done earlier.

The supervisor suggested that the therapist modify her mental attitude towards work with severe cases. Sometimes it was

FIGURE 7

necessary to wait six or seven years before a seriously disturbed patient could take on board a given interpretation. (In Aty's case, this would presuppose acknowledging the therapist's drawings as valid communication.) It had to be accepted that Aty's language was different from that of other children—and different, moreover, from that of the therapist. Aty was an artist of sorts, expressing his inner vision through strange and magical drawings. He thereby gave physical contour to his life with all its drama and hell. Drawing was a response to words and a precondition for others' communication with the boy. Throughout, there was also another person present within him, however—an adolescent who screamed and shouted during treatment sessions and listened to the strident tones of rock music. These facets together formed his personality: there was a monster inside, a dragon, a skeleton, someone screaming, a black person, an Indian. It was in his drawings that he was able to bring together all the manifold strands of his inner world.

The importance of distinguishing between Aty's violent and intrusive approach and true aggression could not be overstated

ALICiA FODiDA
TY ESTÁ MAL
MORRA ALiciA
VEJA AS 'MiNHAS PARTES
MORTAS

VIVA ALiciA
VIVE TY

FIGURE 8

in the supervisor's view. The patient had a need to force violent entry, as would any child who had not had a mother to enter into and be contained within during the first months of life. Aty had come to use invasive strategies to achieve containment and make up for what had been lost.

We noted during supervision that, although the boy attended sessions, part of him nevertheless did not really appreciate the true nature of psychoanalytic therapy. He was still seeking acceptance by the therapist for what he was, and it would be a slow process of years before he could have real faith in her and trust her assertion that he had in fact been accepted. In terms of transference, he needed to be acknowledged as the adopted son he was.

There lay the probable key: Aty wanted to know whether he was believed in, whether he could be accepted for what he was, thereby carrying over the problem of his adoption into the transference situation. In transference, therefore, he would inevitably reiterate the one question underlying all others: was he loved for what he was? In the dialectics and dynamics of transference, he thus replayed the drama of his adoption, acting the Wild Boy or a dragon, a black man or an Indian.

Furthermore, Aty had been afflicted by bouts of acute diarrhoea from when he was a few months old up until the age of

FIGURE 9

three. These attacks left their mark on him, since he had the impression of losing parts of his 'self' in liquid and semi-liquid form. In fact, he had lost parts of this same self several times over: when his mother died, when they tried to kill him, during the diarrhoea episodes, when he did not eat, when his adoptive parents left on a long trip to Europe, and then when a new brother was born upon their return.

Supervision uncovered the coexistence within Aty of a happy and complete child with a crazed and fearsome monster-child. Later, we shall examine other characteristics of the patient in greater detail.

FIGURES 9 and 10 illustrate a ne'er-do-well talking all sorts of nonsense. It is interesting to note that the letters of the words in the picture are pointed, with no curves, suggesting an aggressive mode of communication. (Might the patient have believed real words to be sharp, pointed needles, things capable of inflicting harm; hence his silence?)

The important point to note in FIGURES 7, 9, and 10 is the existence of a fantasy-world of vipers and snakes, punctuated by

swear-words and screams, the implied sound-volume of which appears to be modulated according to the size of the letters.

Aty saw his drawing paper as an intermediary between himself and the external world; nor was the music he listened to at home alien to his creations. Music most certainly functioned as a sound capsule, encasing the ego, as has been noted by Anzieu. David Rosenfeld tells of how certain psychotic patients suffering from hallucinations listen to music through headphones turned to full volume so as to keep down or outdo the hallucinations.

When he shouted, Aty was trying to fling at the therapist accusations and criticism he commonly addressed to himself, and, as such, his behaviour did not amount to true negative therapeutic reaction. Nor, in the supervisor's view, was a situation of deadlock reached; the boy was simply trying to make the therapist experience what he himself was feeling. He wanted to transfer into her head the whole inner world of accusations, insults, and fears whirling round in his own. Such conduct points to a degree of mourning that is too much to bear; hence his sense of being got at. Similar manifestations occur in patients with melancholic mourning who attempt, via insults and accusations, to make the analyst feel what they feel.

Patient's progress and current condition: further suggestions and advice on technique from supervision sessions

We present below selected material from the clinical—and corresponding supervision—sessions that took place in October and December 1988.

Aty came to one of the sessions with short hair. He drew a picture (FIGURE 11) and formed triangular letters with no curves. We noticed that he was beginning to differentiate between masculine and feminine in his pictures. Perhaps that explained why he had cut his hair—like a man—as distinct from the therapist (Alicia). The haircuts in the drawing made it possible to distinguish the woman therapist from the short-haired boy. This appeared to mark the beginnings of the shaping of an independent identity and recognition of a male identification model. This drawing suggests an amorous tie. The short hair might even be interpreted as signalling the physical developments of adolescence. (Such signs of puberty must always be heeded and the incipient sexual development nurtured. A patient's own 'timing' has to be respected; one should not be in a hurry, nor should there be a rush for premature verbal symbolization. Gradually, it will prove possible to perceive indices of adolescent sexuality via the eroticization and sexualization of the patient's relationship with the therapist, who is a young woman. Having clarified the situation at pre-genital level, we shall move on to the genital, oedipal and total-object phases.)

It should be pointed out that in the course of several sessions in the same month, and during one in particular, the patient emitted a sound through his mouth and shook his head. The therapist understood this as meaning that he did not wish to hear mention of holidays or people going away. He apparently wanted to know nothing of separations and goodbyes, since cer-

FIGURE 11

tain areas of his mind were impervious to the significance of
holidays and temporary farewells. If the therapist went away,
that meant she was dead. It was as if there were no place inside
Aty for hope or potential coming together.

Countertransference:
some new ideas on the way to handle countertransference
during the latter phases of treatment

There was an interesting discussion between supervisor and
therapist on the emotional impact on her (countertransference)
of the fact that, whenever she attempted an interpretation, the
patient shook his head, leading her to feel that she was faced
with something impenetrable and unfathomable. The supervisor
pointed out that, apart from whatever else was going on inside
him, this was the patient's way of forcing the therapist to sense
and experience the reality of speaking without there being any

space or container to receive the message. It was as if he wanted to make her feel what he had lived through: 'Your sentiment now that you cannot get inside me is exactly what I experienced as a child when none of my words, none of my tears or fears, met with a mother's body or a loving and receiving containment vessel. I always felt that everything coming from me was rejected, never having the opportunity to witness what I gave out duly received and turned into proper communication. And that is precisely what I now wish to make Alicia feel.'

The supervisor also pointed out that a child cannot remember his first months of life in such a way as to be able to communicate his experience verbally; yet he is capable of making a therapist 'feel' whatever terrible things may have happened to him. In the case of Aty, his childhood story was just as he sought to portray it.

During subsequent sessions, the therapist began to feel that the patient was likely to leave her at any moment. Her very words during supervision were: 'I have an intuition that he is about to abandon me any time. What is more, sessions are becoming shorter and shorter.' According to the supervisor, the anguish the patient was making the therapist experience (the likelihood of being abandoned at any time) was precisely what he had lived through as a child (Barros, 1985, 1987; Levisky, 1987; Mélega, 1984; Osorio, 1984; H. Rosenfeld, 1987).

The whole concept of farewells, holidays, and coming together with others was very difficult for Aty to grasp, for an understanding of such things presupposes a long learning process during childhood. Healthy children are capable of believing that, when a mother's milk stops coming, or when the therapist goes away, these losses are not irremediable; even if they cannot see their mother's smile, they are confident it will return, and when her eyes are turned away, they are sure that she will soon look at them again. This only applies, however, where there has been normal development, which was not the case with Aty. Learning the meaning of saying goodbye and meeting again is an achievement that takes time and entails a fair amount of neurotic pain in the most healthy of individuals. Not only did Aty suffer the loss and disappearance of his primitive objects; parts of his own self seemed to go missing and die in the course of his childhood wrenches. For Aty, then, farewells were the ultimate disaster. The supervisor pointed out that we often wrongly diagnose adult patients as neurotic because we fail to perceive those partial and buried areas of the personality that are operating according to the pattern described above.

During one session, the therapist responded very felicitously and gave the boy a drawing of two faces and two hearts (FIGURE 13), thus communicating to him that she had received a message of affection from the previous picture he had drawn. On some occasions, Aty would play hide-and-seek to ascertain whether the therapist could bear not knowing where he was and to see how upset she would get if she could not find him. He seemed to understand the drawings the therapist gave him in December much better than he had the verbal interpretations three months earlier (words were still difficult for him to integrate into his symbolic code). Notwithstanding, above the heads of some of the figures in his drawings, there began to appear circles containing letters or even words, apparently signifying dialogue or communication between the characters. The presence of these words revealed that a capacity for verbal symbolization was beginning to develop.

Although some of the words were swear-words, the supervisor found the fact that they were 'contained' positive. It was significant that Aty should have enclosed each utterance in a bubble like the ones used in strip cartoons.

Some points regarding technique

The patient's use of words-in-bubbles to communiate

The supervisor noted that, in the drawings produced by the patient a few months before, the swear-words were isolated and written in larger letters, often 'invading' the whole sheet. By December, however, each word had its own bubble. Some of the pictures were still somewhat odd and hard to understand, yet they revealed a symmetrical structure, despite their strangeness; a certain amount of order was being placed on chaos and disorder.

In the case of FIGURE 11, where the patient wrote the word 'Kadela', the therapist noted that the actual letters were structured differently. Aty divided the word according to syllables—Ka–de–la—each part being treated differently. She pointed out that the 'K' was a Freudian slip; his father's name began with a K, whereas here he should have used a C for Cadela.

K being the initial of his father's surname, the analyst's interpretation was that the K stood for the patient's second name, and the A for his first name, Aty.

On another occasion the therapist felt that, as well as linking his father's name to his own first name, Aty was also experimenting with separating the masculine K—his father—from the feminine A, with its smooth curves, which perhaps stood for Alicia, the therapist. These were things he would have found hard to separate from one another, and the written word—with its separate letters—was an attempt to draw a distinction between them.

Around that period we also noticed that Aty had begun to draw curved lines when alluding to the therapist, possibly signalling a softer and smoother transference connection (M. Klein, 1975a, 1975b).

Dragons and monsters:
absence from sessions

Other drawings still revealed aspects of a frightening world, peopled with ghosts, monsters, fearsome dragons, and serpents (e.g. FIGURE 12). Aty's universe always contained a subterranean and mythical dimension, illustrated in masterly fashion.

His absences from sessions were also the subject of discussion in supervision around that time. One of the hypotheses was that in coming some days and not others he was, despite everything, keeping up a rhythm of stable contact. There were sessions he would definitely attend, others he would definitely miss—a pattern to be acknowledged and taken into account. The important point was that he was able to place some kind of structure on time; his own rhythms deserved respect.

FIGURE 12

Some comments on technique and physical disposition

The supervisor stressed that Aty was an adolescent who had 'bled', literally and metaphorically, throughout his first months of life. Emotions poured from him; people died; he was afflicted by real illness, with severe diarrhoea, and had to be given blood transfusions to keep him alive. He experienced emotions and affects in terms of physical bleeding; even looking at people involved outflow. Hence, in order to avoid this sensation of bleeding, of being drained, he would use a piece of furniture as a defensive and retaining wall, or enclose his words in protective bubbles (see chapter eight). The fact that Aty did not express himself through words may have had to do with the primitive psychotic body image (chapter one), since speaking meant losing words and could be equated with the loss of parts of the body. If words were taken as integral parts of the patient's body, talking involved dispersion and loss of those parts. Silence might thus be interpreted as an attempt to keep and preserve various bodily parts, given that speaking equalled bleeding.

In the wake of his childhood experiences, Aty would seem to have learnt not to risk giving himself over emotionally to another person, not to let himself be drained. This involved placing an intermediary object—a piece of furniture or whatever—between himself and the other person and not looking him or her directly in the eye, for that would in some sense mean emptying himself into the other, falling into a gulf or precipice. Other babies and children can look their mothers in the eye, whereas Aty would only hand over a drawing after he had completed it behind the protective wall of a piece of furniture and, even then, he would be cautious and only gingerly slip it sideways to the recipient. That was his way of avoiding being drained emotionally by speaking words that contained too much affection or giving drawings that transmitted too much warmth. This boy had learned to armour-plate himself; avoiding eye contact was a means of self-protection, since pouring himself out in a look could be so painful and dangerous.

In short, the supervisor proposed a hypothetical model of the patient's conduct at this stage, where the fear of emptying himself, of being drained, predominated. Looking at someone or handing over a drawing was tantamount to tearing himself apart, yielding up a segment of his own self. Hence the significance of the measures and precautions taken when presenting his pictures. Hence also his avoidance of eye contact, the sideways glances, and his manner of slipping his drawings across the desk when giving them. Looking into others' eyes, confronting others face-to-face was dangerous. Let us not forget that Aty had never seen into his mother's eyes.

Some more points regarding technique,
communication via the image and transference,
non-verbal messages, and codes in interpretation

The analyst replied to Aty's drawings by reproducing enlarged versions of certain parts, thereby communicating to him that the picture's message had been received. On one occasion, she ventured the following interpretation: 'In yesterday's picture you wrote beast, whore, cadela'—and while saying this she held out her drawings, which were a virtual retracing of what he had written and drawn. She pointed out that all the aggressive words were enclosed and contained within circles, but when she showed them to him he gestured in the negative. She continued: 'Because all the horrific monsters and aggressive words are enclosed and contained within bubbles, we will now probably be able to get closer to one another and communicate more with one another during sessions; we might even be able to create

FIGURE 13

links between our two hearts, as in the drawing'—a drawing she
subsequently copied in larger format, linking the hearts
together as in FIGURE 13. When drawing, the therapist used
strong, unerring strokes, signalling firmness and demonstrating
that she had not been destroyed, but had received the message
and was able to reply.

The supervisor was anxious that the analyst always speak
with a strong voice and draw with a firm hand, thus proving
that she had survived unharmed and was not destroyed. In that
way, over the months and years of analysis, it would be possible
for her to persuade Aty, in transference, that 'this' mother was
not going to die, nor let herself be destroyed, but that she was
strong, alive, and different from his natural mother. This is
important to note, since the therapist's countenance—mainly
without words—would have to show the patient that his drawings of monsters did not harm or kill this particular therapist—
mother. Aty's prime fear, after all, was that anything he
touched would die. Possibly he fled from appointments because
he thought he was hurting or killing the mother-figure in transference. Over and over again, the boy will need to have demon-

strated to him that he can go on indulging his fantasies in transference; no harm will be done, and the real-life therapist will not die. As years go by, this should bring about a total turn-around in his conception of the world; there will be another mother receiving his projections without his having to feel guilty or a murderer, and he will thereby discover that it is possible to find a different containment vessel such as never before existed.

Encounters and farewells,
the notion of time,
encapsulated autism

We now wish to touch upon a fundamental issue. This adolescent boy sought to combat his own scepticism, the belief that everything was a lie, and general object-loss. Several years will need to pass before he can accept that the story of transference can be different from the story of his childhood.

In cases like this, a relationship of trust has to be built up right from the start, underpinned by a sense of constancy, stability, and hope—new concepts *hitherto absent from* the patient's horizon. Hence the long duration of the psychoanalytic process.

The supervisor noted that Aty was beginning to produce abstract drawings of closed, fixed structures, several of which had sharp points extending outwards, as if they might be representing the porcupine within the boy, a prickly thing that had set its spines against a hostile and dangerous outside world. Perhaps Aty was hiding among these spines.

His flinching from physical approaches could equally signal an aggressive stance or a fear of being hurt. The spines of the porcupine could then be interpreted as protecting the patient against emotional stirrings towards a love-object that might be lost, that is, defence in order to avoid suffering. *His time sense was all awry: coming close and loving meant saying farewell; it entailed loss and 'bleeding'.*

In France they say: *'Partir ç'est mourir un peu'* [going away means that something dies a little]. For Aty, however, return already announced departure, farewell, and death. Hence his confusion with regard to notions such as beginning and end, entry and exit. Equally, he was liable to mistake taking away for putting in place, giving for taking.

The word *'fodase'* [piss off] in FIGURE 7 contains the letters 'O' and 'D'. Much to his surprise, the supervisor discovered that, inside the O and the D—which were very close to one another— Aty had drawn two sweet little smiling faces. He pointed out that the comments made with regard to the porcupine at the previous supervision session equally applied here. The two little smiling faces were surrounded by the word *'fodase'*, an exact equivalent of the prickly porcupine. The therapist would need to respond by drawing another picture with two bigger smiling faces, making it quite clear to the patient that they constituted by far the most important dimension and reflected the warmth of his transference.

The therapist did as suggested and drew a larger version of the two little faces.

These faces, smiling as they did in the midst of disaster and reflecting similar tiny recesses within Aty, needed to be amplified over and over. They appeared to symbolize the encapculated nodes where some positive potential still remained preserved, a phenomenon witnessed in cases of adult *secondary encapsulated autism* (Tustin, 1986; S. Klein, 1980; see also chapter two). It will probably not be possible to erase all trace of the terrible things that have happened to Aty in his lifetime, but an attempt can be made to salvage the potential to relate positively that he has kept locked away and encapsulated within him. Patience is of the essence, however; one might be prepared to wait years, for cure does not take place overnight (Aulagnier, 1987; Meltzer et al., 1975).

Hope versus despair:
the linguistics of interpretation

One very interesting dimension of countertransference is the way in which patients are able to inject despair into the analyst.

The supervisor pointed out that, when Aty shouted 'liar' at the therapist, he was not destroying or murdering her, but simply announcing that there was one thing he still did not understand. He was almost praying to her, as if to say: 'Alicia, I beg you, please try to understand; what you said is not true.'

The therapist pointed out that, once he had become used to the medium of his drawings and the paper on which he drew them—an intermediary object—he seemed able to communicate real messages rather than simply transmit aggression. The supervisor felt this amounted to a new development; things had changed since the last session three months previously—although aggression, too, sometimes constituted a message. The point was that the patient was now communicating on a different level whenever possible. An aggressive stance would have involved hiding and refusing to draw or reply. What was now occurring was real communication and should, he urged, provide encouragement for the therapist. The problem is that there are therapists who cannot cope with waiting several years for a system of communication to grow and develop.

One of the main achievements of the supervision of this case was that the therapist regained her belief in the psychoanalytic method. A countertransference reaction grounded in hope is essential for this type of treatment.

Clearly the therapist's morale was boosted when evidence appeared in the drawings that the patient was missing her and wanted her back. Take, for example, the pictures of hearts or mouths linked together, joined by a single line (FIGURE 3).

The first thing the therapist did when she saw this picture was to draw another one for Aty, highlighting the positive communication she had felt at countertransference level. During another session, when Aty seemed to be illustrating mouth-to-mouth communication in one of his drawings, she said to him: 'Aty is ringing me up on the phone.'

At this point, the supervisor intervened with a piece of technical advice. It would be better to say: 'Aty said to me'; 'I, Alicia, say to Aty'; 'Now I am speaking to Aty.' The sentence structure—and hence the linguistic structure of interpretation—should contain a pronoun, the first name of the person speaking, plus the first name of the person who is to receive the message;

that is, the structure of the actual interpretation must encompass the message and both the communicating and the receiving parties. The example given above illustrates this. Another configuration would be: 'Yesterday, Aty said to Alicia . . . and today, Alicia is replying to Aty. . . .' Both parties must always be cited by name. In other words, it needs to be clearly stated what day it is, who is speaking, and who is receiving the message. All the information should then be packaged in a complete sentence to foster the structuring of the psychical apparatus. This is, after all, the way children learn to make straightforward logical connections, and, with seriously disturbed patients, it is vital to adopt such techniques. Conversely, moreover, the psychical apparatus helps in the building of linguistic structures. In Aty's case, no such structural system had ever existed before, and so one had to be constructed from scratch. Extrapolating from this particular example, we contend that this method should nowadays always be applied whenever treating severe cases.

When handling over his drawings, Aty seemed to become more active than otherwise in his efforts to communicate; that was certainly how the therapist perceived things at countertransference level, and the supervisor deemed the point worth noting. The way in which the patient presented his work, where he placed the picture, how quickly he turned over the sheet—all these actions could be viewed as signals within a system of communication (Liberman, 1970–72).

Let us now return to the picture of the two small faces (FIG-URE 7). It also includes a sketch that looks like an old man with a large mouth and an incomplete head. The supervisor suggested that Aty should in future be allowed to go on drawing without interruption; it was not a good idea to keep asking him what such and such an element meant, what associations sprang in his mind. After all, he was not a neurotic patient. That point needed to be made, since insisting on questioning psychotic children often leads to therapeutic failure; patients end up more disturbed than ever, for they feel that they are being subjected to inquisitorial, invasive procedures. Persistent and intrusive interrogation is often experienced in terms of needles or arrows being driven into the head; yet there are analysts who literally bombard children with questions and veritably demand that associations be made. Hence our insistence.

During one session, Aty drew a picture illustrating two faces, linked symbiotically, with one overlapping into the other (FIG-URE 7). In reply, the therapist drew another picture the following session, splitting up the two interlinked faces [FIGURE 8]. She pointed out that there had been tears in the first picture, although the supervisor felt it should be specified that there was really only one tear coming from the single eye shared by both faces, so that he could not honestly say who was weeping.

This episode recalled that of the nail-and-eraser, when Aty had hurled a rubber eraser at the therapist's head—which he had confused with his own—and it confirmed the theory put forward several months previously on the patient's inability to distinguish his head from Alicia's. Ascertaining this was important for the subsequent development of treatment. The supervisor referred to the spaces visible in the pictures and was convinced that, in spite of all the various straight and broken lines, this empty space meant something. Lines of demarcation were seemingly being drawn, dividing off certain areas on the same sheet of paper; these sub-divisions might even be seen as representing the space taken up by an hour-long session. Zones were clearly being marked off within the patient's mind.

Several drawings produced at around this time contained the word 'morro', although it was not clear whether the patient meant 'morro' or 'morra' [die]. The supervisor imagined that when Aty went into the attack and cried: 'Die, Alicia', what he was really trying to say was that part of his own self had died. Our thesis is that a part of Aty's self had died along with his mother—*part of this child had died or else had become lost*. Later, he sustained a second loss when he arrived at the home of his adoptive parents only to find his new mother with child. The third loss occurred at the age of one-and-a-half, when his parents went away to Europe for several weeks. Just try to imagine what it felt like for this boy to learn that his analyst was going on holiday, or that he would not see her for a day or so over the weekend. As we stated earlier, Aty probably had no way of grasping goodbyes or absences as anything other than death.

Attention should also be given to the way in which he began to form the word 'no', with very heavy strokes (FIGURE 5). Perhaps this signalled that he was learning what separation, dissociation, negation meant. *Aty was beginning to learn how to 'erase' verbally* rather than throw an eraser at someone's head. This was a major new departure, since it denoted that he was ready to start expressing himself symbolically. He was now drawing more and more linked figures, indicating a higher level of development of the psychical apparatus.

*   *   *

In conclusion, the supervisor would like to mention a letter he received in April 1989 in which the therapist said how valuable the joint supervision sessions had been. She could not overstate how useful it was to have learned to manage countertransference properly, and she was happy to have had her faith in the psychoanalytic method restored.

Here is an extract from that letter:

Certain things are hard to put into words and some of the lasting impressions of supervision are beyond words. . . .

The patient is doing well and the therapist is now no longer ridden with despair but full of confidence.

PART TWO

PSYCHOSIS, TECHNIQUE, AND BODY IMAGE

CHAPTER SIX

Technique, acting out, and psychosomatics

B y 'acting out' we mean any external behaviour or act motivated by the transference relationship with the analyst (Freud, 1914g).

As Freud (1914g) pointed out, it is a way of remembering by repeating acts instead of recalling them and communicating them in verbal and symbolic language. It is a past that never ceased to be the past. On many occasions, acting out implies recalling, in a continuous present, something that was never a part of the past at all: it is to present the same story, over and over again, on a stage where a drama of the past is unfolding.

As Herbert Rosenfeld (1965) and David Liberman (1978) have pointed out, it is often usual in the course of psychoanalytic treatment to employ a communication style of repertoire including acting.

The difference between using acting as a form of communication or as an attack on the bond depends mainly on the analyst's decoding ability at that moment.

Herbert Rosenfeld (1965) describes and clarifies the difference between normal or neurotic acting out and psychotic acting out, and he relates them to different stages of early development: 'Acting out is a defence against confusional anxieties. Besides, in the case of chronic schizophrenics, there is an additional problem which increases their tendency to act out: the acute state of confusion from which they are constantly trying to defend themselves. If progress is made in analysis and the emotions deriving from the state of confusion emerge in the transference, the patient resorts to excessive acting out as a defence.'

In 1905, in a postscriptum to Dora's case (1905e [1901]), Freud described a model of a number of patterns of behaviour through which the patient expressed her revenge to the very end, by giving up treatment. Therefore, the concept is a metapsychological definition postulated a posteriori of Dora's behaviour. Freud says: '. . . which reminded Dora of Herr K; she took her revenge on me, as she believed herself to have been deceived and deserted by him. Thus she *acted out* an essential part of her recollections and fantasies instead of reproducing it in the treatment.'

In 1905, however, in Dora's case, Freud used a less common word, *agieren* (which also means 'to act' but with a slightly more emphatic connotation), in a technical or specific way. *Agieren* was translated as 'acting out', and, as Sandler (1983) points out, the choice of this English term is likely to have contributed to some changes in the meaning and the concept in the Anglo-American bibliography.

In 'Remembering, Repeating and Working-Through' (1914g), Freud says: 'Further dangers arise from the fact that, in the course of the treatment, new and deeper-lying instinctual impulses, which had not hitherto made themselves felt, may become "repeated". Finally it is possible that the patient's actions outside the transference may do him temporary harm in his ordinary life, or even have been so chosen as permanently to invalidate his prospects of recovery.' In the same paper he wrote that: 'We may say that the patient does not *remember* anything of what he has forgotten and repressed, but *acts it out*. He reproduces it not as a memory but as an action; he *repeats* it, without, of course, knowing that he is repeating it.'

In 1920 Freud related these concepts with highly significant theories such as that of repetition compulsion, in the sense of preserving the pleasure principle (Freud, 1920g).

In 1938, referring to the relationship between transference and acting out, Freud (1940a [1938]) wrote:

> Another advantage of transference, too, is that in it the patient produces before us with plastic clarity an important part of his life-story, of which he would otherwise have probably given us only an insufficient account. He acts it before us, as it were, instead of reporting it to us.

And he added:

> We think it most undesirable if the patient *acts* outside the transference instead of remembering. The ideal conduct for our purposes would be that he should behave as normally as possible outside the treatment and express his abnormal reactions only in the transference.

When we describe a series of behaviour patterns as acting out, we have already interpreted an action or behaviour and worked out its meaning (Lagache, 1968). In other words, when we say that an action is acting out, we have defined and built a model in order to explain a process. The analyst labels and defines it from his own point of view, using the term whenever he is able to discover the unconscious motivations of the act in relation to the transference. Many instances of acting out may be overlooked by the analyst, and the patient then loses the chance to work them through.

In the clinical context, Lagache (1968) uses the term acting out to refer to a dramatic, theatrical representation that conveys, repeats, and displays in space (on the stage) all of the patient's fantasies, wishes, anxieties, bonds, and, in general, his whole inner world, within which we must search for and find the meaning and the message of his communication with the therapist.

To set the scene, we shall start from the clinical basis and present the facts, the type of patients, and the period of the treatment to which we are referring.

Case 1, for example, concerns a patient with ulcerative colitis, and we shall see how a psychosomatic symptom (colitis–diarrhoea) gradually changes or turns into an external acting that we conceptualize as acting out.

In another example (Case 2), we present a clinical vignette of apparently heterosexual acting out in female patients with female analysts, which were often misdiagnosed as hysterical sexual acting out. In my experience as a supervisor and in my discussions with colleagues, the diagnosis of intense homosexual transference in female patients is hard to make and may go unnoticed. This may sometimes be due to the analyst's lack of experience and, at other times, to the display of heterosexual erotic acting out that interferes with an accurate perception of the transference.

The more disturbed the patient is, the more we must endeavour to decipher codes and hidden or highly complex languages.

In the clinical cases I have only considered aspects connected with acting out. I have disregarded other important elements of the psychopathology and the clinical history.

Case 1:
How a case of ulcerative colitis turns into external acting out

This is the clinical description of a patient with a severe psychosomatic symptom, which, with the progress of treatment, turned into acting out where its transference meaning could be understood. I supervised his treatment for three years.

The patient, a 33-year-old business manager, was married and presented with a 10-year history of ulcerative colitis. He was deeply worried at the emergence of strong homosexual fantasies that tortured him day and night. He had recently suffered from a severe episode of ulcerative colitis characterized not only by bloody faeces but also by faecal incontinence, which seriously interfered with his social and business activities.

The patient's only brother was two years younger than he. He described his father as an absent person, and the mother as a domineering, aggressive, and, above all, unpredictable woman: one never knew what her reaction would be. A typical example was that he had never known whether his mother was going to hit him or caress him, or whether she was going to kiss him or throw something at him. In fact, sometimes she had punished her son and thrown clothes hangers at him when she was angry. The patient and his brother had shared a bedroom.

During the first two years of treatment—which was on a four-sessions-a-week basis, from Mondays through Thursdays—in addition to his colitis, the patient had frequent street brawls and incidents at work that made him fail in his job. In his own words, he used to drive his car like a maniac. On the whole, he was a patient with no control and with anal explosions in the different behavioural areas, something like a generalization of his symptom. In one session he talked about his way of driving and expressed his fears:

PATIENT: I drive murderously, something I can't control. If a pedestrian is about to cross the road, I put my foot down to prevent him crossing, but once I drove too near a girl and I got frightened. That's why I bought a pick-up truck. The word that best defines my constant state of mind is 'unfair'. The other day I went back home. The bathroom walls are covered with fungi, my wife doesn't want to stay in that flat. I clean the bathroom, dinner is ready and something goes wrong. I get very cross and throw about everything I can get hold of: pieces of furniture and objects. I throw them about and break them. No control whatsoever.

In the course of that year his transference went along these lines: he believed the session was a fight or a murder (the handling of the countertransference and the technique are very important—for a development of the theme see chapters four and seven). He felt he constantly had to fight his therapist or else she would kill him. Or he felt he himself could kill. As already stated, at the beginning of treatment he had relived in the transference his relationship with his mother, with whom he never knew whether she was going to talk to him or throw something at him. He was being treated by a gastroenterologist but he did not take the medicines the doctor prescribed. Besides, he indulged in self-destructive behaviour such as drinking and smoking.

During the second year of treatment he brought a dream: he was driving a van or a pick-up truck with a square bonnet but a small, round window. He ran into the back of a lorry, and his pick-up truck went under the back of the lorry. The front of his truck was badly damaged, and he mentioned his fear of not being able to stop in time.

The patient brought another important dream: he is

'sitting on the WC, there is a wall behind it, a small door and thousands of cockroaches come out; the floor is covered with them and I'm sitting on the WC, stepping on them. There is a pipe in the wall and the cockroaches are coming out of it. A dreadful disgust wakes me up. The sensation is in my feet. Cockroaches are what I reject most, there is nothing more disgusting. I relate them to homosexual desires and masturbation.'

In the first dream it was possible to see or assume an unchecked violent and destructive anal penetration from behind; in the second something we suspected from the beginning became clear, something close to a persecutory fantasy. The therapist thinks, or thought at that time, that it could possibly mean the murder of the therapist in his anus. In the same way as he crashed into the back of the truck, he seemed to get into his anus where his own self, in turn unable to stop in time, defecated inside the body of the therapist–mother. Possibly the therapist was fragmented into multiple tiny pieces that persecuted him. Then there were thousands of them coming out of the WC and the pipe, persecuting him, and he tried to expel them out of his behind. From behind seems to be the way in which he attempted to possess the therapist, and what came out of his behind were fragmented residues, each with *a life of its own*.

The greater the fragmentation, the smaller the persecutory objects in his delusions.

In the course of the same year there was an increase of anal masturbation fantasies at weekends, when the therapist did not see him. This seemed to be the way in which he got the analyst and the analysis into his anus and, within that space, destroyed them anally. (On a different occasion he put sausages up his anus.) We presume the cockroaches were the fragmentation of this process, which he then tried to expel.

Variations and changes in the colitis–diarrhoea symptom

During the following period (in the fourth year of treatment), the uncontrolled episodes of diarrhoea that paralysed his professional activity showed some variations: they only took place at weekends, when he had no sessions; they were rather more balanced during the week when he had sessions (this corresponded to the fourth year of treatment). This change became apparent only after the dream of the cockroaches, with which he was able to symbolize the persecutory fantasies. This marked the beginning of a change in his communication style: an attempt at a verbal and symbolic level expressed through a dream.

Acting-out period

A year later the acting-out period began; there were no more episodes of diarrhoea or colitis. The acting out had very special characteristics. For instance, once, just before the summer holidays, he bought a motorcycle. From then on the motorcycle became a part of the patient and his permanent partner in his acting out. One of the special features was that, when the acting out with the motorcycle began, the colitis disappeared. The patient seemed to have found an equivalence where the uncontrolled diarrhoea was taken over by the exhaust pipe and by his 'uncontrolled' accidents with the motorcycle. At the same time, there was a gradual change in his communication style and in his somatic expression. This may be illustrated with the following motorcycle episode, in a session that took place eight months after the summer holidays. The patient said:

'It takes a certain degree of madness to ride a motorbike; you ride over a stick, a nail, and that's the end of it. But I can't help competing, driving like a maniac even on wet streets.'

Then he added:

'Could it be that I'm crazier now than before? Maybe it's that now I'm more aware of things. Yesterday I started feeling ill and I was afraid of losing blood. I associated that with the motorbike. I had an accident. I was nearly smashed to pieces, but I can't stop. I was afraid of riding to the beach on the motorbike, but there was no colitis. *MY COLITIS HAS MOVED TO ANOTHER UNIVERSE*. No traces of it.'

To this period belongs the following session, in which the patient changed his behaviour to acting out with the motorcycle:

'I had a little colitis, just a drop of blood. It must be because of my birthday and the crash I had. I have been weight-lifting.'

Later on he said:

'We went to a restaurant, I, my wife, and my son, on the motorbike. After dinner, when we came out, there was this crazy episode. I was on the motorbike, and my son had just got on, but, before my wife could get on, I drove away. My little son was alone behind me, and I almost killed him. My wife hardly realized what had happened (that I had almost killed my son).'

Then he added:

'I don't want to be with my mother on my birthday, I also remembered my grandfather.'

In the following session he said:

'I was in the street, and I shouted when I remembered this accident with the motorbike, when I almost killed my son. I started shouting and screaming when I remembered.'

This was the first time he could cry and shout in the street his madness, his pain, his sadness, hatred, affections, instead of avoiding the mental process and expelling it through is own body as an unchecked diarrhoea. It was the first time he could shout instead of soiling himself. This was another change in his mental structures and communication styles. Perhaps these shouts were the first hint of awareness as regards the murder of his own childish part. Perhaps it was the first time he loved something of his own: his own infantile self.

Concerning this material, I feel the patient was unaware of his need to murder (it was *he,* not his wife, who was not aware of this). His denial is projected onto his wife. He was not aware of the fact that the damaged and murdered part was his own body and his infantile self. Before, he also used to murder an object that persecuted him in his delusion (the therapist, his mother, the cockroaches). His colitis implied expelling: a murder, a murder victim, an infantile self, and blood or liquids that constituted the core of his body image. After the session about the motorcycle there was a change: now he was afraid of killing someone he loved: his son, who was also his infantile part that he was now able to begin to love.

In our view, he tried to expel or defecate or murder his wife with the motorcycle, just as he had done before with the episodes of diarrhoea (the murder of the therapist, reenacting his infantile bonds with his mother in the transference).

In conclusion, after the episode when he became so frightened and shouted and screamed in the street, he decided to sell the motorcycle. During the rest of the year, the psychosomatic picture of ulcerative colitis was well under control (Abraham, 1927; Boyer, 1979, 1982; Grunberger, 1971; D. Rosenfeld, 1985; Zac, 1968; see also chapters two, six, eight, and ten).

Case 2

Celina, a 29-year-old woman who had been married for a year, wanted to start treatment. She was a biochemist with serious conflicts in her professional activities. She also had rather vague problems with her husband, in connection with whom she seemed unable to discriminate roles, and an intolerable mixture of excitement and anxiety when she was on 24-hour duty at the laboratory where she worked. Both her parents were alive; she had a brother and two older sisters.

When she was on the night shift, she sometimes coped with her anxiety by flirting with a colleague.

During the first stage of her analysis, with a psychoanalyst whom I supervised, she appeared to be a young woman trying to achieve self-sufficiency through her narcissistic omnipotence. Sometimes she replaced her female therapist with a lover, particularly on the days when she had no session. There was some material about a homosexual desire for the therapist underlying, in my view, her narcissistic omnipotence.

This was illustrated by the following dream (after a year and a half of treatment):

'I was sleeping with my husband. Suddenly, the door opened, and my lover came in. He got into bed with us, and I made room for him. He was on me in no time. He kept trying to grab me, and I told him to leave me alone. My husband woke up and asked me what was going on. My lover kept pushing us, so hard that my husband fell off the bed. I told my lover to go to the couch. Suddenly, I opened my eyes, and my flat, which is very pretty, was in a mess, full of dirt, worse than it was before we fixed it. It was disgusting. I went back to the bedroom to tell my husband about the condition of the flat.'

These were her associations:

'Yesterday, when I was on the night shift at the lab, we had to work with a patient who was very hard to put up with. He said he was going to commit suicide and kept calling his mother. They said he was a pervert, a psychopath.'

Then she added:

'If I have intercourse with my husband and my lover, who will be the father of my child if I get pregnant? In the dream, the lover seemed to be a pervert. He wanted to do something to me, I don't know what.' (*Silence.*) 'I'm afraid to say this. My lover went to see the film *The Kiss of the Spider Woman,* which is the story of a homosexual. We went on talking, and the subject was homosexuality. He asked me if I had had any homosexual experiences. He told me he had. Are you listening? Did you hear me? And he repeated, "Yes, I've had homosexual experiences".'

Her associations with the dream and the lover on the medical couch were:

'My lover was here yesterday in this house, only in the next room, in your husband's office. He is in a study-group.'

The dream showed three persons on a bed. Dirt and disorder seemed to represent anal elements as well as mental chaos. The first associations concerned a severely ill patient who was referred to as a 'pervert'. The patient's confusion about having a child seemed to be a confusional defence of the roles of infantile dependence as a patient, in the transference. The lover, somebody with actual homosexual experiences, is the key to understanding the dynamics in the transference dream: a homosexual person appeared on a couch, which is important from a linguistic point of view, since the patient no longer uses the word 'bed' but 'couch'. Both in the dream and in the narration of it, there seemed to be a strong homosexual desire to be near the therapist.

It is as if, in her associations, the patient had expressed, dissociated and projected onto the adjacent room the homosexual relationships in a psychoanalytic office, with the therapist's husband. In this case it was the homosexual lover in that office (just as in the dream it was her husband and homosexual lover). This seems to be a mirror-like duplicate of an intense desire to be near the therapist through homosexual eroticization. Her intense homosexual fantasies in connection with the therapist are dissociated and massively projected and duplicated in the outer world by means of male figures.

There is an obvious indiscrimination of persons and sexes representing her own indiscrimination. I feel this illustrates how sometimes the transference with female analysts of female patients with these homosexual fantasies appears in the guise of compulsive attempts at eroticizing the relationship with an object.

The patient looks for her infantile objects in the only way she finds possible—that is, sexuality–homosexuality in the transference (Avenburg, 1975; Bellak, 1965; Chasseguet-Smirgel, 1984; McDougall, 1989; H. Rosenfeld, 1965).

Case 3

I shall describe a special mechanism for the communication of acting out in a patient with psychotic episodes, a mechanism I call projective identification through an intermediary or relay.[1]

Lucy had been in treatment with me for about four years. When she first came to see me, she had just arrived from abroad. She was 25 years old, tall, and rather heavily built; her speech could be fluent, but with sudden severe disturbances of her thinking process, which were due to an infantile psychosis for which she had been treated between the ages of five and nine and from which she had never completely recovered.

She was unable to establish stable bonds with men, friends, or her work. She studied languages.

A talk with her previous analyst, a child therapist, provided me with some interesting information about her childhood analysis. With her we were able to determine the period of her childhood during which she had had several epileptic seizures, because of which she had to take medicines for several years.

The patient thought that during her previous treatment she had remained silent, whereas, in fact, she had spoken endlessly, and with her unchecked verbosity she anxiously and unceasingly expelled words and parts of her mind.

She had had many learning problems at school. As a result of a psychotic episode during her adolescence, while she was living abroad, she was seen by expert psychoanalysts. My diagnosis coincided with that of most of them: psychosis, or severe infantile psychosis with restitutions and formal adjustments to reality.

The patient went to Europe for a few months. She sent me a postcard with the exact date of her arrival. When she returned, she told me about the following acting out: Before leaving Buenos Aires, she had had an erotic flirtation with the mechanic who repaired her parents' car. She promised she would write to him from London. She did so, in the following peculiar manner: once back in Buenos Aires, her friend, who lived in London, would mail every week one of the letters the patient had written and put into an envelope. In this way she would make him believe she was still in London, and flirt with him. When she resumed treatment with me and told me about this, I said that perhaps she had had a flirtation with me and she had attempted to eroticize it on account of her trip and the absence of treatment.

With her usual speech difficulties, the patient said: 'No, no. It's not with you. It's with the mechanic.' I replied those were letters sent from London to somebody she missed in Buenos Aires, and that the person in Buenos Aires could very well be me. She said: 'Ah, no. It's my friend who sends the letters. She goes to the Post Office and mails them. I have nothing, absolutely nothing to do with that.' In this way she revealed her way of thinking. I shall term this piece of acting out projective identification through an intermediary or relay. I believe this is a useful model for certain psychotic mechanisms.

1. Her possibility of establishing an eroticized loving bond at the time of departing does not concern me, but another man.
2. It takes place in distant places.
3. Only when she is back in Buenos Aires does she have the letters sent from London, thus mixing up the geographical places and the place where her self is, so that her stay in a place does not coincide with her transference fantasies.

4. She completely disowns the affective message by saying: 'It's not me, it's my friend who sends the letters.'

5. Finally, she refuses to accept that this is related to the transference relationship.

Affect is dissociated and expressed through a person for another person or persons, who function as intermediary objects or relay stations for the message, while the patient increasingly disowns the share of affect she had initially placed in it. This effect is similar to that of snooker balls: one ball hits the other without any actual link to the initial hit.

I conceptualize these multiple dissociations and projections as projective identification through an intermediary or relay in order to differentiate it from the direct mechanistic effect of mere projective identification. This is recognized by the fact that there is always an intermediary object through which a message is conveyed and then disowned.

For those of us who work with psychotic or highly disturbed patients, the concept of projective identification through an intermediary or relay has been very useful from the technical point of view, in helping to put together the jigsaw puzzle of certain messages. Many phrases that in psychotic patients with multiple characters and twisted messages appear to be disintegrated or confused, devoid of meaning, may be seen from a different perspective if we consider that the various intermediary or relay-like objects that the patient disowns constitute attempts to send a message to the analyst.

Many confused messages in severely disturbed patients may be seen from a different perspective when these mechanisms are taken into account.

One of the features of this mechanism, I am certain, is that, although fragmented into multiple relay objects, it is an attempt at sending a message so that it may be understood (Dufresne, 1985; H. Rosenfeld, 1965; Treurniet, 1987, 1989; Tustin, 1981).

Final comments

The repetition of acting out may indicate that the therapist has been able to detect an important point. At other times the repetition of acting out forms part of the learning system, as in the case of some neurotic adolescents (Aryan, 1985; Rubinstein, 1982; Silverman, 1987).

As regards when acting out may be recoverable and when it may not, it is useful to bear in mind that it is not recoverable if the analyst does not recover it by means of an interpretation that relates it to the transference. A piece of acting out may be easier to recover if the analyst is experienced at decoding it and if the patient cooperates. Therefore, the notion of whether or not acting out is recoverable depends not on when and how it takes place, but on the possibility of its being detected, verbalized, and related to a feeling about the therapist and the treatment (Freud, 1914g; H. Rosenfeld, 1965).

In this chapter we have underlined the importance of putting into verbal symbols the enacting, or acting out, of these types of patients. The technical handling of such cases is described in chapter seven, as is the semantic distortion observed in some clinical cases. Linguistic aspects are discussed in chapter eleven, and ways of handling the countertransferential feelings aroused during the treatment of such patients are shown in chapter four.

NOTE

1. This formulation was suggested by Dr Clifford Scott, as a discussant of this chapter; I am very grateful to him.

The handling
of resistances
in adult patients

I

Among the factors which influence the prospects of
analytic treatment and add to its difficulties in the same
manner as the resistances, must be reckoned not only
the nature of the patient's ego but the individuality of
the analyst.

[Freud, 1937c]

C ompliance with the requirements of the setting—that is,
being punctual, associating freely or pretending to—does
not mean that many of the patients we are going to discuss here may not put the psychoanalytic setting and language
to the service of secret resistances and hidden pregenital pleasures. Perhaps it would be more adequate to say that this is a
certain type of resistance.

From that point of view of the analytic transference, resistances should not be attributed only to the patient. The defini-

157

tion of the term 'resistance' depends on its being detected and defined by the therapist. It exists only when the latter defines it as such (Lagache, 1961). In other words, it depends on the therapist perceiving and defining it in his field.

There is another, new problem: a therapist may think that the therapeutic process is getting on well because the patient appears to respond to what he considers 'good' or adequate answers to his interpretations. But it might happen that this patient has a distorted notion of the meaning of the psychoanalytic cure (semantic distortion). Sometimes it is an apparently formal response, which hides another secret level of using the therapist. At other times, faced with a stereotype of constant 'good' responses and lack of transference conflicts, we must suspect that there is something wrong with the treatment (Liberman, 1970–72).

Sometimes an apparent formal compliance with the fundamental rule and with the setting does not prevent the patient from using speech—verbal tenses, tone of voice, questions, etc.—with purposes that are very different from those we know of as adult communication. We are interested in investigating this use of verbal and bodily communications in the service of resistance. In many cases this resistance may be subtle, insidious, or hidden, that is to say, more disguised than, or different from, those described by Freud (Freud, 1895d) in some of his first papers as resistance against speaking, evolving memories, associating: all these are easily observable signs, which help the therapist to be on the alert. We are interested in exploring the communicational approach, that is, what the messages and speech modalities of the patient are, what they convey and contain, and, above all, how they are perceived (uncoded and decoded) by the therapist, and from this vantage point to be in a better position to detect resistances, especially those that are not so obvious (Liberman, 1970–72).

As Freud (1916–17) pointed out, these resistances 'include so much of the most important material from the patient's past and bring it back in so convincing a fashion that they become some of the best supports of the analysis if a skilful technique knows how to give them the right turn.'

It should also be stressed that overcoming resistances is not to be equated with an attempt to force the patient to evoke memories or to speak, because some of these patients tend to see it as a command or a requirement to be fulfilled (likely to be used for resistance purposes by obsessives and melancholics) or to provide material in order to appease a persecuting figure or else to repeat the game so as to feel forced once more, even intrusively.

It is from this vantage point that in the following sections we are going to deal with the points we want to prove, together with the presentation of the clinical material.

All the clinical examples presented here have some elements in common: one of these, for instance, is that resistances are based on a distortion of the meaning attributed to the psycho-analytic cure (semantic distortion) in order to maintain an illusory balance. It is something similar to what Nunberg (1931) calls 'pathological fantasy of cure', which the patient himself maintains and which leads him to this process of semantic distortion. ('We want to suggest that the study of human communication can be subdivided into the same three areas of syntactics, semantics, and pragmatics established by Morris, and followed by Carnap (1942) for the study of semiotics—the general theory of signs and languages— . . . These problems [of transmitting information] are primarily *syntactical* ones. . . . Meaning is the main concern of *semantics*. While it is perfectly possible to transmit strings of symbols with syntactical accuracy, they would remain meaningless unless sender and receiver had agreed beforehand on their significance. In this sense, all shared information presupposes semantic convention. Finally, communication affects behaviour, and this is its *pragmatic* aspect. While a clear conceptual separation is thus possible of the three areas, they are nevertheless interdependent' [Watzlawick et al., 1967, p. 20–21]).

Another common element is that such a distortion is based on misinterpreting the therapist's interpretations and changing them into a violation or an intrusion. In one case the patient's goal is to bring about such violation (Section II), in another the violation situation is reversed (Section III). In the 'Rat Man' these general guidelines can be observed throughout the original records and in Freud's own interpretations, since, as I always stress, sometimes it is the therapist himself who brings about this type of situation.

It will be seen that the stress is laid here on the effect some patients try to produce or bring about. Sometimes it is the therapist who, with his inquisitive attitude, may become the (sexual) partner, quite often unwittingly. In this case, the patient uses the therapist to avoid all knowledge about his unconscious.

With these patients we try to offer technical suggestions and handling procedures that are relevant to their common characteristics. It is our belief that the psychoanalytic technique must try to detect and differentiate this type of problem very carefully; it is not wise to inquire or ask too 'actively' in order to get the patient to talk, to remember, or to associate, in all the different stages within the course of a treatment. We should bear in mind that these patients put the rules of the psychoanalytic setting to the service of their own goals, distorting the semantic meaning of the setting and, therefore, the meaning of the psychoanalytic cure and thus maintaining their pathogenic defences. (For instance, when a patient speaks about a current event but uses the past tense, he actually avoids contact with the therapist in the here-and-now of the session—see Maldavsky, 1977; D. Rosenfeld, 1975).

In a different context, Freud (1916–17) warned us that the first thing we achieve by setting up this fundamental technical rule is that it becomes the target for the attacks of the resistance. Freud also teaches us that certain obsessional patients and those suffering from anxiety hysteria may render the fundamental rule useless and take it to absurd extremes. 'Thus at times one has an impression that the patient has entirely replaced his better intention of making an end to his illness by the alternative one of putting the doctor in the wrong, of making him realize his impotence and of triumphing over him.' Freud himself wonders whether there are cases of neurosis in which associations may fail for other reasons.

For example, we suspect there is resistance, as Greenson (1967) points out, when the patient rigidly and monotonously repeats the same thing over and over again. But we also regard it as a sign of resistance when the whole treatment goes 'too smoothly' and without conflict: everything seems too perfect; or when, from a phonological point of view, the music of the story shows a voice that is monotonous or lacking in emotions (Guiard, 1977).

We are particularly interested in studying the microscopic level—for instance, verbal tenses and the syntactic structure—in addition to the macoscopic level suggested by Greenson (1967).

On the whole, we are trying to recover the minor details of what takes place between therapist and patient, as Freud (1909b) taught us, by carefully mentioning all the occasions on which that resistance emerged or in detecting the non-verbal language (pain) in the case of Elizabeth von R. (Avenburg, 1975; Baranger & Baranger, 1969; Bleger, 1967; Fenichel, 1957; Freud, 1895d, 1896b, 1909b, 1919e; Meltzer, 1973).

II

In two of my four female cases an elaborate
superstructure of daydreams, which was of great
significance for the life of the person concerned, had
grown up over the masochistic beating phantasy. The
function of this superstructure was to make possible a
feeling of satisfied excitation, even though the
masturbatory act was abstained from.

[Freud, 1919h]

In this section I present material about a female patient who hides and 'constipates' her material. As soon as the therapist asks a question or adopts an inquisitive attitude, he is involved in a resistance game. In this way the patient tries to induce the therapist to rape her; later on it will be seen that she repeats her behaviour outside the office.

J., a 21-year-old university student, sought treatment. Her

sexual life was promiscuous, and she lacked moderating parental figures.

After five months of treatment, the patient told a dream that has deeply impressed her:

Neither her father nor her eldest brother were present. Her younger brother was in their parents' bed and she bade him: 'Caress me', and he masturbated her. The mother realized what was going on and asked them what they were doing. The patient answered: 'It's nothing, nothing.'

In her associations, she remembered that the previous night she had been in her room with her boyfriend, that he wanted to caress her and she had said no, that it made no sense. She added: 'Perhaps I wanted him to, really. I don't know.'

Then the patient added that since she was 11 she had dreamt of forced sexual relationships: she was forced, assaulted, and then she couldn't help having intercourse, but then she got married, that is, she was not abandoned. After a long silence, she added that when she was 11 and she masturbated, she did not feel there was anything wrong about it and did not try to avoid it either.

Her answer in the dream—'I said: it's nothing, nothing'—is habitual in this patient and is used to try to avoid all kinds of emotions and thoughts.

During the following session the patient would not produce any material; she remained silent, 'constipated', trying to set going the childish circuit aiming at rape. This silent attitude was an attempt to force me to act and intrude upon her to grab her material (Meltzer, 1966). The session developed in the following way:

J (*long silence*): At the beginning, if you ask me nothing, I don't speak.' (*Another long silence.*) 'I'm very constipated. I only have a bowel movement every 10 or 15 days, or sometimes once a week. At least it's been so for three years.'

I asked her what she had been like before and she answered: 'I don't remember anything about that time.

After a moment's silence, she added:

> 'I want to go to London again and see *Hair* at the theatre. I
> had an affair with a Negro there. There's good people there. I
> saw good faces, smiling faces. They give everything, they give
> everything they have without any avarice: they gave me
> handkerchiefs, necklaces, they even gave me marijuana.'

We may infer that being constipated for 15 days in the course of
psychoanalytic treatment does not imply the need for a small
enema but of a large violating enema to force her to 'let go' of
the material.

I feel that by asking her a question I take part in the patient's
unconscious game. My question was experienced as an intrusion, an enema designed to extract from her what was hidden
inside her. Through the mere fact of asking her I helped to trig
ger the abovementioned mechanism. The structure of her
answer to my question: 'I don't remember anything . . .' is similar to the answer she gave to her mother in the dream: 'It's
nothing, nothing.'

After my question, the patient went far away, to London,
which for her implied taking shelter in her masturbatory fantasies: drugs, sex, anal excitation, and anal coitus, *Hair,* the
Negro boyfriend, which generously gives her all sorts of satisfac-
tions. Thus she would rather have anal excitation and her over-
valued faeces as a way of disparaging the analytic bond (H.
Rosenfeld, 1969, 1975).

Three months later, her mother had her uterus removed,
which intensified the patient's need of being raped, in an acting
out that was pre-announced long before.

In the course of this session the patient said that she agreed
to go for a drive with some young men. She also went to the
house of one of them. She described them as aristocrats and
Nazis. She said: 'In the house of that guy I kept crying and
pleading not to have sexual intercourse with him, until I fell on
my knees, still crying. This lasted for more than an hour, and
then I said yes.' She did outside the analytic setting what she
had announced three months before: that she would try to act
out being raped. One of these announcements corresponded to

the session in which she said that she would remain silent unless I took the material away from her by force, and that if I did not do so she would try to put into practice her anal orgiastic fantasies in London with *Hair* and the Negro boyfriend.

Her acting out of her raping fantasies expresses her need for a violation, together with her need for punishment, in view of her ill-treatment and destruction in her fantasy of the therapist's head through her withholding material or missing a session and, before that, against her mother's body. She seduced and used people in order to make her transference fantasy real.

Technical handling: This type of resistance in the transference may become stereotyped if the therapist, due to his own desire to know what is secret and hidden, adopts an actively inquisitive attitude. It is here that we may say that it is not advisable to ask too actively. In any case, here the analyst faces a dilemma as to his therapeutic role (Boyer, 1983, 1987).

Using silence, the patient tries to induce the therapist to respond. The important thing here is to discover the type of response the patient expects from the therapist—that is, we would like to insist that the stress should be laid on the effect these patients try to induce in the therapist: curiosity, despair, a desire to know what is hidden, loneliness and childish abandonment. That is, the therapist's capacity to be alone with himself is perhaps the countertransference attitude that allows him to start thinking about these problems in the analytic field.

This resistance becomes stereotyped if, and only if, the therapist cannot overcome this disturbed communication circuit (Abraham, 1919; Grinberg, 1965; Liberman, 1978; H. Rosenfeld, 1965).

III

> In the frightening scene in childhood, Coppelius, after
> sparing Nathaniel's eyes, had screwed off his arms and
> legs as an experiment; that is, he had worked on him as
> a mechanician would on a doll.
>
> [Freud, 1919h]

> We remember that in their early games children do not
> distinguish at all sharply between living and inanimate
> objects, and that they are especially fond of treating
> their dolls like live people.
>
> [Freud, 1919h]

First, I describe a resistance based on a distortion of the meaning of the psychoanalytic cure (semantic distortion), which
consisted, as in the other cases already described, of a fantasy of
raping/being raped. In this game the patient reverses the situation and tries to change his passivity into activity, that is, he
tries to get into the therapist's head in order to inoculate orders
or perversely enjoy that penetration or necking. The patient's
linguistic style is described; he also presents a pragmatic distortion. Second, the session to be transcribed shows how the patient
induces the therapist to respond like a doll or an automaton,
and, if the therapist gives in, he becomes involved in the
patient's sexual game. Third, some remarks concerning the technical handling of this type of resistances are made.

1

The patient has a pre-genital, perverse personality structure.
The complete case history is irrelevant to this chapter, and
therefore I take into account only the part of it that the patient
repeated in the transference and the way in which he put it to
the service of his resistance.

The patient used to masturbate with small dolls he made
himself and which he dressed and undressed in a kind of strip-
tease that aroused him frantically; on other occasions he
resorted to photographs. Years before that he used to mastur-

bate in front of a mirror, dressed as a woman. At this time there predominated masturbation while watching women with binoculars and his activities as a '*frotteur*' in public transport vehicles. The psychoanalytic relationship was of a pregenital nature, including the attempt to secure a violation, but reversing the situation, that is, this patient's behaviour amounted to raping or rubbing against the interpretation or the therapist's head, thus obtaining a masturbatory pleasure. In this way he partially enacted his perversion with the analyst, a fact that required exhausting months of detailed analysis before the therapist was able to detect it and conceptualize it. The pattern of the relationship would be the following: the analyst would interpret a piece of material fairly adequately, and the patient would reverse the relationship by saying: 'To be able to say that, Dr Rosenfeld, you surely must have thought of this other thing, because what you had in your mind was some thought related to something you were feeling.' This was accompanied by irrepressible manic and joyful laughter. That is to say, he got into my head and felt sexually aroused by that penetration. At the level of the patient–therapist communication, Liberman (1972, 1978) refers to this as a pragmatic disturbance, an instance of positive entropy, since it aims at doing away with the asymmetry that should characterize the therapist–patient relationship. Pragmatic perturbation is that which implies a distorted use of signs, which very often, as in this case, employs an apparently informative language in order to induce responsive actions in the listener.

After this defensive resistance system was detected and it became possible to show the patient that this was his way of reversing the situation and, among other things, magically transforming mental pain into a new mental state of excitation, he would leave the consulting-room, buy some magazines with pictures of women, and masturbate between one session and the next. On other occasions, after an interpretation that caused him minimum suffering, he would get on a bus and act out his *frotteur* behaviour.

At the linguistic level, what we are describing manifested itself in the structure of his utterances, which were mainly based on the second pronoun singular; the verbs were sometimes verbs of thought, mood, or feeling, but used in order to induce me to make an interpretation; on other occasions they were verbs of action. In moments of maximum excitation I was able to count, for instance, the word 'ass' eleven times in the first ten minutes of the session. From a phonological point of view, his laughter showed a state of excitation, the intensity of which increased constantly. The same may be said about the rhythm and speed of his speech. This defensive system of resistance designed to avoid all knowledge about his unconscious has characteristics that are more perverse than those of the other cases presented, but also some elements in common with them. As already mentioned, the patient reversed the relationship and tried to be the one who becomes sexually aroused and rubs within my head. It seemed that the therapist became for him an inanimate object, like the dolls with which he used to masturbate.

If the therapist does not become aware of this resistance game and does not correct the distorted meaning attributed by the patient to the psychoanalytic cure, each interpretation contributes to his becoming a sexual partner. This gives rise to a repetitive resistance system that is chronic and silent.

This patient had never differentiated between his body and that of his mother. After his father's death, when the patient was 14 years old, his mother used to take him to her bed, ask him to sleep with her, and to caress her hair from behind.

In the analytic relationship this patient reversed the situation which in the other cases presented here amounted to securing an anal enema designed to extract the 'constipated' material. Sometimes he shouted at the therapist to make him interpret: 'Speak more, Rosenfeld, say something, speak more, speak!' One of the meanings this had for the patient was that of a violating enema designed to rape me and extract from me what I had hidden in my head. Sometimes his demand became part of a perverse sexual game, where, by responding like an automaton to his demand, I became a doll that aroused him sexually, like the dolls he used to undress. When the therapist was able to show the patient that he remained autonomous, that is, silent, the patient became panicky. On other occasions panic had to do with the fact that, in his eyes, I also acquired the qualities of an agonizing object which he tried to keep alive (Etchegoyen, 1991; Gillespie, 1956; M. Klein, 1948; Klein et al., 1952; Segal, 1950, 1973; Zac, 1968).

Many changes took place when the therapist became independent, that is, did not comply with his demand for him to respond like a doll.

2

This session illustrates the way in which the patient subtly induces me to talk, that is, to be a doll that must respond according to his wishes.

The patient arrived:

PATIENT: You placed the cushion higher, its more comfortable like this. Last time I left saying, 'Of course, of course, I was creating a whole mental structure on the basis of what I attributed to you'. I attribute emotions to you, but you told me each thing to get a special effect. Above all it was felt in a perverse way. Last time you interpreted my perverse pleasure, and I thought you were enjoying yourself perversely when you pronounced the word 'pleasure'. It's funny how my identity changes here, and I tell my wife, what I do during the session is not conscious. I was speaking about my sexual problem with my prick, and last time when I left I was thinking that you paid no attention to my prick.

Then I remembered I am always accusing my wife of the same thing. She pays no attention to my prick. I remembered I had fucked with my wife in front of a mirror, on the floor, looking at the mirror; I couldn't see the prick get into the vagina, I saw the buttocks, everything . . . both of us. I think of masturbatory things so as not to think during the session.

It is dangerous for my clients. Well? Come on! Speak! You pay no attention to my problem with my wife, to my complaints about her, you didn't say a word, . . . well . . . it must be the way I see it. . . . Of course, you interpret me. . . . Of course, I thought I told my wife everything because in this way I evacuate what happens here. I remembered my father, who had a shop on street XX number XX, I can remember that, I even remember the phone number, the number, I used to call him to ask him to get things for me near the place where he had the shop; once he gave me some tools I asked him for.

THERAPIST (*I only managed to say a few words about how he can change from the sexual theme to the father, and . . .*)

PATIENT (*interrupting*):   I had the feeling that you were smiling.

THERAPIST (*I remain silent, somewhat surprised.*)

PATIENT: I have an image of you with a benevolent smile; my father used to call me KID, I associate that with my brother who used to sing to me but in a disparaging way or as if he were making fun of me.'

THERAPIST: When I try to speak, you are already getting into my head and then if I remain silent I become someone who smiles or makes fun of you. But I don't seem to be an analyst who is listening to you.

PATIENT: Yes, I feel that quite clearly. Well, the other things I said you will interpret afterwards. I remember that last session you put everything together into one single interpretation, that I forced you and my wife and now I've got into your head. I was trying to guess what you might be thinking. I was thinking for you. I feel persecuted because you don't appreciate what I said. Oh, well, I won't go on speaking. You pay no attention to me. You reject me. When I arrived you greeted me in a friendly way. Of course, last time you did pay attention. But I felt you should do something else, say something else. Last session I was late. I have funny ideas, that I speak too much and you never interpret. I said to myself all right, you'll have to go on by yourself.

THERAPIST (*I point out that this is his typical code: first he accuses me of not giving him anything, then he inoculates devaluation in order to make me react, and then, by means of a subliminal order, forces me to talk or interpret, but only when he wants me to. I remind him of my first interpretation that session.)*

PATIENT: Once a friend of my father's, who was called A., he was very kind, once he drove me in his car, a very expensive car; I must have been 10. At that time the police were there checking on shops, they asked everybody their names. I still have my father's image and I took hold of the ruler to . . . but from within your head I thought that you were already associating I took it to measure my prick. I think more than you think. I think my prick is short, and I feel persecuted.

3

Analytic technique.
Difficulties and vicissitudes in the handling of resistances in the treatment of patients with these symptoms.

With this kind of patient it is important to avoid the symmetry they try to create, since their aim is to do away with all differences between patient and therapist; for instance, when I make an interpretation, he starts speaking of what is happening to me. That is his way of distorting the analytic relationship. If this communication circuit is not overcome, the therapist may never be able to inform the patient of what happens to him. By trying to avoid asymmetry, these patients try to eliminate, at all levels, the differences between patient/therapist, man/woman, near/far, son/father, penis/non-penis, etc. This coincides with the pragmatic distortion. As stated before, by reversing the relationship this patient loses all notion of source and destination of the message, and the limits of the self and the object become blurred (Liberman, 1970–72). This is expressed here in terms of the theory of communication and coincides with what Herbert Rosenfeld (1969) describes when he deals with the different types and qualities of projective identification which lead to self-object fusion, blurring of limits in order to deny envy, and useful dependence. Since the limits of the source and the destination are lost, there comes about a gross distortion of communication, as Rosenfeld points out in his paper. (After the publication of Melanie Klein's works [1948], Herbert Rosenfeld drew very useful distinctions. One type of projective identification is that used by the psychotic so that the analyst may contain his anxieties, that they may lose their frightening and intolerable quality and acquire meaning, and that the analyst may put them into words. This provides an experience of mental union which favours the development of introjection and of the ego processes. This is the type of projective identification used for communication. A second type of projective identification is that used to get rid of parts rejected by the self. The psychotic uses this type of projective identification to split off parts of his own self, to expel the disturbing mental aspects they contain, and to deny psychotic reality. According to Herbert Rosenfeld there is a third type of projective identification—namely, the type used to control the analyst's mind and body. It is an omnipotent projective identification, based on a very early type of object relationship, which interferes with the ability for verbal and abstract thinking, brings about a concretion of the mental processes, and leads to confusion between fantasy and reality. The omnipotent ego penetrates into the analyst, and this gives rise to confusion or fusion with him. This third type is at the root of the omnipotent narcissistic structure.)

It is very important to detect the numerous and sophisticated ways in which such patients try to inoculate the therapist and make him play their resistance game (Bick, 1968; Green, 1973; Joseph, 1971; Resnik, 1973; Searles, 1963, 1974, 1979).

One of these ways consisted of jumping suddenly from a story that was linguistically monotonous, slow, lacking in philological nuances, to a flash-like vivid description of his sexual behaviour or his perverse activities; then he would fall back on monotony, and finally he would start another vivid description, accompanied by many gestures. This linguistic modality is designed to leave everything else in the dark and thus enhance and illuminate the sexual element into which he wants to trap the therapist (Freud, 1909a; Mordo, 1976; D. Rosenfeld, 1975, 1976; D. Rosenfeld & Mordo, 1973; D. Rosenfeld & Schenquerman, 1977).

If the therapist simply remains silent, the patient regards him as a partner in his game; for instance, he imagines the therapist is masturbating, as in the following session:

PATIENT: My prick is this big (*gestures with his hands*), and my wife's buttocks are like this (*another gesture with his hands*) this big . . . and I screwed her like this (*gesture with his hands*), and she was in this position (*gesture with his hands to describe the position*).

If the therapist makes an interpretation and in so doing uses words like, for instance, sexual pleasure or intercourse, the patient believes the therapist is included in the act. This raises a very difficult problem concerning the psychoanalytic technique. A true dilemma. The most convenient solution is to adopt an obsessive interpretive style, with an optimal schizoid distance, using words that are significant from a linguistic point of view but abstract enough for the patient to be able to listen to them.

I would like to stress that perhaps the most important element in order to start handling this type of resistance is the therapist's countertransference.

In this way it is easier to respond to the patient's demands and inoculations and even easier to become a voyeur of his perverse sexual descriptions, which allows both the therapist and the patient to avoid going together through painful mourning processes.

IV

October 11.   Violent struggle, bad day. Resistance, because I requested him yesterday to bring a photograph of the lady with him—i.e. to give up his reticence about her. Conflict as to whether he should abandon the treatment or surrender his secrets. [Freud, 1909b, p. 260]

It was still hard enough. After a struggle and assertion by him that my undertaking to show that all the material concerned only himself looked like anxiety on my part, he surrendered the first of his ideas. [ibid., p. 281]

I would like to show here how the patient distorts the reception of the analytic nourishment and turns it into an anal penetration. Sometimes it is the therapist himself who promotes, creates, determines, through his attitudes and interpretations, this special type of resistance.

The element in common with the other sections is the semantic distortion consisting of transforming the analytic relationship into a violation, in this case through the anus.

I will use the 'Original Records' that Freud employed for his paper on the 'Rat Man' (1909b).

We might suspect that the patient already had some psychological knowledge when he first met Freud. It should also be added that at that time psychoanalysis did not attach much importance to the re-enactment in transference, as it would later on.

We are interested in giving transference meaning to a large part of the verbal communication between Freud and the 'Rat Man'. We will select the material, which we find rich and significant, in order to explore it on the basis of what Freud told us about the unconscious life and of the clinical experiences of later years.

In the first session Freud himself draws attention to the patient's initial words, which Freud related to a homosexual object choice: a friend to whom he used to go when he felt guilty. We might suspect he felt he had to give a detailed history of his childhood sexual experiences because he thought Freud was interested in and concerned with these subjects. That is to say, we do not think it was really free association. From the point of view of the theory of communication these stories are not without value, but perhaps what is more important is the intense transference search for the friend–man–therapist, so that the latter may feel satisfied and find him 'good', since, by talking about these things, he complies with the therapist's wishes.

Concerning the second session, it may be assumed that the story about rats told by the patient does not only concern the remote encounter between the patient and the sadistic officer but may also indicate a manifestation in transference of his fear of anal penetration by Freud, whether with his penis, with rats, or with interpretations. Sometimes it is the therapist himself who promotes and induces these fears, which already exist in the patient. It is our belief that Freud unwittingly did so when, in the course of the second session, he requested him to bring a photograph of the lady with him and surrender his secrets. This request to a patient with such psychopathological characteristics may bring about a special type of resistance and a conflict concerning the fear of being penetrated and forced to surrender his secrets. Near the end of the same session there is a linguistic formulation which I regard as a transference response to what the patient experiences as a violation when, speaking about the professor in the Sanatorium room, he says: 'May he be struck dead for it' (Freud, 1909b, p. 261).

Some patients manage to make the therapist express their problems, and thus they finally come to the conclusion that they are the therapist's problems. This is the kind of resistance psychoanalysts often play into, quite unwittingly. For example, when the 'Rat Man' talks about the rat punishment, he achieves his purpose, that is, that Freud should get into his anus:

> 'a pot was turned upside down on his buttocks . . . some *rats* were put into it . . . and they . . .'—he had again got up, and was showing every sign of horror and resistance—'. . . *bored their way in.* . . .' Into his anus, I helped him out. [Freud, 1909b, p. 166]

Thus, the patient forces the analyst to pronounce the word 'anus', which might be understood as meaning that Freud is already inside the patient's anus (Kanzer, 1952).

Unlike the other cases presented here, this patient does not exclusively aim at being penetrated and violated, but reacts with ambivalence since, as Freud clearly points out, the expression in his face showed a mixture of horror and pleasure. This would support the hypothesis of ambivalence: fear of penetration and, on the other hand, longing for anal penetration as an infantile mode of object relationship. There are fragments where Freud is seen as a friend, and others in which he has the role of the cruel captain. *I feel that the intensification of the obsessive crises and the story of rats coincide with specific moments in the transference relationship with Freud* and express a fantasy of transference rape.

In the session of 21 November the patient induces the therapist to become a sort of enema, which, after a forty-minute struggle, violates him and forces the hidden material out. Let us remember what happens in this session: The patient says that while he was on a tram, he had a frightful idea he could not possibly tell Freud, for he thought he would be turned out as the idea concerned the relationship with him. I think the patient 'makes up' a forty-minute struggle in order to induce the therapist to force his way inside him. This same resistance as a defensive system includes pregenital pleasures. It should be borne in mind that Freud points out that 'by refusing to tell me and by giving up the treatment he would be taking a more outright revenge on me than by telling me'. One of the Original Records which allows me to illustrate how these patients manage to generate specific moods in the therapist refers to the session of 21 November. Freud says: 'all the material concerned only himself and looked like anxiety on my part' (Freud, 1909b, p. 281).

This countertransference reaction shows how the patient induces in the therapist longing, desperation to know the hidden material. With some patients, the therapist is the recipient of these very primitive types of projections (Bion, 1963). In the session of 21 November, when the patient speaks of the naked bottom, he refers then to lice, worms; this patient is adopting a seductive attitude by referring to the anus and worms getting into it and forcing Freud to ask him. In my opinion, it is a typical example of the way in which the patient exhibits his anus for the therapist to get into it. The patient tried to inoculate Freud with his own erotic curiosity. On an oedipal level, this might amount to a homosexual search for the father, but there is another level, that of the pathological mourning when he was 4 years old, a time when he reacted with a defensive erotization: he managed to revive and be his little sister in the session, while the therapist was his own curious self (as he puts it, 'for looking at his sister's buttocks').

The therapist becomes the self of the desperate patient and may be used in order to bring about an intrusive violation.

The session of 23 November shows the most regressive fantasies, which he feels to be quite concrete. The story about rats boring into his anus, mentioned in connection with the past, appears now intensely in transference. This happens when he walks around the consulting-room protecting his head with his hands from blows of terrible violence. Faced with this inter-pretation: 'Hasn't it ever occurred to you that if your mother died you would be freed from all conflicts, since you would be able to marry?' the patient answers: 'You are forcing me into this, because you want to revenge yourself on me' (Freud, 1909b, p. 283). The patient now uses the words 'forcing me' in connec-tion with Freud, in the same way as he had previously referred to the rats, when in a *lapsus linguae* the patient calls the thera-pist 'Captain'.

Session of the Herring: In connection with this session, I intend to show that the concrete food (herrings) Freud gives the patient is experienced by the latter as an anal penetration. I want to draw attention to certain resistance elements associated with the fantasy of violation. In some cases the patient makes a defensive erotization of his relationship with the therapist, and the bond then becomes an anal pleasure. In other cases what must be detected is a different nucleus, as in the case of the 'Rat Man', basically related, I believe, to his mourning over his dead sister and his homosexual longing for his father, perhaps some-how fostered by the parents. (His parents may have forced him to assume the role of the dead little sister, with all the logical implications concerning his confused sexual identity.)

It should be remembered that in this session of 28 December, the patient started by saying he 'is hungry', and Freud fed him. Then he goes on to say that his passing 'from one point to another' and talking 'a lot of nonsense' is a way of rejecting a person. This is important from the point of view of analytic tech-nique because very often a patient makes false associations, and so, if the therapist accepts them at their face value, he is actually translating instead of interpreting. This sometimes is used by a patient to defeat and even destroy a therapist (Liber-man, 1970–72, 1978).

The next subject the patient brings up is a transference fan-tasy in which there are two women, Freud's wife and Freud's mother, and between them a herring was stretched, extending from the anus of one to that of the other. Then a girl cut it in two, upon which the two pieces fell away. Then the patient makes an association and says that he dislikes herrings and that when he was fed recently he had been given a herring and left it untouched. I think that this is a transformed manifestation of how the patient received the food Freud gave him, but above all, concerning the objectives of this chapter, I believe it shows how a patient may transform analytic nourishment into an anal penetration. In this vivid description, where the patient appears dissociated and identified with women, he expresses what analysis is to him: the way in which Freud gets into him, so that feeding him (giving him interpretations) amounts to an anal penetration.

In the session of 2 January 1908, after asking questions about parasites and an enema, Freud told the Rat Man that 'the story about the herring reminded me very much of the enemas' (Freud, 1909b, p. 308). I think Freud was right, since both when giving the patient the herring and when asking questions Freud may be equated with somebody who penetrates like an enema.

On another level, I think that the herring theme is just another way of expressing in transference the delusion of rats boring into the patient's anus. The difference here is that it is a dead animal. Perhaps that is the reason why it is not a mere coincidence that in the same session there should appear some material that very few authors related to the transference fantasy of the herring. I am referring to the fact that at that moment the patient speaks of a stuffed bird on his mother's hat and mentions that, while he was running along with it in his hands, its wings moved, and he was terrified that it had come to life again, and so he threw it down. *I believe that, by means of that association the patient actually explains that the same thing happened to him when Freud gave him the herring, that is, he was afraid it was a stuffed animal that might come back to life and transform itself into rats that get into his anus to gnaw at him and devour him.* Another element to support my hypothesis would be that at that moment he also remembered that 'he felt that the rat was gnawing at his anus'.

Besides, I believe he also wanted to split off his feminine parts—which in that fantasy appear as the two women—when in the following session he says that if the food had been prepared by two women, that meant bringing women into the session. It is then that Freud says: 'When I brought him something to eat he thought at once that it had been prepared by two women' (Freud, 1909b, p. 308).

On the whole, this patient shows an ambivalent attitude in that he wants food or his father's penis and he also runs away in fear. In this way he expresses his ambivalent libidinal drives, as Freud points out. The patient's infantile sexual theories allow Freud to establish a relationship between rat, parasite, and penis and also allows him to explain the infantile hypothesis that coitus involved the anus and that marriage consisted of people showing each other their bottoms (Freud, 1908b, 1909b, 1920g, 1923b, 1926d, 1940; see also Abraham, 1919; Chasseguet-Smirgel, 1975; Grunberger, 1967; Laplanche & Pontalis, 1973; Racker, 1957; Zetzel, 1967).

Epilogue

It is important that the reader should take note of the technical indications in the handling of specific resistances, and at the same time see how we can pass from the clinical basis to a medium-range theory (empiric generalization). This type of patient makes the analyst despair of ever effecting a cure. The analyst looks upon it as an immovable resistance, and what really happens is that he has not detected this semantic distortion. We are interested in investigating the specific linguistic expression of the patient, his manner of communication, and, naturally, his feelings.

We use the concept of the three areas (semantic, syntactic, and pragmatic) in human communication (Watzlawick et al., 1967), and above all we insist that the semantic area has to do with the sense or meaning of human communication and is connected with the theory of values or axiology, and this is related to superego and ego ideal, and to superego/ego ideal synchronization.

This development, which could be applied to the clinical field, could result in subtle diagnoses. This is the outcome of Liberman's investigations and teaching. But all the psychoanalytic techniques and methods will become as nothing without the affective and human understanding of the analyst.

CHAPTER EIGHT

Hypochondrias, somatic delusion and body image

Knowledge in the psychological field is different from that in the physical sciences, in that it does not consist of discovering physical objects and processes that are already in existence to be uncovered. Rather, it is made of detailed observation of, combined with empathic responsiveness to, another person's states, so that a *construction* which has sufficient consonance with the nature of those states can be formed, making it possible to describe them to other people who have had something like the same experiences. Thus, those readers who have not had deep experiences with psychotic children may have found this a somewhat incomprehensible book, for we have been immersed in states which are not part of everyday experience.

[Frances Tustin, 1981]

Introduction

In this chapter I attempt to describe the various clinical ways in which hypochondriac pictures become manifest in psychoanalytic practice. It is not my purpose to create new

179

entities or abstract terminology, but rather to offer a description that is mainly based on the clinical experience of the variations a hypochondriac picture may present; the realization that different dynamics prevail in each of them may prove useful for their technical and therapeutic handling in psychoanalytic practice. The mechanisms underlying hypochondria are predominant modes of functioning, which does not imply they never change: they may change, become altered, and alternate with others. What I want to stress is that there is a prevailing dynamics, as well as its relationship with generic–developmental levels. Likewise, I discuss the conceptions of body scheme predominant in each type of hypochondria.

The first part of the chapter describes the picture of the somatic delusions. It then deals with a clinical variety of hypochondria based on autistic mechanisms; finally, I discuss ideas concerning hypochondrias whose pathology is based on a special type of conception of the body scheme.

Hypochondria, traditionally described as a constant preoccupation with one's own health, with self-observation of organs that are thought to be diseased, may be regarded as varyingly severe, ranging from *chronic hypochondria,* which is closer to psychosis, to transient hypochondriac *states.* The latter include genitalized neurotic and also confusional and psychotic elements. They are quite common in periods of change, bodily growth, migrations, etc. (H. Rosenfeld, 1965). They also have a defensive function at the onset of paranoid psychotic pictures, as discussed by Freud in 1911. Schilder (1935) dealt with the subject of hypochondria and the boundaries of the body scheme. Clifford Scott made original contributions in connection with the mobile and changing body image (1980).

Hypochondrias predominantly based on projections onto the outer world: the somatic delusion

The basic characteristic of the *somatic delusion* is a delusion of self-reference involving others, which may be focused or else spread over body areas; in any case, what matters here is the disturbance of the social bonds. This can lead to the *isolation* to which the subject resorts in the belief that he is being watched, since he thinks everyone looks at him and knows of his bodily defect. Thus, Pablo, the patient discussed in this chapter, begins to withdraw because he thinks that everyone outside keeps staring at his lips and cheeks, which. he thinks, are like a woman's. In the case of another patient, an elderly man I shall call Mr G, I found that his isolation and social ostracism were based on the somatic delusion that his body was filled with putrid and filthy matter, and he acted accordingly: he never went out for a walk or attended a social gathering, because he thought everyone stared at him and smelt the foul smell coming out from inside his body. Mr G kept all this half-hidden until he was finally able to communicate it through a narration in which he said he had stepped on an insect that smelt bad. This allowed him to describe his own conception of the inside of his body and made it possible for me to get more acquainted with his somatic delusion. Unlike the encapsulated–autistic type of hypochondria, where social ties are not disturbing, the opposite happens with the somatic delusion. In the somatic delusion the patient sometimes keeps it hidden from others; he does act it out, and, therefore, his whole life is organized on that basis. There are intermediate states, which are not clearly delineated. What concerns us in psychoanalysis is to try to discover this at microscopic levels, to use data that we sometimes derive from the linguistic structure and the repetition of utterances that refer to concerns over the body projected on to the outside (Liberman, 1970–72).

For some authors (Meltzer, 1964), the meta-psychological conception of the somatic delusion is that of a split in the self, where one split-off part takes hold of a bodily part. This split-off and projected part of the self is felt to exist independently and by itself, alienated from the ego and interfering with the good object relationships, and the somatic delusion may reappear when there is an attempt to reincorporate the split-off part of the self. As Resnik (1973) says, it is an egocentric conception of the world 'where there are no others except Him as the centre of the universe'. It is an attempt at re-establishing ties. Besides the splitting or severe dissociation, another mechanism in the somatic delusion—massive projective identification—is likely to include fragmentations and faulty dissociations with confusional anxieties. The re-internalization of the delusion may take place in one bodily area, in which case it may be accompanied by a marked increase of paranoia. This process might be understood as follows:

1. The process begins with what we would call a classic hypochondria: the patient expelling a part of his ties with his internal world on to an external object.

2. He re-introjects what has been previously projected (libido, sadism, confusional anxiety) and localizes it in a bodily area.

3. Hypochondria may thus become established in a bodily area. This is the type of hypochondria based on re-introjection and confusional anxiety, as described by Herbert Rosenfeld (1965).

4. There is a second projection or re-projection with a special ego de-structuring quality: the conflicts and ties of the inner world that were placed in that hypochondriac area become intolerable. There is an attempt at re-projecting them, that is, what used to happen with an organ or bodily area now takes place with an external object: the somatic delusion becomes established. Here the reality sense is already lost. The delusion is the patient's pathological attempt to re-establish his ties with the outside and thus compensate for his end-of-the-world feelings and the de-structuring of his self. The somatic delusion develops as an effort to endow the self with meaning and organization.

5. There may be a second re-introjection: the delusion is re-introjected, and there is a marked increase of paranoia. In Pablo's case the patient feels persecuted on account of his lips and cheeks and runs away down the street. All this is localized (for the second time) in a bodily area. It is my belief that this re-introjection of the somatic delusion that includes the loss of reality, of partial and whole objects, is the key to

understanding the cases of severe hypochondria that may eventually commit suicide.

6. The patient may also try to project his delusion on to the therapist and thus establish a delusional or psychotic transference. Technically, this the most difficult situation for the analyst.

7. Likewise, the patient may try, as regards this hypochondriac delusional nucleus:

(a)   to remove it, amputate it, get rid of it; Pablo wanted to tear off his lips;

(b)   to commit suicide in the cases in which homosexual elements are added to paranoia. The objective is to kill an unbearable tie localized in the body and taken for the individual's life itself. It is my belief that in these cases there has been a previous somatic delusion. At a linguistic level, the patient expresses this in a persecutory way by using the singular or plural third person: 'the pain persecutes me', 'it wants to drive me mad', 'this pain wants to kill me'.

Of course, at the onset of schizophrenia there may be delusions of self-reference, hallucinations, and preoccupations with the body, hypochondriac delusion or a restricted hypochondria, as signs that mark the onset of a psychotic episode (Pichon Rivière, 1970).

Clinical presentation:
Pablo

The patient, Pablo, whose somatic delusion became manifest in the course of his treatment, sought help in order to be cured and helped to recover his lost inner objects: he also expressed his concern over his body, which, nevertheless, did not prevent him from doing well in his work. As the treatment developed, transference became more and more regressive, thus showing the patient's relationships with aspects of the mother and the father in connection with parts of his body (lips, cheeks, penis). Pablo started speaking about his pre-occupation with his ideas about his own face. He was 39 years old and, when he was 8, his father, who was then 43, had died. The mother died when she was 53 and Pablo 18. There was a brother, five years older than Pablo. The patient married when he was 29; a year later he became the father of a girl and, five years afterwards, of a boy they named Pablo. When the boy was 2 years old, Pablo and his wife decided to divorce. The patient pointed out that when his daughter was born, he felt left out of his wife's life. When evoking his youth, he remarked that for a time he lived alone with his brother, but when he was 18 he was absolutely alone; he added that, after living with an uncle for six months, he had decided to enter university and work in the summer to pay for his studies. He said he had difficulties with his girl-friends and that he ran away from people because he thought he was homosexual, and that is why he decided to grow a beard. After some time he stopped having sexual relationships with his wife. In turn, his wife became reluctant to leave the house after the little girl was born. The same happened when the second baby was born, but to a lesser degree. Pablo then said that, while at a party, he felt terribly jealous because his wife was flirting with other men; he felt hurt and 'slighted' by his wife and, because of her behaviour, weak in the eyes of the other men. The second baby was born severely ill. Pablo thought that his painful situation would solve his marital conflicts. His wife thought that an injection was the cause of the infection from which the boy suffered. In the course of a trip, Pablo caught gonorrhea from a prostitute and told his wife about this affair, in a show of childish rebelliousness against her. He felt that in connection with his wife the choice was between a kind of filial submission and divorce. They decided on divorce, and the children remained with their mother. Pablo remarked that his relationship with his wife was cold, that there was no emotional surrender on her part, and that he had felt free when they divorced.

In the course of his analysis it became more and more obvious that the patient imagined things that happened in other people's faces and minds—for instance, when he imagined that others stared at him. At a microscopic level there were subtler signs. For instance, in one of the sessions he said: 'You must be worried because I'm crying.' He thus projected onto me his own sorrow and worry over his crying, and he saw his own worry in me. Sometimes I had the countertransference feeling that Pablo's material was something between unreal and dream-like, for instance when he spoke about the party in which his wife tried to seduce all the men there (Schafer, 1983). The events narrated might have been constructed as an episode of hysterical provocation on the part of his wife; instead, he conveyed with much more realism and conviction his feeling of weakness as a man, which he sometimes expressed as 'muscle weakness'.

In another session during the first month of treatment he told me a dream: 'I hadn't remembered a dream for more than twenty years.' In the dream he saw an old friend called Davis: 'He was just an ordinary fellow, not too good and not at all interesting, whom I met in the army.' *Pablo, his two children and Davis, who was the driver, were in a lorry that caught fire and fell down a deep ravine.* This dream was analysed in the course of several sessions in the context of the transference by relating it to what we had seen at the beginning of his treatment: his fear of surrendering to somebody who cannot 'drive' him well and may thus destroy and set fire to his infantile male and female parts (symbolized in his dream by his two children). His distrust of my ability as the driver of the analysis–lorry seems obvious, and the same may be said of the association of Davis with David, my own name. At that time the therapist was for him a father who could abandon him or a madman who could lead him towards an uncertain future. In later sessions we realized that the dream also represented his childhood history. After the dream he said he liked reading and added that when he was a child he studied Hebrew in the afternoon; he added that he would like to be with his children for the following holidays (Passover).

In another session Pablo talked about his father, whom he stopped seeing when he was 4, although he met him once four years afterwards not long before his father's death. They were separated from the father because of the war and the Nazi persecution in Europe. He added that when he was a child, he went to a synagogue near Buenos Aires with a cousin of his; and he thought of his mother, whom he described as a wonderful woman, full of affection, a hard-working, tenacious person, who seemed to be weak but who was really hard and tender at the same time. The mother went through periods of severe depression after her husband's death and was hospitalized once. Several years later she started a relationship with a man. The patient felt very guilty about this: 'Guilt, I felt very guilty, because we put that man out of the house; that guilt is always persecuting me.' Spontaneously he went back to the time when he and his mother fled from Europe in the middle of the war: 'I remember that one night many planes came, they said they were English; we hid in a basement for 24 hours; I wanted to draw a curtain and I felt a slap on my face because they could see the light' (here the cheek already appears as an important locus for representations). I asked him a question, and he added that he remembered that 'They took my brother out of his bed, we slept in the shelter and he kept jumping up and down'. He remembered something about that period: 'Mother asked me to buy some cakes, and I lost them because they were white, and when they fell on the snow everything was white and I could never find them, and Mother couldn't either.' He also remembered his nursery school: the teacher complained to his mother that he was rebellious, and he felt very ashamed on account of that. While he was alone with his father, he was an *enfant terrible,* he added. I interpreted that perhaps he now recalled his own infantile parts he thought he had lost in the dream, the two small children, and the patient answered in a sadder tone: 'I remember that the young Nazis hit my mother and my brother for being Jewish.' He then remembered how his father managed to run away only a couple of years after they had. I went on with the interpretation and pointed out that the lorry on fire seemed to represent Pablo with all his infantile world, which he now remembered in the session and he feared had been lost and destroyed. He also feared that I, the driver, would not be there to save him from falling down the ravine, from a mental breakdown.

Later on we saw that the truck that catches fire and falls down the ravine already heralded his ego breakdown and the emergence of the somatic delusion. In his recollection of the 'cakes that cannot be found' we find the model of his internal relationship with objects—an object difficult to retain: when he took something he lost it. I thought he had learned to retain things, but then they slipped through his fingers. After this dream it became obvious that his hypochondriac area, the lips and cheeks, began to invade the rest of the face. (His cheeks are also loci for the primitive skin-to-skin relationships of the baby who rests his skin on his mother's breast. The baby looks first at the breast–nipple and introjects it through his eyes; when this becomes very persecutory it may be expressed as nipples or spears or knives that hurt his eyes—in this case, his contact lenses.) He let his beard grow longer and longer as his delusion invaded his eyebrows, his forehead and then his whole head and face: he feared people in the street might think he had the face of a woman or of a homosexual. When in the midst of his delusion he showed his lips, he said they are woman's lips, then the cheeks, and the same with the rest of his face. It seemed to be a desperate case of searching for and missing his mother, his own sexual identity, localized in a bodily area—that is, his own face. On another occasion he touched his penis and said: 'My circumcised penis is the same as my father's', as if establishing an equation: my penis is like my father's, and I am like Father. At that moment his speech seemed to become more coherent. In that period of full-fledged delusion, as he walked to my office, he would sometimes hallucinate people telling him that he had a woman's face, that he was a homosexual, and then he would start running towards my office.

In another session he dealt with a different aspect of his hypochondria, in this case connected to his eyes. *He spoke insistently about his eyes,* about how they ached, and added that the contact lenses made them sore. He said: 'My eyes ache so much I want to tear them out.' The interpretation centred upon his wish to tear out the perceptual apparatus in order not to see reality (closing his eyes, closing the windows to a dangerous and painful reality). But in later sessions there reappeared the fantasy of tearing off part of his body: his insistence upon having woman's lips and the way people looked at him in the street because they noticed led him to consider 'tearing off my lips or having them removed'. There were also fantasies about people who persecuted him. I thought he seemed to want to tear off his ties with his primitive objects localized in bodily areas. He tried to fuse with his mother as a means of recovering his infantile ties, but at the expense of mistaking his body for that of his mother/woman/female/homosexual. There were also melancholy aspects with their sequel of pathological mourning and persecution by the parents, re-introjected and experienced in bodily areas (Abraham, 1924). At that time my interpretations were rejected when transference was very regressive (delusional or psychotic transference levels) since I turned into somebody who wanted to drive him mad; I became those who persecuted him in the street. It was a way of enacting in transference and projecting on to me his homosexual fears and the madness that was beginning to invade him. During that period he sat on the couch and had to control me by looking at me. On other occasions he clung to me as if looking for a father who might save him from 'the bombardment of crazy ideas'. The protection was sometimes idealized. Ideas hinted at in the first interview began to reappear: The outside world persecuted him, hurt him: 'It is society that makes me a homosexual.' 'The man thought I was a homosexual.' The material became organized with paranoid structures. Even the story about 'people in the street' near my office who told him he was a homosexual made us think that that, in fact, also happened in my office during the session, when after saying that he remained silent (Dupetit, personal communication).

Hypochondria predominantly based on autistic mechanisms

From a clinical point of view, this type of hypochondria is silent, chronic, and more rigid. It reappears in the course of time at intervals of varying lengths and is closely related to autistic objects and an autistic nucleus. This encapsulated nucleus has very little connection with the outer world, unlike the somatic delusion, which is wholly involved with it. Since these patients rely very little on projective identification, the likelihood of massive projective identification is remote, and the same may be said of the transformation of the encapsulated hypochondria into a somatic delusion. Clinically there prevails an apparent control of the hypochondriac nucleus, in contrast with the hypochondria based on confusional mechanisms, where control is not complete. Unlike the latter, it also seems to show a more clear-cut differentiation between self and object. Within a different framework (Bion, 1963), the rigidity of this encapsulation can be tentatively accounted for on the basis of a severe splitting. This is not an openly expressed hypochondria, but, rather, it is opaque, hidden, silent, quiet, and dormant. It awakes at intervals in the course of many years, but when it does, it sometimes has a disruptive effect on the therapist due to the bizarre way in which it emerges. There are not many fantasies about the hypochondriac nucleus, and these are sometimes expressed without any semantic or linguistic variation. The patient projects that over-sensitive autistic nucleus with his autistic objects. His speech is more controlled or marked by long silences, which may serve at times as a linguistic clue for the diagnosis of this type of hypochondria. If these hypochondriac nuclei are mobilized, there may emerge psychosomatic pictures, which in my view indicate improvement and change, since they show that the patient is beginning to use a new style of communication and expression (Liberman, 1970–72). They create an armour where the conflict with the objects becomes encapsulated in a bodily area, something very similar to what psychotic autistic children do. The encapsulated area is sometimes seen as almost alien, non-ego, and at other times as an inanimate foreign object. On other occasions the patient functions as an autistic child would with his toy or autistic object in his own world of sensations.

For this type of patient, his body scheme contains something, while in the other types of hypochondrias the hypochondriac nucleus is more often seen as active, as the cause of pain and illness (Baranger & Baranger, 1969; D. Rosenfeld, 1990; S. Klein, 1980; Ríos, 1980; Wilson & Mintz, 1989).

More often than not he experiences his body scheme as containing empty or hollow areas, unlike hypochondriacs who rely on confusional mechanisms and who experience their body scheme as containing blood, muscles, and sometimes skin. Such encapsulation, used as a defence against the underlying conflict, is so rigid that they appear not to need the help an analytic treatment can provide. Just like pathological autism in autistic children, this type of hypochondria becomes self-sufficient, perpetuates itself through the years, and becomes chronic (Tustin, 1981).

Hypochondria predominantly based on the primitive psychotic body image

In order to explain this clinical variety of hypochondria I shall start by stating the notions of body scheme I will be using. I shall be dealing with two different unconscious notions of the body scheme: a neurotic one and a psychotic or primitive one. Those patients who function with a neurotic body scheme retain the normal coating, the psychological feeling of a warm skin that protects and envelops, with the experience of having protective parents. Those patients functioning with a *primitive psychotic body image* have lost the psychological notion of skin and, above all, feel that their body scheme is a vital fluid, sometimes conceptualized as blood, contained by a weak membrane or wall. This is a way of expressing through the body scheme how the patient's ego becomes de-structured, liquified. These two schemes are present in an alternating and mobile way; they are not static and rigid modes of mental functioning but rather alternative prevailing conceptions of one's own body image (D. Rosenfeld, 1982b).

These are methodological models, useful for the time being in order to understand and organize the huge mass of clinical data from psychotic and severely disturbed patients. The methodological use of a model implies certain risks, since the model is created in order to explain something that is hidden from sight and perception. But subtle clues allow us to assume that there is an underlying mechanism. The model may be changed if new data indicate it should be modified. The notion of a body scheme, which I shall call primitive psychotic, is the extreme notion with which one's own body scheme may be conceived of: a liquid mass with the qualities of a vital fluid and which some more highly developed patients re-conceptualize later on with intellectual elements and call blood. The walls of this membrane are sometimes conceptualized and experienced as the arterial walls. Thanks to Avenburg (personal communication) we were able to compare the great similarity between that which I am describing and Freud's concept of stagnated libido [*Stauung*], which conveys the image that what becomes stagnated is a liquid. It is a process of fluidization, loss of quality, of differentiation. A later level of conceptualization, even more highly developed and reached only by those who have attained a certain level or style of aesthetic or hysterical expression, is that of the patient who can express the notions of blood in terms of red and blue: red arterial walls, on the one hand, and blue venous walls, on the other. This notion of the body scheme usually predominates in the acute episodes of schizophrenic patients but also in patients who are well adapted to reality, like psychosomatic ones. It is my belief that many psychosomatic pictures may be understood in a different way if we work on the hypothesis that they function with the conception of the primitive body scheme (D. Rosenfeld, 1976). I would like to stress again that personalities that function with a neurotic body scheme close to normality may, in the midst of a personal crisis, change abruptly to another body image, and that happens when the notion of primitive body scheme emerges and invades the mind.

Hypochondriac ideas concerning the primitive body scheme may appear: suffering from leukaemia, from haemophilia. Sometimes, these are clinically neurotic pictures, which at that moment function with a primitive body scheme. Every hypochondriac picture localized in the primitive body scheme should alert us to the possibility of a suicidal attempt or an accident of a suicidal nature. I suggest we should adopt the same attitude as regards the danger of suicide in the cases of drug-addiction that function basically with the primitive body scheme, for instance, the intravenous administration of drugs. The same warning should be taken into account when patients have the hypochondriac fantasy of a blood infection, for instance, a patient who administers himself antibiotics intravenously on the basis of that hypochondriac fantasy (Bucahi, personal communication). Some patients take diuretics in large doses in order to expel persecutory objects that have become anchored in the body fluids. At present I feel that every time that persecutory objects are expelled through the body fluids (blood, urine, etc.), one has to be much more on the alert as regards the possibility of the patient committing suicide. This also applies to drug-addicts when the fantasy accompanying the introjection of the drug is the belief that the drug will help them to expel parts of the body that prevent them from thinking (urine, faeces). Becoming empty of the body fluids or of blood corresponding to a primitive body scheme may even be expressed verbally, but when it is localized in the body, without any kind of verbal symbolization, then there emerge certain psychosomatic pictures, which find concrete bodily expression in the form of an illness. For another patient, Inés, every object loss or every separation from her therapist was expressed through a loss of blood through the skin and mucosae with necrotic lesions (D. Rosenfeld, 1982b). She saw her body as a weak arterial wall which became emptied of blood. This shows how the conception of the primitive body scheme, by becoming *chronic* and rigid, grows pathological, just like the infantile autism in which what once was primary normal autism becomes pathological later on (Tustin, 1972). What I have been able to observe is that after many years of treatment, instead of a loss of body fluids or blood, the patient who improves begins to have fantasies in which he is emptied of elements that are increasingly solid, like dreams in which he loses oil and then hard faeces. In my view, it is only then that the elements of object retention begin to express themselves at the anal-retentive level, which implies a new conception of the body scheme. I will give an example taken from Inés in the sixth year of her analysis.

Inés is a patient in whose functioning the primitive psychotic body image prevails, a fact that is expressed through body language in a psychosomatic illness. This case was supervised by me for many years; the analyst is a woman. The patient, a 26-year-old woman, said that she became aware of her illness after she and her boyfriend had broken up. She wanted to be treated because 'I am depressed, I want to die'. The patient said that her illness consisted in necrosed sores in various parts of the mucosae and the skin and that, according to the many doctors who have already seen her, its origin was unknown. Some of these physicians had suggested a diagnosis on the basis of biopsic tests. As a matter of fact, she was considered a hopeless case in view of the severity of her illness: when there was an anxiety or an emotional crisis, the vascular inflammation and necrosis of the mucosae of the mouth, the larynx, and the lips was indeed severe. On one of these occasions, she was unable to speak for six months, and, as she could not eat either, she had to be fed intravenously. One acute crisis resulted in a coma that lasted three days. The patient added that 'there is no longer a prognosis for my illness', and 'at this moment I don't have so many necrotic sores on my legs'.

I would like to sum up a few basic ideas. The possibility of detecting in the transference relationship what Inés feels every time she is abandoned was essential for understanding that bleeding amounted to becoming empty and/or losing an object relationship. This emotional wound seemed to turn into a definite injury, that is, her body's boundaries, at the level of the psychotic body image, were only a weak arterial wall that, as a membrane, surrounds and contains blood. The boundaries of her body were not the skin, the muscles, the skeleton, etc., but only arterial walls which play the role of the external skin and which become empty of blood when there is an anxiety crisis and lack of contention. Her body language expressed how her self becomes emptied of the nucleus of the psychotic body image, which was the blood that oozes out and is lost in the outside world.

From 1976 onwards, a better understanding of the nature of the patient's transference made it possible to study more thoroughly, almost microscopically, the origin of her bleeding, sores, and necrosis, which were correlated with specific stages in the analytic transference. Only now Inés may say that she feels 'something *before*' the appearance of her sores. This was the first step—a small one, indeed. She began to perceive affects instead of expressing them concretely through her body. That same year she had to undergo plastic surgery in order to re-shape her mouth and lips, distorted by the severe skin and mucosal necrosis. Here we can study in greater detail material associated with the relationship between the nipple and the mouth, that is, her transference relationship.

(1) Due to the lack of boundaries between her body and the breast, every separation or loss seemed to imply that the nipple takes or tears away fragments of her skin. The nipple skins her, deprives her of her body's outer boundaries. (2) There is a murderous attack on the objects that abandon her. (3) The lost object takes away with it pieces of the membrane, and she bleeds through perforated pores (the skin of her legs, face, etc.). (4) The confusion subject–object–lips–nipple leads to the attack on the object in a space within her non-differentiated body; therefore, to attack the nipple implies an attack against her own lips. The lack of boundaries (fusion) (Mahler, 1968; Searles, 1979) is the reason why, by attacking the object that abandons her, she becomes identified with parts of her own body's surface (Kafka, 1967; Pao, 1967). In this case, *the arterial and venous walls take over the function that should be fulfilled by the normal skin.*

Before the 1976 holidays there was a new intensification of the feeling of becoming empty of blood, manifested mainly in bodily terms—sores and necrosis—during the therapist's absence.

I would like to stress that in this paper I deal with the psychological experience of the notion of a protective skin that covers and protects the body. The same applies to the psychological notion that her body is a kind of large artery or vein about to be perforated, but in no way do I refer to the organic concrete body, or to its anatomy, such as can be studied in anatomy or histology.

In my opinion, the type of hypochondria centred on and expressed as a phantasy through the psychotic body image—in the case of this patient, a phantasy that she had leukemia—is different from all others, not only because it concerns the blood or the psychotic body image, but also because in my experience it implies the danger of accidents or suicidal attempts. Everything concerning the psychotic body image corresponds to a more primitive and psychotic level. Here, as in the case of other patients, the fantasy of suffering from leukaemia is an example of a hypochondriac disturbance centred on the psychotic body image. It may indicate anything from becoming empty of blood to a severe persecutory delusion in connection with monsters or organisms that eat away the blood, or an attempt at achieving hypochondriac control. These delusions sometimes bring about suicidal attempts, such as cutting one's veins to expel and get rid of persecutory objects that have already invaded the psychotic body image. Transient hypochondriac fantasies concerning blood may emerge in every neurotic personality.

I will illustrate this point by presenting dream material from Inés. It should be noticed that in the case of severely disturbed patients dreams may appear only after a long period of treatment. The first dream, five years after the beginning of treatment, *concerns some chewing gum the patient has and keeps in her mouth*. This is the first time there is a representation of something she keeps. Besides, it is semi-solid—different from the fluid that oozes out through all her pores—and, also, it is centred on a circumscribed erogenous zone: the mouth.

In 1977 there was a period during which she could symbolize her fantasies through her dreams, while the disturbances of the body image were expressed on a linguistic level in a very peculiar way; for instance, the orifices did not appear in her skin but in her speech, which began to lose the normal lingistic structure, that is, 'the social skin'. At a linguistic level, speech disorganization may express de-structuration of the body image. During this period the patient dreamt of '*a little woollen dress, knitted with holes and given as a present to a little girl*': fragments of skin-dress that cover her. The dream represents the dress/new skin—the protective envelope she has received from the therapist after so many years of treatment. The fact that the dream material shows that the loss or emptiness is not related to liquid or blood and that more solid materials, which are easier to retain—for instance, solid faeces—begin to appear, is a very important clue that marks the beginning—though only the beginning—of her functioning on the basis of the neurotic body image and shows that the psychotic body image is not so dominant. In this dream the body is also emptied of its contents, but this time they are not only liquids or blood, but also faeces,

faeces which are hard and seen as a penis. Besides being more solid, they are contained or introduced inside an orifice in her own body (vagina), which contains it. In connection with the psychotic body image, this is expressed at a different developmental level. The patient says in the course of a session:

> . . . Oh! I remembered a dream. . . . I was in the waiting-room, laughing to myself, when I remembered. Is the session over? (*she laughs*) I took out a . . . I don't know what to call it . . . puf . . . ouch . . . oof . . . (*she makes noises*). I kept quiet to see the expression on your face.

The therapist points out that he is *not* alarmed—like the patient is—and that he is not afraid. Then the patient seems to believe in the therapist's contention and goes on:

> Well, shit [faeces] came out, a very long one. . . . My God! It wasn't sticky, it was not disintegrated . . . to put it into my vagina . . . what a masturbation fantasy!

In this chapter I would like to stress particularly the importance of modifications in the conception of the body scheme as something liquid that becomes semi-solid and then solid, as the patient improves; for instance, when Inés stopped losing blood through the skin and started feeling something solid inside her like in the above-mentioned dream about a hard stool, which, besides, came out through a circumscribed erogenous zone. In turn, these transformations and improvements concerning the body scheme are experienced as internal modifications that generate new and different hypochondriac defences.[1]

In November 1979 the patient brought a dream including material related to the loss of blood associated with menstruation, in which she showed that the towel was not stained with menstrual blood. But menstruation was not expressed as before—that is, when she believed that it implied bleeding through all the pores (we are reminded here of her sores every month). The important thing now was that she could dream of this and symbolize it. Previously, she had expressed through the psychotic body image her feeling of being emptied through her skin injuries. When an inner space may be created (Bick, 1968) and also a mental space between the patient and the therapist (D. Anzieu, 1974; Winnicott, 1971), another stage has begun. In a patient with such a severe illness, this stage brings with it the hope that the struggle or the battle will cease to be expressed through the body and will reach mental transference levels.

We hope, as Shakespeare says, that

> if God doth give successful end to this debate that bleedeth at our doors, we will our youth lead on to higher fields. . . . [*Henry IV*, Part 2, Act IV, Scene 4]

Final conclusions

These different types of hypochondria are not static and fixed; rather they fluctuate from one to another. It is common for a patient to start with a delusion of self-reference (where he thinks he is the centre of the world) or a somatic one, then change to a hypochondria of a different kind, and then develop another type of hypochondriac preoccupation localized, for instance, in his primitive psychotic body image, where he believes that he suffers from haemophilia or is bleeding to death. This, in turn, may change to a somewhat more stable picture where the patient denies some of the organs or parts of his body (a picture I refer to as Cotard's syndrome); for instance, in one such hypochondriac fluctuation, a patient stated he did not have a heart; another asserted he had no bowels; a female patient I had the chance to study very thoroughly swore she had neither a vagina nor any other hole; a psychotic patient still says he had no blood or any other organ except his heart.

When studying the clinical picture we call hypochondria, it becomes obvious it is not uniform. We try to account for the differences on the basis of new theoretical models with which we attempt to explain the underlying (dynamic and genetic) structure that is beyond mere phenomenic observation.

What I have presented are observation models that may be of use to analysts in the course of their psychoanalytic work. Scientific models are ways of conceptualizing reality through a theory designed to explain what is behind appearances. If by means of a new model I can account for what presents itself in the course of an analysis—for instance, transient or temporary hypochondrias—and show that they are not all alike, that only some of them are based on neurotic or paranoid mechanisms while find a clearer explanation in an autistic mechanism, then this theory, in turn, helps me increasingly to refine the diagnosis and differentiate it better.

When the empirical basis or clinical practice confirm the proposed models, this may lead to modifying what in methodology we call a taxonomy—that is, a classification.

NOTE

1. Clifford Scott (1991) suggested very interesting ideas about this theory. He wrote to me: 'Later on the page you compare liquids and solids, but do not add gas. In my later thinking gas, fluid, and solids and their mixtures and the way they are distinguished play an important role. Of course, the baby would not live if it did not establish its capacity to breathe and be related to air after birth and this continues throughout life.' . . . 'At the beginning you talk about psychotic body image containing liquid blood but you do not give enough attention, I think, to the many gases, fluids, and solids, that are inside whatever the patient begins to use as a container. It takes the infant some time to separate air and milk. . . .'

PART THREE

DRUG ADDICTION, IMPULSIONS, AND LINGUISTICS

CHAPTER NINE

Drug abuse
and inanimate objects

I n this chapter I describe the psychoanalytic study of the psychopathological changes that can be detected in the treatment of drug addicts, based on the clinical evolution of several such patients. In this evolution, I have found a number of characteristics that, in my experience, can be generalized. I attempt, then, to show the evolutional steps detectable in the course of the clinical treatment of these patients, the approach being similar to that previously used in my study of successive stages in a therapeutic group (D. Rosenfeld, 1988). I also advance new concepts explained on the basis of the theory of the primitive psychotic body image (p. 235), as well as the idea that addicts are in a continuous search for primitive autistic sensations (p. 256), and I develop new ideas related to life, death, and suicide in addicted patients (p. 247). I also propose a new classification of three different types of these patients.

The management of the patient who is addicted to drugs is particularly difficult because the analyst is dealing not only with a specific set of symptoms, but also at the same time with the combination of a mental state and the intoxication and confusion derived from drug use. In view of the length, difficulties, and vicissitudes of the treatment of drug addicts, I found it important to be able to establish milestones in order to find my way along the evolutionary course of transference neurosis and psychosis, which is of basic importance in the treatment of these cases. 'The understanding of the specific psychopathology of drug addiction must result from the study of the transference neurosis and psychosis, always within the psychoanalytic setting' (Bleger, 1967).

In order to illustrate some of my ideas, I describe certain characteristics observed during the psychoanalytic treatment of a female drug addict.

In my experience with these types of patients, I have been able to detect a series of stages of clinical–therapeutic evolution. These stages may be summarized as follows:

Stage 1

Indiscriminate use of any drug, drink, or object as a drug equivalent: this stage is characterized by a marked lack of discrimination between the patient's own identity and that of his analyst, and promiscuous or perverse behaviour is usually observed. Suicide is a risk when the patient is in a dreamlike, confused state. In these cases it is extremely difficult to interpret the material: the patient's ego at this point is not receptive to interpretation, nor is it a dependable source of free association. In this first stage, interpretation aiming at discriminating between the patient and the analyst, and between different spans of time and space, etc., is more important than word-for-word interpretation of what the patient says. The patient shows strong resistance to therapeutic dependence. There are several case histories (Dupetit, 1985) of drug addicts whose initial stage of treatment fits this description. Drug addiction appears as being determined by multiple causes, which are perverse and confused.

Stage 2

In this stage the patient typically selects a favourite drug, which plays the role of an anti-drug. The patient classifies drugs as 'good' (idealized) and 'bad' (persecutory). Thus, he uses some drugs to defend himself against others. In other words, he resorts to a new addiction to drugs in order to fight drug addiction. Nevertheless this represents a first attempt towards discrimination within a previously more confused totality. The therapist becomes identified with one or other of these drug classifications, either alternately or simultaneously.

Stage 3

Drugs arc used only in specific situations, especially when the patient faces experiences that he finds unbearably distressing: weekends, holidays, etc. This can be recorded as progress to the extent that the patient begins to cope with therapeutic dependence and its resulting frustrations. At this stage the therapist becomes the chief unconscious motivation of drug addiction. Drugs are now a substitute for the analyst–breast function when the analyst is absent. The patient's experience is that of either 'being in or being a total vacuum' or 'being full of drugs or full of the therapist'. There are no intermediate situations. In other words, the patient faces each separation by repeating the primitive prototypes of separation from the breast, where the infant rejects the breast and replaces it by thumb-sucking until he goes to sleep.

Stage 4

At this stage there are successful attempts to give up drug addiction. It is possible to approach an object possessing more vital qualities than drugs. It is usual for patients to begin to start collecting certain objects: toys, musical instruments (guitars, flutes), sculpture or other artistic pieces, which play the role of companion objects and at the same time of intermediary objects, very often with fetishist qualities. These objects permit a greater degree of reparation but run no risk of dying, because they are not really live objects. Mild signs of a depressive approach to the analyst begin to appear in the analytic relationship. The analyst no longer acts as breast–toilet, but, rather, as an object to be cherished. At this stage the patient becomes more clear-minded, and there is a greater risk of suicide. It may occur without any previous warnings appearing in the material, since what emerges is in fact a narcissistic, omnipotent aspect, expressed through dissociated, often highly suicidal fantasies. It is not suicide during a dreamlike, confused state, as in the first stage, but rather it may show the characteristics of a mega-lomaniac assertion of identity. This must be borne in mind because although this aspect of the problem is not greatly stressed in the existing theory, it is an ever-present risk during this stage.

Stage 5

The patient begins a determined analysis of the structures underlying drug addiction, which, due to the failure to achieve intrapsychic balance, had given rise to his addiction.

In some cases the patient, who had so far never attempted to shake hands with the therapist on entering and leaving the consulting room, begins to do so.

In fact, after many years of treatment, some features that I call 'addiction equivalents', and which can sometimes be disguised as habits, may be recognized. They can be detected in the patient as a preference for a certain food or drink, a preference which, if studied more closely, appears as a craving for certain objects that the patient cannot do without. There are other types of equivalents, among these, for example, the shift from drug dependence to extreme dependence on paying monthly instalments—for the purchase of a television set, a record player, a flat, a real estate plot, for example. I must point out here that what the drug addict acquires are objects rather than vital, real experiences (courses, lectures, travels). This way of life can lead patients of this type to actual economic disaster. Another drug addiction equivalent is unbridled voracity in connection with all kinds of tasks. The patient then becomes addicted to 'not missing any task or job'. The danger in this case is that the patient accepts work deadlines that he cannot possibly meet. In that sense this stage resembles the first one, during which the patient makes an indiscriminate use of drugs.

* * *

My final remark regarding the description of the successive treatment stages is that the passage from each stage to the next one is a sign of evolution and a favourable prognosis for the psychoanalytic treatment. Each stage must not be considered as being fixed, but rather as a dynamic, dialectic process in which psychopathological changes take place with progress and regression between one stage and the next. It is particularly important for the patient to enter the third stage, that is to say, to resort to drugs only when facing situations with the therapist he finds difficult to cope with. The patient wants to make the analyst feel like an inanimate object or a drug, and it is most important that the analyst take this into account to manage the counter-transferential feelings. (See chapter four.)

Some clinical generalizations

In the treatment of drug addicts I have traced a series of common characteristics that can be added to existing data on the behaviour and unconscious fantasies of these patients.

In the personal history of drug addicts there is frequently a deeply frustrating relationship with their mother during the earliest stages of development. For the child, this lack of a real mother is a reinforcement of inner fantasies about an inner mother who cannot accept the changes in her child's mood. The young child learns to manage with substitute mothers, but without working through his melancholy mourning over the lost mother–breast (Gálvez, 1980).

Drug addiction appears as an attempt by the patient to find the affective nourishment or breast which may thus control his changing mood. But drug taking also constitutes an attack on the analyst and on the maternal breast of the patient's childhood, since it functions as a substitute of this human and present analyst he is leaving, changing him for an inanimate drug. Later on, the drug loses its magic, its idealization, and sometimes becomes the internalized representation of a mother who does not accept his changes in mood. Therefore, with the drug, the patient reenacts the behaviour he had previously suffered from his inner mother. This is a determining circumstance of the struggle in transference, in which the patient tends to imagine and to attach to the therapist the meaning of a mother who returns his anxiety twofold, instead of helping him to cope with it. In the course of treatment, the analyst must show (and the analysand discover) that he may be utilized as a useful container who permits the working-through of emotions.

Technique

The analyst's use and implementation of a communication style different from the one the patient received from his parents during childhood was named by Liberman 'complementary style' (1970–72). The so-called 'complementary styles' are the different phonological, linguistic, and emotional communication styles a therapist has to use, depending on the type of patient under treatment. The firmness of this setting, which implies containment and stability, is another variable to be used in the 'complementary style'. Thus, for example, if the patient is a hysterical, seductive woman, the analyst's linguistic style must be measured and accurate, with an almost distant, cold, and schizoid attitude. In particular if the therapist is a man, he must be very careful when using words or terms of affection or of affectionate support, for she may decode them as a sexual approach. On the other hand, if the patient is a mourning or depressive adolescent who is constantly seeking demonstrations of affection, the analyst's complementary style should be almost the opposite of the one described above: the phonology should convey emotion, affection, and containment. Calling the patient by name may be useful in these cases. The complementary style used with a schizoid or distant patient must be a close and concrete affectionate language. Moreover, when dealing with an obsessive patient, the therapist's complementary style should penetrate through the holes left by these patients as body gestures and slips of the tongue, and he should not interpret the material in a tidy, orderly language, purified of any anal filth (Liberman, 1970–72; Radó, 1933; Reich, 1950).

Drug: technique

I believe that drug addiction is an attempt to recapture the primitive sensations of glow and warmth aroused by skin-to-skin contact with the mother (Baranger & Baranger, 1969).

The notion of the skin is the psychological notion of a containing enevelope which is introjected only when the mother and the father, enveloping and containing the mind and affects of the child, can be felt and internalized.

The psychological notion of the skin is the result of a more or less acceptable development, but sometimes this notion does not materialize. The ensuing disturbances, in patients who have lost their notion of the skin and function with a primitive psychotic body image, have been dealt with.

In turn, this creates some complications in the transference, to the extent that the patient may tend to compare the analyst's interpretations with the drug, instead of accepting them as something equivalent to the original breast and not to its degraded, object-turned substitute, a pill. I try not to be inquisitive. I avoid asking, for example, whether the patient has taken drugs on the previous day, and if so, how much. Many patients usually get paranoid, so my experience has taught me to wait.

I have further found that by means of certain stimulants the drug addict attempts to achieve an increase in the respiratory rate. This is correlated with magic fantasies about introjecting the inexhaustible breast—air and the simultaneous expulsion of its negative aspects in exhaling. Pleasure is derived from inhaling and exhaling air at an increasing rate. By breathing in this way, the patient is attempting to reproduce a manic movement of loss, hunger, and recovery of the object. The drug addict feels that his ego and his inner object are alive rather than dead. He tries to recover and reexperience, by means of air, the primitive object relations, with loss and recovery of both the object and the links. This particular way of carrying out the respiratory function can be detected before, during, and especially after taking the drug: above all, once the initial effect has waned. It is important to watch drug addicts closely when the drug becomes a highly persecutory object. At this time they need to expel the introjected object, for which purpose they resort to a type of behaviour I have called 'expulsive nasal tic', which consists in the sudden expulsion of air through the nose.

This behaviour can be detected in drug-addicted patients in certain paranoid moments, as well as in other patients facing similar situations. This can be taken as an indication of the patient's response to certain interpretations made by the analyst. Basically, it consists in the material expression of a fantasy in which they expel a persecuting mother. Within this framework, I wonder if, from the clinical standpoint, it would not be useful to postulate the existence of a 'respiratory pre-oral stage'.

In these patients we can detect an unbridled voracity towards all kind of objects. The suicide attempt is expressed through the intake of drugs, as a way of obtaining the annihilation of a disorganizing inner object. This is one of the reasons that have possibly led to stressing the manic-depressive element in these cases.

The narcissistic organization at the origin of addiction becomes pathologically powered by the effects of drug intake and makes any discrimination more difficult.

Herbert Rosenfeld (1965) places the point of fixation of drug addicts in the paranoid–schizoid stage, and he adds, further, that these patients partially reach the depressive stage. I contend that one important feature in these cases is a specific aspect of manic defence, the degradation and devaluing of the object. According to the Barangers (1969), this defence has specificity as a system, whether it operates in the paranoid–schizoid or the depressive stage; what is specific in this defence is the devaluing or degradation of the object. When discussing the relationship between drug addiction and manic-depressive pictures, Herbert Rosenfeld (1965), following Melanie Klein (1975, vol. 3), refers to the correlation between manic triumph and destructive omnipotence connected with primary envy.

Countertransference

When dealing with addicted patients, the therapist's most difficult task regarding his countertransference is to stop feeling like, and being, the drug or inanimate object, since this is the role these patients continuously force on him. With respect to countertransference, when a therapist starts to feel that he is answering mechanically, that he is an inanimate object, or when he realizes that he is speaking or answering when the patient wants him to, he must be capable of using these counter-transferential signs to escape this error and save himself as an analyst and as a human being. If the therapist detects these countertransferential characteristics in time, he may be able to save the treatment from monotony, inflexibility in roles, and lack of interpretation of transgressive and psychotic aspects, which lead to long and ineffective pseudo-treatments. An example of this will help to illustrate my point. The complementary style with drug-addicted patients consists in doing just the opposite of what the mother of one of my drug-addicted patients did: if the boy arrived from school in a state of anguish, instead of talking to him and containing him, the mother gave him an aspirin or a sedative. If he asked her for understanding and advice about a personal crisis in his relationship with his friends, she brushed him off, asking him not to disturb her, as she was with some friends.

A more extreme example is the following: a patient with a history of suicide attempts was being treated by a colleague (S. Dupetit, personal communication).

One day the boy, who was a drug addict, took a large number of pills. The maid found him and, most sensibly, telephoned his mother. Despite the seriousness of the case and the maid's distressed and desperate call, the woman answered in this way: 'I can't possibly leave before dessert, what will these elegant people I'm dining with think?' The end was quite dramatic: the boy died.

Clinical material: Irene

Most of the theoretical generalizations included here have been drawn from the treatment of drug-addicted patients. In the following, I present a case history for the sole purpose of commenting upon and illustrating some of my opinions. This material shows quite clearly the theoretical model suggested for the evolution of a drug-addicted patient, even though we have not included here all the points that we developed as theoretical generalizations.

I supervised the case in question over three and one-half years. The therapist was a woman.

After the presentation of some data on the patient, some important aspects in the evolution of her treatment are given. Out of the numerous sessions recorded I have selected those in which the material is clearer as the patient was not in a marked dreamlike confusional state.

Some data about the patient

A series of traumatic events in Irene's life proved to be significant elements in the second complementary series, in determining her tendency to react to conflicts in a way that, in turn, increased her frustration and her inability to solve them. She had been breast-fed by her mother for a week, after which she was fed by a paid wet-nurse. The lack of skin-to-skin contact with her mother can be inferred from some childhood symptoms—for example, eczema and boils. (On severe psychosomatic disturbances of the skin see Rosenfeld, 1988, p. 65: During the first year of his life, this patient lived in a province with a wet-nurse. From that time onward he has suffered from eczema and desquamation.) Irene, in turn, apparently developed obsessive techniques to compensate for the lack of affection, as can be observed in the early development of language as a substitute means of contact: the patient said that her mother talked to her from a long distance. Another aspect related to the early development of obsessive controls is connected with the development of motor faculties. According to the patient, she was forced to walk too early.

First stage:
confused and indiscriminate relationships

When Irene came for treatment, she was 23 years old and a university student; she was an active drug addict. She took amphetamines, sedatives, and alcohol indiscriminately and had a promiscuous sex life. All these behaviour patterns became considerably more serious after a traumatic event: her mother had undergone brain surgery a short time earlier. Irene, who was placed under psychiatric treatment with electro-shock, attempted suicide by slashing her wrists with a razor-blade.

The onset of her illness can be summarized by means of actual comments made by the patient. At one point she showed the cuts in her wrists and went on:

'My other friends and I form a closed group. The others in the class stay outside, and there is one girl who is a skeleton, so ugly, lifeless, skinny. But we need Lito to make the group complete.' Shortly afterwards she adds, referring to two of her friends: 'To those two I am like "the Guest", by Simone de Beauvoir.' Then she says: 'The boys die laughing together; the boys say no to the fees the English teacher wants to set.' Finally, before the end of the session, she describes a dream: 'I asked Fernandez to sleep with me, and he kept saying no. The bed is a rat-hole. I felt very lonely again, now and in the future (*pause, deep intake of breath*). Mom nags me all day; we've given her the name "she who was born to suffer". I'm fed up with her. I wish I were far away, so I wouldn't have to see her. Today she cut her finger and went on for three hours, saying, "I want my head to bleed so I feel better and it is my finger that bleeds instead". If she says that, it means she is ill, and there she was staining everything with her blood and again her stubborness appeared and she won't see the doctor.'

The patient was attempting to project an 'inert', devitalized inner object and to form 'closed group' with a narcissistic part of her self. Nevertheless, there was weakness in her defensive system: one friend (a lost aspect of herself) was needed for the group to be complete. One of her pathological fantasies of recovery would be to recapture that lost part of the self. In this way she might continue to maintain outside herself an aspect of her dissociated self which contains her private, frustrated, sicker aspects.

The rejection of therapeutic dependence (the 'no' to the fees, etc.) is equivalent to the rejection of her own dissociated aspect. From inside an omnipotent inner object she degrades the object on which she is beginning to depend.

Through the dream, however, she accepts a certain degree of dependence which is displaced from an oral to a genital level. The dream also shows her fantasy that whenever she asks for something she will be refused, which seems to motivate her defence against therapeutic dependence. The request to Fernandez was also a sign of defence against her fear of being alone in a dark room (the baby's cot) as well as her fear to lie on the couch and talk in private to her therapist. Her fear of the bed as a rathole expresses, through a comment made in a wakeful state, the 'nameless fear' (Bion, 1966) of a child who is afraid of being devoured by monstrous rodents, which contain the impatience and also the oral aggressiveness of the patient. According to Resnik (1969), there is a topographical displacement from the top towards the bottom. It is an oral–assimilative relationship which displaces itself towards the pregenital use of the sex organs as a way of degrading this model of relationship. In these cases the object relation is precociously eroticized and thus prevents the exploratory questioning process. Finally she reintrojects with the air (she breathes deeply) the object she is searching and calling for. When in the session Irene recognizes that she feels lonely, she paradoxically begins to suffer less from her loneliness, as she admits it in a loud voice after a deep intake of breath, with which she introjects the air–good object. In this last fragment the rodents are humanized: an inner mother, attacked with a razor-blade when she tried to commit suicide, later persecutes her and reproaches her stubbornly. The patient is invaded by that dying, reproachful mother, who stains everything with her blood. It is a dying inner object which coincides with the real mother who underwent surgery for a brain tumour and who now has a bleeding cut in one finger. In addition, this cut strengthens the omnipotent fantasy that her suicide attempt was an actual equivalent to cutting and chopping up a ceaselessly reproachful mother, causing her to bleed. In other words, actual events concerning her mother provided her with the perception that her own suicide attempt had been an effort to murder an internal and external mother as well as her link with her.

Beginning with this first session, the patient reported on her indiscriminate addiction to alcohol and amphetamines, her sexual activity, and her intensive use of sedatives. The session we have just described is an example of the use she made of all these elements, though they are replaced by a group of friends, whose company enabled the patient to exclude and dissociate a sick part of her self. Through sexuality she expresses deeper and more psychotic conflicts. The fact that they are expressed in an apparently sexual context does not mean that they correspond to that level (Liberman, 1970–72, 1978).

The patient arrived at several sessions in a dreamlike state that interfered with the progress of treatment. She seemed to be indiscriminately searching for an idealized breast that she identified with faeces (equivalent to the group mentioned during the first session). These sessions alternated with others, during which the patient was more clear-minded and was able to ask for help and, through her verbalization, show the state she was in. These latter sessions correlated with the therapist's attempt to discriminate herself from Irene and to distinguish times and spaces that were confused in her. Simultaneously with this progress in the quality of the information she supplied, some early phobias became incipiently reactivated. These phobias appeared to the extent that the therapist was able to discriminate herself and appear as an object from which Irene separated, and which she also approached with conflicting feelings (D. Rosenfeld, 1976).

During one session she said:

'In class I sweated while I talked. . . . I would need more sessions. . . . You know, I fell in the street. There was a taxi coming at full speed, I got a nasty bang, at home another bang. . . . The street is bad, and I was crossing the street as if

I were walking in my sleep.' Later she relates a dream: 'My cousin was getting married, she was coming down the stairs of the house and then at the table my aunt would not let me drink wine. . . . There was a little girl, a little dark kid from the orphanage, she had no mother, no father, and she was always looking out of the window. And then my pals and I decided to let her come in because it was awfully hot. Then she ran errands for us. The little kid first wanted the programme for the wedding, all full of little drawings; then with some razor blades she made two little cuts on my hand and told me she would read my fortune. She told me I would get married that day . . . and my parents were coming for me and I didn't want to leave. It was raining and the little girl looked prettier and prettier, and cleaner, and she was no longer my enemy but she became my friend.'

In this passage we can observe Irene's early phobias of walking. Walking is represented in this context by her being forced to part with the therapist while she is not yet ready. The intense anxiety created by any separation is one motivation for her indiscriminate addiction to alcohol, drugs, sedatives, promiscuous sexual activity, or for her becoming submerged in a group of 'friends'. The importance of the hand is evident in the dream. When a small child begins to walk, his hand becomes, among other things, an instrument for the search of contact, or a buffer which protects him from being hurt on the face or the head. In contrast, the hand did not have that function in our patient, because she had projected into it an idealized relationship with a little girl who, at the same time, attacked her. This girl (an idealized sadistic aspect of herself) was the object that dominated her future, her fate. In the first session, she appeared in the shape of a skinny, skeleton-like classmate. She felt excluded from an oral primary scene. The orphan girl was the equivalent of the part of herself that, through voracity, envy, or jealousy, had killed the breast–hand by means of a dental attack, which later turned against herself and triggered her suicide attempt. The depressive elements (crying) are represented in the dream by means of rain (and by the mention of sweating in her account). The patient's anxiety before the persecutory object (the girl) is hidden under her friendly attitude.

Transferentially the therapist appears as an omniscient object. Irene's questions about the future of her treatment appear in the dream in the shape of answers. The question marks refer especially to her bond with this dissociated orphaned aspect. In her dream, as she identifies with the therapist, she lets this aspect into the consulting room. Nevertheless she fears that her gratitude and her dependence on the analyst may be used by the latter to gain absolute control over her will and her life. In other words, she panics at the thought of creating an addiction rather than a bond.

In a later session, during a painful moment in which she told about her self-destructive link with her mother, she uttered an exclamation in which she mentioned the therapist's name for the first time ('Ah, Isabel!'). Her exclamation is an appeal to the therapist to defend her against her inner self-destructive organization. She is like a child uttering the word 'Mother' to be protected. In addition, the fact that she is speaking the therapist's name implies a certain degree of discrimination of people and roles, of independent times and spaces. This allows the patient to gratify herself, at least occasionally, with the 'analytic breast'.

One Monday she related a dream:

'When my class-mate from the university stayed for dinner, my mother made chicken casserole and I was dreaming that I went to the kitchen at night and saw them inside two jars, a big one and a smaller one. Strange, because at home we don't make pickled chicken, only fish. I told my mother many times to put in more oil to preserve it from botulism.'

The patient struggles to prevent her psychoanalytic foods—interpretations from turning into something rotten (faeces). Previously she would transform food into faeces and illusorily feed on them. She degraded the analytic breast, transformed it into her own faeces as an idealized, omnipotent, and inexhaustible breast. At those times drugs played a certain role. Now we can observe the patient's struggle against bacilli (her self-destructive aspect) by means of a protecting liquid that permits the analytic food to withstand the passing of time and its resulting impatience. In addition, we can see those aspects of the patient that are not yet ready to defend the food received. The two jars—the breasts—represent at the same time the part of the patient that is capable of continence, of differentiation between the self and the others, between good and bad, between the inner and the outer world. We must remember that this patient had serious problems in her skin-to-skin contact, which compounded her difficulty to differentiate her self from the outer world (Bick, 1970).

In transference this differentiation emerges as a recognition of the difference between the analytic week (in which there was as equivalent to skin-to-skin contact) and the weekend (Zac, 1968).

In a later session she again referred to the problem of the inner self-destructive bond by means of a dream:

'I was going to a place for a massage and a very strange gym class, with a very strange character. I met a big man and he asked us if we wanted to visit the building. In each room there was a child with a physical handicap. A big one moved on his back, and I went with five small kittens. I couldn't find the smallest one; it always got away from me like Speedy Gonzalez.'

The massage and the gym class represent the concrete experience of the analytic treatment as a mother who surrounds her and holds her in her arms. The sensation of something strange and queer is the result of an incipient change in the way she perceives herself and the others, a consequence of the introjection of analytic experiences. The reference to the children with a physical handicap is related to the memories of her stay in a psychiatric hospital and the crises connected with that stage. She fears that these crises will be reactivated by the approaching separation from the therapist during the analytic holidays in February. She is, however, capable of controlling certain infantile aspects (five kittens). When she compares one of the kittens with Speedy Gonzalez—a mouse running away from a cat—she seems to be condensing both 'characters' from her inner world. They stand for the self-destructive relationship between one part of herself that impatiently attacks another part in an oral–sadistic dental fashion. This other part represents the analytic breast and her own infantile aspects, which are predisposed to development.

The increase in the patient's inner continence was evident in the frequency with which she described her dreams. These dreams expressed an implicit request for help, especially because the summer holidays were drawing near. The following dream is an example of this:

'This dream has to do with something I mentioned to my aunt and it was about a boat: the wind blows it against a rock and opens a seven-metre gash in it. It was a grounded boat that had to be turned over in order to be fixed. One of the people fixing it was my father, and another person, but it had to be turned over.'

The boat represents the patient struggling to repair herself and to avoid being psychotically shipwrecked for the rest of her life. The opening in the boat is equivalent to her inability for continence. The seven-metre gash refers to the fact that the year 1970 was beginning (the session is that of 2 January 1970). The number 7 also represents her anus, whose 'sphincter' was not yet properly regulating (at the mental level) her relationship with reality and the retention or supply of material depending on her own needs during the session. The fact that the boat has to be turned over is related to the patent's sensation that she has reversed her perception of reality and, at the same time, the sense of that reality. She had initially projected the future into her hand (which was really her past: the cuts), reversing the notion of temporality (past considered as future). Similarly, she attached an illusory reversed sense to her experiences. Now she felt that she (the ship) had to place herself again 'right side up' in order to overcome the risk of shipwreck. In addition, if she kept within the realm of illusion, she would be in constant danger of deterioration through increasing loss of her vital strength, which was escaping her like diarrhoea, together with her valuable objects. Respiratory and continent abilities are related to the sublimated genital function of the paternal penis (heir to the good breast), to which she can resort in search for help in the presence of the maternal figure which, at the moment, appears as the sign of her deterioration. She wishes to contain the analytic past as a good object, to take it with her to the future. In another sense, the grounded ship represents the patient at the time of her psychiatric confinement, when 'they made her a hole seven metres wide'.

Besides, her problems related to the discrimination of the erogenous zones begin to emerge. The hole in the ship represents the indiscriminated cloaca. The patient's inability to differentiate between her anal and vaginal openings is related to her difficulties to retain what she has incorporated and to learn from experience. The fact that the ship was being repaired is the indication that the patient's therapeutic dependence is beginning to appear. Nevertheless, the fact that the ship was still aground is due to her feelings that the separation over the summer holidays interrupted her treatment and left her without adequate resources to continue to navigate on her own. All this was compounded by her own anal self-destructive attacks (the rocks against which the ship crashes).

In mid-January she said:

'I am always dreaming about kittens. I remember that once we took a cat to the country, she had four kittens. She wanted to keep them all. She had them in a box. There was one that was very cold and I told her he would die. And when she went to take a bath he died in my hand and I cried a lot. Now I have dreamed again that I was with a lot of kittens or maybe baby mice, and only two were alive. When I held one, I lost the other. The kitten was very tiny, I could hold him in my hand. It had a fine skin, soft, very soft, like an otter, only much softer than an otter.'

The separation over the holidays was felt, on a very infantile level, as an absolute, final, and total loss of contact with the therapist. As was the case with the mother's skin, this feeling is expressed as coldness. This, in turn, originates a feeling of death due to the intensity of her aggressive attack on the containing object. The death of the object also entailed the death of the patient contained in it. This is the expression, in the treatment, of the patient's suicidal attacks to free herself from her aggressive inner mother. In addition, the dream once again shows the condensation and confusion between persecuted and persecutory objects, since she held in her hands a kitten and, at times, a mouse.

However, Irene cannot yet keep alive in her hands the two kitten–breasts. We may infer that during her childhood she had an elusive relationship with the maternal breasts, in the sense that, in making contact with one, she would lose the other. This initial instability must have been one of the factors that determined her intense greed to avoid the loss. This experience was one of the reasons that drove her into sexual promiscuity and drug addiction. She sought to compensate for coldness with alcohol and drugs—which provided glow and warmth of the skin—and with sexual embraces, since she could not tolerate the depression and hatred she felt when she was abandoned. She made up for her bodily sensation of emptiness by filling herself up with concrete objects, drugs.

Fantasies associated with drug use

I would like to enlarge upon the unconscious fantasies associated with drugs and drug use, and upon the pharmacological effects that intensify paranoid–schizoid and manic mechanisms (omnipotence, control, degradation, exaggerated dissociation, projective identification of ego-parts that create dissociation, and weakness in the ego).

In the case of another patient it was found that, at a given moment of the analytic process, he equated drug taking with the search for his dead grandfather. In a dream he looked for drugs in a drawer of his grandfather's desk. This was the drawer where he kept his valuables. When his grandfather was very ill, the drawer was used to keep the medicines he had to take during his long agony. The patient went to get the inanimate-dead (a pill), but he wanted to extract life-stimulation from that drawer in dark wood, which the patient himself associated with the colour of a coffin. From the inanimate he wants to extract stimulating effects that will trigger live reactions. This is an identification with the sick or dead object. The patient revived the dead object by means of his addiction to drugs and the fact that he took medicines just like his grandfather.

We must be aware of the danger involved in the possibility of suicidal doses taken as a result of this mechanism, for example during the anniversary of the death of a loved one. The reason for this is that, besides reintrojecting the dead object, the patient reintrojects his own hatred placed and dissociated in the object, which returns through the drug.

A different clinical case shows the symbolic meaning of drugs. This patient is a young adolescent, an active drug addict who got marijuana ('dope' or 'grass') in a place where hippie groups meet. In fact, the important thing is to obtain the drug in a specific place, behind the high walls of a cemetery. This represents the search for his father, who died very near that cemetery. A further warning: in this case the danger lies in the fact that, due to the guilt the patient feels over his infantile hatred of his father, he will end up identifying himself with the illness and behaviour of his father or looking for him underground in a psychotic fantasy of reencountering the lost object.

With respect to the first period of great confusion and perversion in their relation with drugs, other patients, who do not evolve as Irene did, show violent behaviour with intensely destructive acting out against the therapist, either inside or outside the session. If they find it impossible to stop this persistent behaviour, they usually give up treatment. In other patients, I was able to observe either an increase in mythomania, or its emergence, which can only be detected in transference as an exaggeration and modification of a story that seems to be true. The mechanism underlying this behaviour is an increase in projective identification, so that the story has a greater impact on the therapist.

While clearly under the effect of drugs, the patient may well claim that he has not taken drugs for a long time, or he may distort an actual event by omitting or exaggerating a detail.

Second stage:
use of an antidrug drug

During this stage Irene continued to take drugs, but with a special quality: she took a drug (Antabus), which was supposed to prevent her from taking drugs and alcohol. Irene persuaded the psychiatrist to give her the medication. This happened shortly before the holidays and was an attempt to keep near herself an analyst who will not forsake her and who will help her fight the drug. This was a transitional situation: the patient accepted and denied separation and dependence, struggled against drug addiction, and gave in to it. Irene remarked that the drug caused 'some lipothymia', which was the expression of her inner emptiness resulting from the loss of the breast–therapist. At the same time we find an indication of confusional anxieties leading her to feelings of estrangement (parts of the body image perceived as belonging to somebody else) and depersonalization (one part of the ego not recognized by another part as belonging to it). These were transient feelings which, to a certain extent, were already present in the preceding stage.

During the first session following the holidays, Irene mentioned that she was on a diet that enabled her to lose several kilos of excess weight. She told the analyst that she dreamed about José, a former lover who was a married man. In the dream he left on a ship, and she tried to commit suicide, to make him feel guilty.

(*Pause.*) 'My sister was late and there was a great fuss at home. Besides, I was a bit afraid to go out and meet José. By the way, one night during the Carnival I saw him get into his father's car, and his brother and his pregnant wife were also there. They had a boy.'

Then she mentioned her studies and a course she was taking on the problems of labour and of the female genital tract. She added:

'I never told anybody at home about my anguish. I wanted to manage on my own.'

Then she mentioned some friends she had lately found she disliked. She was trying to get away from them. She said:

'I prefer to go out with nice people, or with my uncles and aunts, but not with Federico. It is a gruesome relationship. . . . It's a bit like taking care of myself. Also, Federico attacked me with the death of Oscar, who committed suicide, which he knew upset me. Now Luisa, the girl I study with, she asked me if she could come. Well, if she really wants to study, it's OK, but sometimes she cries, and if you ask her something she bursts into tears.'

The first dream, in which José left on a ship, corresponds somewhat with the dream about the grounded ship the patient described before the holidays. We can understand now that the previous dream also represented an attack on the therapist–container (she was pregnant in Irene's fantasy), who took with her the father's penis and left her all alone. At all events she no longer tries to carry out the fantasies of suicide but rather dreams about them; that is to say, she has internalized a series of words (furnished by the interpretations) which, through the dream-work, become plastic images.

The patient's attempts to manage on her own are also significant. These are a consequence of her greater continence, so that when she talks about her things she does not do it in an expulsive way, as if trying to expel them out of her self. Previously her compulsive search for company had led her to damage herself in her relationship with other people. She was unable to assume a critical attitude towards others and herself, and thus protect herself, as if it were the same thing to feed on faeces or on the breast. Now, instead, she tends to select her friends better and tries to set up alarm signals (Freud, 1926d).

Through Luisa she expresses her doubts about letting herself be flooded by depression, or else trying to differentiate herself from the object over which she is mourning and thus have an independent life (Freud, 1917e).

A few sessions later, after saying that she had passed a very difficult examination for which she had prepared very carefully, Irene told about a dream:

'I was cleaning up the refrigerator. Mum is in the habit of keeping food bits and leftovers. I was cleaning and collecting all the leftovers in order. Mum always leaves a lot of saucers in the fridge because she cannot see them due to the tumour. Then I fixed things, one by one, about half of them, and there the dream ended.'

Later she went on:

'I took Antabus so as not to drink alcohol.'

And then:

'Last night several times I got up to drink milk, and two or three times it was sour and I couldn't stand it any more. Sour milk makes me sick. Father throws away all the leftovers, it's a bad habit of Daddy's. Mum fixes a meal, leaves it for the evening and Daddy finds it stale and throws it away.'

The weight-loss over the holidays might correspond to the inner order that Irene was attempting to make, as was the case in the dream about the refrigerator. She was trying not to be like her mother, who did not see the untidiness, and she was trying to tidy up her insides. This dream also represents her attempts at gathering together the dispersion of her self during the holidays, provided that the attempts take place within an adequate and nourishing container (refrigerator–treatment). These attempts seem to correspond to an effort to recognize and repair her own body. The numerous saucers appear as the various parts of the breast (with parts of Irene's self) which the patient was trying to discriminate. In this way she was attempting, as in the previous stage, to separate the rotten parts (faeces) from the real nourishment (the breast on which she depended). Success (passing an examination) turns into bitter triumph (sour milk), since, by succeeding, she has tried to give life to and repair her external mother. In view of her failure, this was equivalent to suckling from a breast with the meaning of faeces. Success was experienced as a manic triumph over the mother who dies to give her life.

We will later describe the patient's evolution in connection with the discrimination of the dying object.

Irene related 'two dreams with a clear interpretation'. In the first there were two women. The patient was in a gynecological ward. A woman's prolapse had to be closed.

'What I had said during the exam, only I did not know the name. Each professor gives it his own name, and the woman doctor asked me to be the one to close the vaginal opening. Well, I suppose it was like a part of the examination and, besides, my sexual part. (*Brief pause.*) Then there was an argument at home because I wanted to have my hair cut, and I can't make up my mind. This length is ugly. I like to wear it long, but this in-between length bothers me. In the second dream I dreamed that I had cut my hair around here, the opposite of where my mother has the tumour, because I saw her head shaved when she was operated on. My hair would not grow again, and there were scabs and I squeezed them and something white came out, as if my brain were coming out through a little opening . . . and then it was quite bald; in another place it grew.'

Later she added:

'Mum has urinary incontinence and prolapse'.

Later she associated:

'I have a problem with pee. At night I go to pee again and again: a few drops only, I go back to bed, and immediately I get up again, and every few minutes I have to get out of bed and go. When I do have a big pee I go to sleep like a baby goes to sleep after it has peed. I want to control myself, but I can't go to sleep. Before it didn't happen because I took Mandrax and fell asleep at once.'

Later she added that she wanted to stop dyeing her hair.

The patient's intolerance to retain her own contents at a urinary level is expressed in her speech, which is like an unending jet of urine. She needs to 'have a big pee' to feel relieved in her couch–cot and to be able to relax and express her feelings. Incontinence is also experienced as fantasies of miscarriage of a urinary pregnancy. These fantasies are correlated with the fantasies about the therapist's pregnancy during the holidays.

The dream about her hair is a reference to her partial identification with the mother with a tumour. If she cuts her hair–tumour, there is no longer a problem, it will not grow again. She fears the tumour will grow again and invade or kill her, and she will thus remain identified with her mother. When the patient mentions her short hair, she is in fact referring to the attempts she made, when she identified with her mother, to remove the tumour from her own head in a pathological attempt at reparation and in a splitting of the dying object. She asks for the therapist's help to close up the prolapse (the opening in the grounded ship). This would be an attempt to know and repair her own insides by recovering the possibilities of learning sphincter-control and, at the same time, to discriminate the objects contained inside her, and also her inside and her outside.

Her reference to hair is connected with the wish for contact by means of the skin. In this case, hair represents her repaired (gratified) skin. On the other hand, the unrepaired part is represented by the half of her head with scabs, from which a white substance is oozing out, as if through this substance she were losing her brain. This part corresponds to the aspect of the patient that has not yet worked through the mourning over the object she is losing, plus the aspects of her own self that are being lost with it.

A few sessions later the patient said:

'I'm afraid: now that Aunt Matilde is gone, my phobias are coming back. When she is there my parents don't argue, and there is peace. It was a peaceful week because of my Aunt's presence.'

Describing other periods of her life, she added:

'Sometimes I'm afraid to go home, a phobia of how I'll find my house, which takes me back to the time when I was seventeen. The two [father and mother] had bigger fights than these; these are over money problems, they argue over the gas bill and every day they complain more. I told Daddy: "You're getting old." All those things upset me, I wish I had a calmer home.'

Later she continued:

'This is the first year I have studied at home. Whenever there is someone else in between my phobia disappears, and now my phobia appears, Matilde should go and everything be as before.'

Later she said:

'As my father was a travelling salesman, we used to live at my Aunt Matilde's. I have the image of Mother and Mariana [the patient's younger sister], whom they took to the paid wet-nurse. It was enough to leave my Aunt's house for the harmony to be broken. I never wanted to ride in the car with them. But before I used to be Daddy's pet, like the little dog is now. From the time before my sister was born I remember they got on well together; I used to sleep with Aunt Maria. The paternal house was big, about a quarter block. There we spent eight years of Mother's marriage. The day they were nursing my sister was always a cause for uneasiness.'

Then she said that she gave Mariana some chemistry lessons. She taught her a 'mother formula'. Then she added:

'Mariana was always very sickly, with eczema all over her body and boils. At eight months she talked like a parrot, just like now. They told her: "Turn off the radio." But she had a deficit in her motor faculties.'

This material begins with a reference to an attempt to reestablish the usefulness of the anxiety signal. Her mention of Aunt Matilde refers to the patient's wish to interpose between herself and the object that makes urgent demands on her (dental oral sadism) another object, which will act as a protection. In other words, she tries to interpose an ability for delay she hopes will contain the impatience of the object which up to now had victimized her. We find here an attempt to elaborate the function of the hand, which serves as a buffer against invasion by other objects, or against falls. The recovery of the hand function is particularly important to the extent that the hand had appeared as closely connected with the idealized object and to its attacks (the breast).

Mariana represents a part of the patient that experienced the pathological link between the parents in a way similar to hers: lack of skin-to-skin contact (eczema), verborrhage (in which she equates speech with urine), and, like herself, a deficit in the motor faculties that might have allowed her to put a distance between herself and the home, and to become independent from pathological and frustrating objects. Irene's knowledge of the formula with which her mother used to react appears in the expression she uses to describe what she explained in chemistry (the mother formula). The reference to her frustrating way of feeding herself (pathological introjection with greed, hatred, and distrust) seems to be related to a nursing period with ambivalent feelings and a constant fear of being abandoned.

Nevertheless the material about the paternal house contains a reference to moments in which she felt partially contained by the mother who, in turn, was gratified by the father. We can find here a motivation for the crisis that triggered the addiction, since at that time the father was less able to face his wife's difficulties. As a consequence, during this period the father did not act as a protective penis between her and her mother. To the extent that, through analytic treatment, the patient can recover a reparatory internal parental couple in which the father plays the role of protector, Irene's vital experiences will become more satisfactory.

Third stage:
recovery of protecting inner objects,
exclusive use of sedatives

As we have seen during the preceding stage, Irene's ability to ask for and receive therapeutic help increased. This was evinced by a change in the drug situation. She began to take only sedatives, and only when she felt that anxiety overwhelmed her. However, in dealing with drug addicts, it is important not to be deceived, and to detect the sadistic use of drug taking, whatever the drug used. The drug is identified with destructive objects which, once taken, persecute the ego and the good objects. Besides, the pharmacological-toxic effect is used to strengthen the power of destructive impulses against external objects which turn against inner objects and the ego itself (H. Rosenfeld, 1965). In some clinical cases the sedative can serve, for example, to lull and dissociate a part of the ego, so that the patient does not feel either pain or anxiety over his destructive orgy. For this reason, it is important to remember that every patient who takes drugs functions with an exaggerated dissociation and, thus, in the course of treatment, the analyst must be prepared to detect 'what he does not bring', which is often constituted by acting out or suicidal fantasies.

At these times our patient resorted to sedatives as an equivalent of the therapist's function when, for various reasons, the latter was not sufficient to her. This also showed that the degree of her disorganization had markedly decreased, and that the analytic relationship had a tranquillizing quality, similar to the one the patient longed for during the previous stage, when she referred to the times of family peace in her childhood. During this period the patient was still struggling to achieve that inner 'family peace', but, by means of her motility, she could now search elsewhere and independently for what she could not find near her primary objects.

During a session following a holiday, Irene said:

'Mother asked me why I had her operated on, and cried all over me.'

She added:

'I have a terrible cold. I lay down on Norberto's bed when he got up. Mother hits the roof, but the relationship with Daddy is getting better and better and the problem I have now is that my hand trembles.'

'And last night I had a dream. I dreamed I was looking for a doll, a Topo Gigio.'

Later she added:

Ah, another thing I did was to show the room upstairs. First I told Norberto not to tell Esteban about seeing the room upstairs, but he knows that I keep it nice and I showed it to him, but he did not say anything. Every day I get up at seven and go to bed at midnight: that's why I've been hiding the trembling when I eat for the last four days.'

Then she added:

'I was anxious to come. . . . I lay down for a nap and the first hour I could not sleep, but then I could.'

Then she went on:

'I'm afraid to have to study at home. About the hand, I was actually carrying something very heavy in it. . . . Oh, I know, my mother had prepared things to eat at the boys', a big package like this: I also bought a buzzer, a colander, and in the other hand I was carrying an old round picture frame painted white for a mirror, and it was too much to carry. Oh, and some nights I got up to eat.'

Later she said:

'And another thing I did with this hand was to paint what I like, something that at home they think is sick, because at that time I used to paint shelves.'

The session shows that the patient has taken another step in her wish towards inner self-continence and also shows her possibilities and limitations to achieve this. She is making efforts to find inner objects that are capable of lessening the impact of her pathological relationship with her mother. For this reason she seeks the protection of masculine objects that can help her work through the pain over the loss of her mother. The reference to the trembling of her hand is related to her attempt to transform it again into an object serving her self-preservation, and to the difficulties she had in doing this.

The fear of studying at home has to do with primitive experiences of feeling ambivalently nourished within the endogamic group. The search for other companions and other environments is an attempt to repair what she could not do during her childhood, that is to say, to have sufficient independence to gratify herself in other areas, using, for this purpose, her striated motoricity. In other cases, the fact that patients who used to take drugs individually and alone now take them in groups sometimes indicates change.

The fact that she showed the little room upstairs (the mind) has to do with the sensation of being more repaired and in a condition that bears observation from others, with its valuable and beautiful qualities.

The dream I have just described has a very special value. The figure of Topo Gigio, towards the end of this period and especially during the following one, incorporates multiple meanings. Therefore I discuss this aspect when dealing with the following stage.

Fourth stage:
disappearance of drug addiction
and emergence of a transitional and accompaning object

About this time Irene bought a Topo Gigio, a toy mouse-doll, which replaced the drug at times of anxiety, especially when she went to bed at night and during weekends.

This is an intermediary object, alive and dead at the same time, but more reparable, since it is a doll that can be looked after, rather than a drug. Through this toy the patient gratifies her need to make contact with a silky and warm object onto which she simultaneously projects her own conflictive parts: the toy expresses someone else's opinions, and is manipulated by strings moved by somebody else's hands. This is the way the patient felt at times owing to therapeutic dependence, experienced as slavery. Inasmuch as she did not feel that she was voicing her own opinions, she could not gratify herself totally because she was unable to ask for things. Moreover, the purchase of the Topo Gigio was an indication that, to a certain extent, the patient was beginning to discriminate this conflictive aspect of herself and to overcome it.

The following material belongs to this stage. The patient begins to talk about a 'rather unpleasant' acquaintance with 'grotesque features', extremely obese and with a 'big bosom':

'One could tell that she was a girl who had had many conflicts in the past.'

Then she added:

'We were eating at home and we saw the little dog appear, the sign that Daddy had come to lunch, and it turned out that it was his birthday and I had forgotten all about it. My father was terribly nice to Norberto, he was euphoric about the partridges. They sent me to the garage for soda water and I had an ugly shock when I saw three gutted hares, which reminded me of the times when I used to go hunting with Father. The lazybones would shoot from the car and send me

off to fetch the partridge, and I learnt to shoot with Daddy
when I was very young. I remember once he shot at a hare,
and when I picked it up it pissed, because it was relaxed and
we had to hit it on the muzzle to kill it. Then I learnt to make
them escape. While I was walking I would make a little noise;
like this. (*She reproduces it.*) When we went to Cordoba I did
not want them killed and I never said anything. I just walked
on, stepping noisily or else I would whistle softly to scare
them away.'

The patient's vital potentialities are connected to the fantasy of
rebirth of personal aspects that had remained undeveloped for a
long time. This is symbolized by the father's birthday. The obese
girl represents the patient herself when she used to resort to
drug addiction, compulsive eating, drinking, and genital hyper-
excitement, as a defence against pathological mourning. As we
now understand it, at that time, through her own constantly
growing tissues, she had tried to recapture the firmness of the
breast lost during infancy, a loss that was revived in the presence of her mother's increasing deterioration. In addition, when
the patient talks about the gutted hares, she is also alluding to
her female castration anxiety. She begins to feel phobic anxieties about heterosexuality, about the penis, to the extent that
the latter appears as identified with an expulsive organ, shooting faeces–bullets that destroy her inside. When she says that at
one time she learned to shoot with her father, she is referring to
her previous identification with the persecutor, a defence she
resorted to in periods previous to the analysis, when she was
functioning as an object that destructively attacked the envied
and fertile inside of others (remember the dream of the
grounded ship, for example). Now, on the contrary, she tries to
defend her own fertile parts and to resort to the anxiety signal
in order to protect herself. We can place along these lines her
references to how she whistled to get the hares to escape—the
hares representing her own womb and the feminine condition of
fecundity that begins to emerge as a result of the analytic process. At the same time, it represents the part of herself that
accepts her need for other people and is able to have adult relationships of dependence or interdependence.

We can also suppose that, at this time, the patient sees in the therapist the figure of her potentially dangerous father (the therapist, hunter of fantasies), before whom she must make 'little noises' to overcome danger in the face of the penis–gun. This reveals an increase in her anxieties about the transference. In fact, as her treatment progressed, Irene developed new latent tendencies towards a closer approach to the therapist as a penis (heir to the breast on which she depended). This circumstance aroused strong phobic anxieties in her. The working-through of these anxieties led to new changes and to the fifth stage in her analysis.

Fifth stage:
the present stage

After several years of treatment, the patient has begun to shake hands on coming in and out of the session. This is an indication that she is much more capable of accepting that she is the aggressive individual who attempts to attack and destroy the hand–breast of the therapist with her dental oral-sadistic fantasies (remember the dream at the beginning of the treatment about the razor-blade that cuts the hand). If she can recognize these fantasies, it is because she can also look after the object better. She also recognizes time and space limits, because shaking hands in coming in and going out after the session implies leaving behind the magic omnipotent belief that sessions are never-ending. Shaking hands implies accepting that she must do it not only when coming in, but also when going out. In this context, one of the interpretations that the therapist repeated was that she was able better to withstand the pain of parting, as well as the anxieties connected with their meeting again. Earlier she used to come to the sessions with the fantasy of having an idealized omnipotent breast, made up by the drug she was carrying inside. At that time no one left her. Now, shaking hands also implies that she was able to gratify herself through skin-to-skin contact with the therapist. Before this, the patient was identified with her frustrated infantile aspect in the presence of an emotionally remote mother, whom she attacked in an oral–sadistic way. Not shaking hands implied her inability to feel needed: she did not have to receive or steal anything from anybody, since she herself—by means of her drugs—had everything that was valuable and desirable. The aspect of herself that is able to receive the maternal breast (the analyst's hand) into her mouth (the patient's hand) and take what the breast offers emerges during this period.

Other remarks

Throughout this chapter we can detect fantasies related to drug-taking and to the body image. It is of interest to detect these fantasies in patients, since this allows us to diagnose the evolutive period and the seriousness of the case, and thus to determine which of the five stages the patient has reached. If we determine that a patient is in the first stage, our interpretation will be along technical and even medico-legal lines, different from the one used in the case of a patient who is going through the third stage.

We have also seen how certain signs allow us to establish the seriousness and prognosis of the case: using drugs as a container, through skin sensations, is sometimes less serious and entails a better prognosis than other cases, in which, through drugs, the patient creates an autistic and psychotic world— where the characteristic sensations of this stage are favoured. Even these cases are less serious than those in which the drug addict resorts to intravenous injections, which is characteristic of patients who function within the primitive psychotic body image and lack the notion of skin, the arteries and the veins being their body limits.

I would like to emphasize again the importance of considering these evolutionary stages in drug-addicted patients. In order to make an accurate diagnosis and prognosis and efficient interpretations, the therapist must determine which of the five stages the patient has reached.

Body image, inanimate objects, and drug abuse

I deem it necessary to enlarge on the study of the primitive psychotic body image in addictions. I refer particularly to those patients who, using syringes, intravenously inject drugs into their blood-stream. Besides seeking the effect of the drug itself, those patients inject a liquid into a body they feel empty of blood. One of the main pleasures they attempt to get is to feel a renewed shock or stimulus in their blood-stream, which makes them feel that their heart and arterial walls do exist and, therefore, that their bodies are not empty of liquids. The fantasies that accompany the act of intravenous drug-injection may be explained by the primitive psychotic body image theory.

I found these hypotheses particularly beneficial, because through them I was able to gain insight into adolescent addicts. The significant fact is that certain groups of addicts do not use drugs requiring intravenous injection but feel a need to fill their veins with liquids, such as saline solution, nasal drops, liquefied analgesics, or other euphoriants. Such observation allows us to infer that these patients are not seeking pleasure in the drug itself, but in filling their veins with 10 or 20 square centimeters of liquid and, thus, feel their arteries and heart pounding (a patient referred to the pleasure of feeling a sort of shock when the drug reached his heart).

It is very useful to consider these hypotheses, for, in this case, drug-taking is not due to oral voracity. If the analyst's interpretation is focused on oral voracity, he will probably attain no therapeutical effect, whereas I believe that changes will occur if the analyst interprets the fantasies related to the PPBI. From the technical point of view, this hypothesis has led to useful results, because these patients feel themselves empty; they want to fill themselves with liquids (and in this way they express the psychotic body image notion). In connection with these cases I consider it ineffective (or useless from the technical point of view) to make a theoretical conceptualization related to orality or skin sensations. Neither the idea of the erogenous zone nor that of the skin as a body limit exists in these patients, but only the notion of a body full or empty of such liquids. Hence their need to inject themselves.

I want to take this opportunity to mention another characteristic I have observed in certain groups of addicts. Sometimes gangs require candidates to show that their arms are pricked as a condition of becoming a member of the group. Gang members usually inject themselves in groups, sharing the same syringe. In these ritual situations, there is always a fantasy of creating blood bonds, through blood mingling. This idea is similar to that of the blood pacts that were very frequent in medieval secret sects and in fraternal orders of the Romantic era.

That is why it is often useless and ineffective to suggest to these groups that they take hygienic measures to prevent the spreading of disease. These patients lack the notion of future, danger, or death; they are interested only in belonging to a group joined by blood bonds, and they are ready to do anything in order not to be left alone and alienated.

The indiscrimination of the identity of these patients includes perturbed and distorted notions of their own body image, with an evident lack of limits between their own body and that of the therapist.

The management of an addicted patient is particularly difficult because the analyst is dealing not only with a specific picture, but also with the combination of a mental state and the intoxication and confusion derived from drug use. Due to this danger, it is important to define better the states of confusion in clinical practice. These states can be found in a range of patients, from those who are decaying, in the most extreme cases, to those who evince the same clinical picture, because their psychopathological mechanisms are nearer to borderline cases. In these patients we observe predominant confusional anxieties, oneiric states from which they cannot emerge, residual states of intoxication, and vital crises handled in a chronic way. It is of particular interest to study this last topic in the psychoanalitic clinic with patients who seem to manage good neurotic mechanisms but later start to evince confusional mechanisms (e.g. because of withdrawal or the set-in of menopause); these states can also be observed in the vital crises suffered by young people, e.g. before getting married.

The lack of a limit to their body image is correlative to those mental states. Now I believe that we can interpret both the mental state and the disorder and lack of limits of the self, as expressed through the lack of limits to the body image.

The choice of a favourite drug coincides with the choice of a part of the body as an erogenous zone, used for the administration of the drug. Patients usually 'create'—delimit—a part of the body as an erogenous zone, which behaves as such and is physiologically determined, even if it does not function according to neurotic or normal standards.

I want to stop here to consider these psychological sensations in greater detail. They are very important because they coincide with the patients' personal experience of the self in which they show how their body image functions. It is important to remember that only some, not all, patients express their deepest and most intense personal experiences through the plastic manifestations of their body image.

This psychological sensation 'of being empty or of being a total vacuum' is based on the notion of an 'empty', 'bloodless', 'organless' body image, and sometimes a body 'having merely an enveloping shell'.

We soon realize that these concrete experiences are traits of what I have called the 'primitive psychotic body image' (D. Rosenfeld, 1988; see also chapter eight). As I said, acute psychotic crises appear in patients who believe they are being drained of blood or are completely bloodless.

The image or notion that the body contains nothing but liquids or blood and is enveloped by one or more arterial or venous walls is the extreme limit of what may be called the primitive psychotic body image. These walls carry out the psychological task that the real skin, the muscles, and the skeleton should perform. In episodes of acute psychosis, the experience of draining of blood and being emptied corresponds to the breakdown of this psychological image of a wall or membrane containing liquid or blood. In those cases there are not even arterial walls, which were the ultimate containers of the PPBI. Thus, blood seems to be the ultimate limit of the body representation when the arterial or venous walls, which replaced the external skin, are broken. Sometimes this 'emptying-out' is linguistically expressed in a fast, uncheckable way of speaking, in a true 'verbosity' in which the voice of the patient overlaps the therapist's (see chapter eleven). The notion of 'liquids that spread out' is a material frequently found in schizophrenic patients when they express feelings of being emptied out at the level of the primitive psychotic body image. This emptying-out is at a narcissistic level, it does not appear through an erogenous zone, but through all pores of the body image.

Drug addiction and inanimate links

In psychotic patients with serious disturbances in the early object relation with their mothers, we realized that their link with living objects is not stable, because living objects are confused with inanimate objects. This pathological relation is based on the fact that the patient considers all objects as inanimate objects. This is one of the characteristics of a psychotic patient's object relations. The physical relation, the skin-to-skin contact with their mother is so disturbed, so vitiated, so spurious and bizarre, that the patient is indifferent to whether he is with a warm-skinned mother or with an inanimate lifeless object (drugs, for instance, are inanimate).

Some babies reject the breast; they prefer to suck their thumbs. This mental organization reappears in the transference when the patient prefers the drug to the therapist's nourishment. It is interesting to observe that, at a deeper level, the parts of the parents' body, or sexual objects, are considered as a part of the body of an inanimate object, which can be possessed, owned, or used (Dufresne, 1990).

There is a wide variety of patients who function within this primitive mental pattern, from schizophrenics and some drug addicts to the more organized extreme: psychopaths who take others as objects that they can use and dominate at will.

This somewhat complicated explanation is useful to attempt a more extensive re-approach to the genetic evolution of drug-addicted patients and, specifically, to the origin and history of their relations with inanimate objects.

When the addict starts his fifth treatment stage, he is ready to analyse the structures that underly drug addiction, those that, due to the previous failure in their attempt to achieve intrapsychical balance, gave rise to addiction.

As I already mentioned from a technical point of view, at this fifth stage we are no longer dealing with the analysis of the addiction itself, which now becomes a relevant subject rather than a basic acting out. We find, instead, that the patient becomes an individual with a psychology that evinces the neurotic and/or psychotic traits usually found in psychoanalytic treatment.

It is of the utmost importance to take into consideration the addict's physical relation with the analyst, with the consulting-room couch and furniture. As we have already stated, pieces of furniture may give us some guidelines about the patient's relations with inanimate objects. Furthermore, affective relations expressed through gestures or words are as important as their body image fantasies, for they express, in another language, what occurs in the self.

In other patients, the approach to the therapist is more complex: for example, the patient may show hatred and more violent aggression during the session, but may later come to acknowledge that someone helped him through difficult moments. This change in the relation is a hint that he is recovering the good parts of the therapist. In all these cases there is a real willingness on the patient's part to accept the analyst as an independent being whom he has sought with the purpose of obtaining help, with all the conflicts implicit in a therapeutic relation.

The patient plans for the future on a more realistic basis, which implies becoming objective towards his past whenever the future forces him to ask himself what he will be and what he was. Lacan (1966) claims that what evolves in the history is not the past that was, but, rather, the future antecedent to what will have been and what will be. The personal history is not what was or what has been accomplished, but rather the future perfect, what the patient will have been in relation to what he will be in the future. Lacan (1966) also refers to time dialectics, following Heidegger and Husserl's ideas. Even though at this stage there is no addiction to drugs proper, we may observe some vicissitudes similar to those characteristic of the period of active drug addiction or intake.

In fact, when treating an addict for several years, we usually detect some traits—'addiction equivalents'—which can sometimes be disguised as habits. At present I believe that the term 'addiction equivalent' is a true clinical finding. It is very useful in the analysis of and research on patients who temporarily give up drugs, but in whom we can detect an 'addicted' relation with certain objects the patient cannot do without: food, drink, inanimate objects, the need to pay in instalments. An unbridled voracity in connection with any kind of task may be another 'equivalent'.

When supervising students, it is actually useful and fascinating to follow this course, this guideline or clue for research. This phenomenon can also be observed in obese patients who, especially during periods of weight loss, buy objects and become workaholics, instead of experiencing vital, real things.

I further insist upon the importance of detecting manic defence mechanisms, whether in their aspects connected with denial of persecution, idealization, and denial of depressive anxieties, or in their destructive, triumphant, and derogatory ones, which, through the guilt they arouse, force a reintrojection of the destroyed or dead object, as well as of the sadistic and aggressive parts of the self, through drug use.

David Liberman (1970–72) has traced a correlation between impulsiveness, drug addiction, and defence against depressive affects. He states:

> The impulsive nature of perversions gives rise to the type of transference relation commonly observed in the various psychopathic pictures and in other forms of neurotic impulsions. In this group we may include patients who have certain habits which, in the particular case of pharmacothymia, involve the handling and use of external objects, from alcohol and intravenous morphine to coffee and tobacco, for defensive purposes aiming at blocking depressive affects or pain in certain situations. . . . How can we detect the impulsive nature of something? Because the patient sees it as urgent. An addict does not go to the cinema like everybody else, but rather feels an

irrepressible impulse to go to the cinema, and even reproaches himself later for his addiction to films. An impulsive action is geared by an irrepressible urge to do something 'pleasant'. For our purposes, impulsion refers both to sexual perversions and to drug addiction, as well as to cases denoting certain types of antisocial behaviour.

What some addicts are seeking, through the pharmacological effect of drugs, is to achieve a certain vasodilation, sensations of warmth, and a glow of the skin as an attempt to recreate a container in the form of the skin in moments of extreme fragmentation. This is the sensorial world of the autistic patient, who creates objects through sensations that are not object relations (Tustin, 1990); these are bodily sensations that represent the patient's own world. In this way he attempts to restore a link with primitive lost objects, associated with sensations and fantasies involving the skin and the air. But the attempt is carried out in such a destructive and envious manner (with rejection of the dependence on the real external object, such as the analyst) that the result is a container that is destroyed from the outset or will not survive for long, and a vicious circle is created.

Why does an addict use drugs? It is because drugs enable him to interrelate physical sensations, sometimes representing object relations. As a last resort, sometimes he is attempting to achieve unity through a very precarious organizer, that is, a drug that functions as a poor-quality paste or glue but represents a real striving to find something which will provide a structure. This is similar to the use of precocious pseudo-sexuality in certain cases where this also functions as a poor-quality glue, as well as, for example, in the case of certain types of perversion, nymphomania, promiscuity, and so on.

The addict has gone through a highly pathological paranoid–schizoid phase with a particularly exaggerated and violent splitting and projective identification. For fear of relapsing into hatred and envy, he is thus prevented from re-introjecting and assimilating the helpful aspects of his own self which were previously expelled, together with sensory impressions. Consequently, he is prevented from establishing the firm basis of good objects on which the growth of the ego depends.

My experience of certain drug-addicted and psychotic patients, as well as of some psychotic adolescents, has shown me
how drugs are used to eliminate any early signs of depressive
anxiety, which is thereby dissociated and expelled. The effect of
drugs is to help a very weak ego to effect a very special form of
splitting and so to escape from the intolerable depressive
anxiety, and the associated suffering and guilt (H. Rosenfeld,
1987).

The result is that the addict sometimes functions in a chronic
state, in which he cannot either break down in psychosis or
manage to tolerate the depressive anxiety and, hence, to believe
in the possibility of reparation and care. I would add that this
does not apply to frank psychotic or neurotic states, but to a
state in which the patient is like a robot or zombie, as one of my
patients described herself, or like 'Frankenstein'.

Linguistically, we can see how drug addicts adopt a way of
speaking that is neither dead nor alive, repeating certain words
in a mechanical, fetishist, robot-like way. These words fulfil the
function of an object that is neither dead nor alive, or of a precarious integrative nipple.

The addict often uses a pivotal word to express reality, just as
linguistically we may speak of pivotal verbs and nouns. It may
not always be a word; it may be a gesture, a whistle, a recurring
phrase used as a drug through which the patient tries to articu-
late and organize his mind.

The manner of speaking, which sometimes appears neither
dead nor alive, is often in a low metallic voice, measured and
sepulchral, revealing the projection of panic, while the voice is
allowed to rise, as if it were a sphincter being tightened through
fear of being drained into the air. The same applies to breaking
wind, defecation, or blowing of the nose, which may become
really terrifying acts when the addict is not able to avoid them.

The way of dealing with air is of particular importance. It is a
primitive object, which can be expelled violently (as well as
introjected). At a level of greater abstraction we could relate this
to a projective identification of persecutory objects and of the
parts of the self associated with them. If what is expelled is a
defined part-object, we can conceptualize it as having succeeded
in using the mechanism of dissociation. This is one example of

how, from clinical observation of the way of dealing with air in drug addicts, we can progress to theoretical levels of greater abstraction.

According to Piaget (1926), pivotal words are found in children from the age of 32 months. As I have said, the repetition of certain pivotal words functions in the addict as a bad glue, an ineffectual way of organizing self and reality. Sometimes there is no break between words. It is rather like a piece of chewing-gum, which can be stretched indefinitely, something sticky or elastic. It is difficult to see where one word ends and the next begins. In this it is possible to discern the lack of limits. There is a further characteristic, which is that when they are extremely confused, addicts tend to use verbs only in the infinitive: this is an indication of a state of depersonalization, in which even at the linguistic level there is a transformation into something non-personal, neither dead nor alive. There is also a failure to discriminate between subject and object, between past, present, and future, as well as between different verbal moods (subjunctive, imperative, etc.), with their different meanings. This indicates a deeper, confusional anxiety underlying the style of speech.

Insofar as the function of time is concerned, drugs have one very specific characteristic. According to Bleger (1967), it is characteristic of perversions to last for a limited period, during which the patient gets rid of the psychotic part through a perverse act and is then left with the more neurotic part, which can function in a more or less organized manner. In the same way, drugs can at certain times fulfil a similar function, to the extent that many addicts try to find a drug which will have an effect for a limited, measurable time. This is of the greatest importance, and I have seen it in patients who smoke marijuana, in particular. They choose marijuana or other drugs on account of a fantasy in which marijuana is perceived as a container into which they can discharge their sadism, perversions, and the search for something magical or idealized, but only for a given time. During this period under the influence of the drug, there is a violent expulsion of the psychotic part. After a limited period of discharge, as in the case of perversion, the addict often experiences relief in the neurotic part of his personality.

My experience in the past few years with patients who use cocaine, crack, hashish, heroine, iris tea, Brazilian mushrooms and cacti from the north of Argentina or Mexico, has led me to understand that they use it in their phantasies for a limited period of time and in a limited setting. Mushrooms called 'cocumelos' are infused with tea or coffee; they are usually sold in the streets during the carnival in Brazil. A very common cactus, called 'San Pedro' or 'San Pedrito', is infused like tea; it is usually found in the North of Argentina and in Bolivia. In Mexico, one of the cactuses used for this purpose is called 'peyote'.

Clinical example:
Cocaine patient: Philip

I will now give examples of the above using some excerpts of clinical material from a 40-year-old addict, whom we shall call Philip. This patient started treatment with me in 1982, and, after a break of approximately two years, he resumed analysis. One year after resuming therapy, he brought a highly emotional and significant piece of material, with the following characteristics: he was able to verbalize the deep sorrow, the psychic pain, and the true suffering he felt on account of the death of one of his daughters and his younger brother in an accident before he started therapy, as well as the death of his father. This patient, just like his brother, used to drive his car at speeds of some 140 miles per hour.

It was very important for the patient to discover that it was difficult for him to tolerate such profound pain, and he even realized that during the whole treatment he had hardly ever mentioned the name of his daughter Florence.

On that occasion, my intervention consisted in pointing out to him that he was only now able to mention his daughter's name, her death, and her burial, in a deeply moved voice, which I had never heard him use before. Towards the end of that session, and also in a highly emotional tone, which was quite unusual for him, he said: 'Maybe you are right, maybe I take cocaine to feel stimuli, to get wound up and not to feel dead as my daughter and my brother. . . .' Then he added: 'But what I do know is that if I go over the daily doses, it causes isolation, I do not tune in and I abandon myself, and thus I get on very badly with my son, little Philip'. I must point out that this son, whom the patient had named after him, sometimes represented his own growing infantile aspects.

Isolation

Throughout years of treating addicted patients, on many occasions I have listened to similar reports, referring to the search for intense and peculiar effects by taking cocaine. Actually, many of these patients are seeking isolation—a sort of capsule that envelops them, causing a feeling of isolation, which prevents them from tuning in, from communicating with the other person. Philip is one of the patients who best managed to describe the cocaine-induced effects that he was attempting to obtain.

Effects sought with cocaine

Philip had gone through three well-differentiated stages in drug use: The first stage corresponds to the time in which he smoked marijuana and sniffed cocaine when he was younger, together with his brother; this was the brother who later died while driving a car at high speed. The usual, most frequent circumstance was taking marijuana at some sex party with one, two, or three women he shared with his brother. The second stage came after his father died and consisted in the use of LSD on two or three occasions, also together with his brother. Philip's father also died in a car accident, while driving at high speed, a few years before his brother died. The third stage came after his brother's death and corresponded to the frequent and massive use of cocaine. It is worth noting that during the first years of his therapy with me, drug addiction was not a central problem for the patient; rather, he considered that the problem was a source of concern only for the analyst (Joseph, 1960; Krakov, 1987).

On certain occasions, when I interpreted some material or dream related to mourning, the patient would irritatedly answer that 'everything that happened was not necessarily due to mourning', thus suggesting that I change and interpret something funnier. This is, on the other hand, an answer typical of the manic defense of an addicted patient.

The cocaine doses increased at the same pace as his marital problems, which resulted in divorce. Regarding the *increase in the doses,* I believe it is important to point out a key aspect. Consumption of increasingly large doses seems to be due to the patients' need to obtain bodily and psychic sensations to feel they exist, to feel they are alive and not dead. This applies to patients who identify with dead objects, or are undergoing periods of pathological mourning, as in Philip's case. For example, when he raced his car, it was usual for me to interpret that he was trying to feel as his father or brother had felt before dying, and Philip would make a reference that confirmed my interpretation. Many times he would risk his life or need to have an extreme experience of the limit between life and death in order to feel that he was alive. This means that if he managed to survive a risky, dangerous situation, such as walking along a high cornice, driving fast or taking large doses of drugs, he felt he was alive and not dead, like his father and brother. It seemed to be a resuscitation, a sort of victory over death.

When in 1988 Philip exhumed his daughter's body, he discovered with great sadness, for the first time, what he actually was covering up with drugs. He said: 'Maybe you are right, maybe I take cocaine to feel stimuli, to get wound up and not to feel dead as my daughter and my brother. But what I do know is that if I go over the daily doses, it causes isolation. I do not tune in and I abandon myself, and thus, I get on very badly with my son, little Philip.' There is an excessive disconnection (autistic capsule) with his infantile self.

Threshold Stimuli

We may infer that the patient needs the stimuli and the feelings of anxiety and fear to be extreme, so that he may overcome a threshold and be able to feel 'something'; because these great stimuli make him feel alive. I must point out that this is a sensorial world similar to that of autistic children.

I repeat this key notion, as it is of great clinical significance: *This type of patient seeks stimuli to feel alive, but those stimuli must overcome an extremely high threshold, which normal or neurotic people cannot even conceive.* This behaviour is beyond the understanding of many people, who cannot even think of such perturbed and mysterious workings of the mind. These patients seek the maximum, the extreme limit, for the sole purpose of feeling 'something': be it fear, anxiety, panic, terror, or apparently pleasant sensations in orgies with drugs and alcohol, where their main goal is always to feel 'something'. The threshold or barrier to be overcome by the stimuli is such that some psychoanalysts do not believe it possible. Some patients do not perceive the warning signs of suicidal risks, even if this has been interpreted to them.

My clinical experience in the treatment and supervision of seriously disturbed patients has taught me that this search for danger arises from two particular motives:

1. Certain patients have no prospective notion; they cannot conceive in their minds the idea of the future. The defects in their logical relations are so severe that they damage the logical connection between cause and effect. This is the reason why they can drive a car at top speed or walk along a cornice without realizing the risk involved. These situations are perceived as dangerous only by those (normal or neurotic) people who have a notion of the future and know that a certain cause may well produce a certain effect, because their logical train of thought includes causative relations. For example, during the first year of a child's life, it is usual for the baby to realize that the breast, the mother with her caresses, smells, warmth, and voice, goes away and then returns and, through this experience, to learn the meaning of presence and absence, present and future; because this is the basic and essential way of learning a sequence from which the child manages to conceive the passage of time—the past, the present, and the future. Now and then, certain very disturbed patients have not had this experience in their childhood and, therefore, have not managed to build this mental

notion of the future or the passage of time. It is as if they were children who throw an object into the air and cannot imagine that later that object will fall back down upon them. I have observed this during the treatment of psychotic children, who cannot conceive that their mother goes away and comes back later. The space–time notion and the notion of return and future are learnt simultaneously.

2. Certain patients are surrounded by a thick armour, as Tustin (1986) points out for autistic children, whom she describes as crustaceans with a shell in which they clam up, encapsulate, and protect themselves from a world they fear. This defence system has been useful to them for a long time, but when this mechanism is compounded by the identification or confusion with dead objects, it acquires an extremely dangerous quality, since the barrier becomes more intense when the patient attempts to come out of his autistic isolation. It is as if after locking himself up in a castle to take shelter from a Barbarian invasion, a medieval knight attempted to establish contact with and receive stimuli from the outside world; his projective force to break and pass through that wall would have to be very intense.

Even though this model has not yet been sufficiently developed, it does allow me to create hypotheses to attempt a further explanation of intense drug addiction. The dialectic interplay between these two poles creates the spectrum within which these patients oscillate.

For example, through the excessive use of cocaine, Philip sometimes attempts to overcome the stimulation threshold (the wall of the castle); on other occasions he attempts to lock himself up, to isolate himself, to clam up. Significantly, this does not depend only on drugs themselves, but also on whatever fantasies predominate at the time they are taken.

Return to treatment after an overdose

Let us now go back to our patient. It is worth noting a significant event. When Philip resumed therapy after a two-year break, he did so because he was almost killed by a cocaine over-dose which severely intoxicated him and resulted in serious res-piratory and cardiac disturbances. A year before finishing his analysis with me, the patient had to undergo gall-bladder sur-gery, and on that occasion I insisted that he report his drug addiction to the surgeon. Philip did so, and the doctor said he should absolutely refrain from using drugs after the operation.

Before the operation he brought to the session a dream in which he was afraid of dying because of the anaesthesia. The fact that I was able to show the patient the relation between that dream and his emergency hospitalization due to the cocaine overdose was very important for the treatment. It seems that on that occasion he had an experience of death, but he was only now becoming aware of the possibility of dying, and that fear meant that he was slowly becoming aware of the fact that he could have died due to the cocaine intoxication. Before surgery, however, there was a persistent acting-out in which he con-cealed (until he told me about it) the fact that he was taking 'very small doses of cocaine, but only as a digestive'.

Clinical example:
Drug sniffing: Julia

It is extremely important to point out the meaning, the con-notation for certain addicted patients, of sniffing drugs or chemical substances to achieve psychic and bodily sensations. In order to stress the importance of air and smell in drug use I will now give a small clinical vignette about a patient whom we shall call Julia. She is 37 and single. Julia constantly sniffs spray, acetone compounds, synthetic glue, and stimulants with a chemical compound she obtains from an unscrupulous supplier. During her treatment the meaning of her search of olfactory sensations became very clear to me: she wanted to recover the primary relationship with her mother, which she did not have during most of the first two years of her life, as her mother had been hospitalized with a psychotic condition at the time. Her father travelled abroad frequently, and the only support for her was provided by a housemaid with remarkable affective qualities.

In my opinion, as I have previously described, in this case it was very clear that air was conceived or fantasized as an object that was introjected or expelled through the nose. Air and the well-known smells of the breast and of the mother are the first objects, the first models, in the hypothesis I am describing here. In normal evolution, the infant conceives his mother's smells as objects which he introjects by breathing.

Like Julia these types of addicted patients had no opportunity to experience the pleasant and comforting sensations in the mother's smells, coming from a stable, constant, present mother, as normally experienced by a child. The experience of a mother is a harmonious set of sensations of smell, skin, voice, and food, which conveys affection and containment. Drug addicts have not had these experiences; so, by sniffing drugs, many of them attempt to introduce a vital object magically through the air. They attempt to turn the air into a vital object in which they seek the smells and the sensations of a mother they never had. Then they engulf themselves in their surrounding world of sensations, because this is the only way in which they feel they exist. This is similar to what autistic children do: they obtain sensations by licking a rough wall or sitting on a pointed object to feel their anus. Many times, as Meltzer and colleagues (1975) point out, they also clutch, touch, or surround themselves with hard, semi-solid, or liquid elements. The body image theory (D. Rosenfeld & Luna, 1983) is used by many analysts working with autistic children in order to detect fantasies of the primary psychotic body image (solid, semi-solid, or liquid).

Internal and external space

Let us now go back to Julia's case. When the patient discovered that her father was living abroad with another woman, she started to take amphetamines, without which, she argued, 'she could not work or study'. After her mother's death, when she was about 20, the patient created a neoneed, according to J. McDougall's nomenclature (1985, 1989). In fact, Julia fabricated an exterior stage on which she dramatized all the infantile needs of her inner world; she built a scenario in which she tried to reproduce her mother's smells, containment, and lap. In preparation for using drugs, she created a scene: she locked herself into a room, she sniffed a synthetic glue which stimulated her and sometimes gave her hallucinations, while she listened to music at top volume, surrounded by 3 or 4 dozen very beautiful and comfortable cushions she herself had embroidered. The music she listened to was from her mother's country of origin, and the cushions were a substitute for her mother's lap, in which she sought to be contained as she had not been contained during her early life. It is obvious that she was staging the whole imaginary world of her relationship with her mother, in her quest for containment and stimulation. We must also mention the hate and vengefulness deployed by this ritual, since the patient preferred drugs to a useful dependence on a living being, be it her father rushing to her rescue or her analyst and his team. Revenge on a mother who abandoned her and on a father who left her lies at the root of the hate the analyst reports on transference.

We must remember that addicts, as Herbert Rosenfeld points out (1987), prefer sucking their thumbs to sucking the breast. They prefer drugs to the analyst, and this is the root of the amount of hate and vengefulness they sometimes show in the transference, because they need a living object.

Dependence and transference

When treating severe cases, it is important to bear in mind that, for them, having to depend on somebody to take care of them may be something terrible, catastrophic, and even dangerous, because they have no real childhood experience in this, and, therefore, they have not been able to develop the notion of useful dependence on being helped. I repeat, therefore, that one gets the impression that these patients seem to have sworn never again to depend on a living being, because their actual childhood experience has showed them that it may be something terrifying.

Time and containment

Let us now go back to Julia's case. Sometimes she telephoned, saying that she had no desire to live, that she would sniff drugs or commit suicide. At those times, it was very important to offer rapid containment and the presence of the therapist and his team.

The contributions made by Searles (1979) and Liberman (1970–72) are extremely valuable, since they remind us that it takes a long time to create in the mind a notion or concept that has never existed before. The patient must gradually discover that there may exist a constant and stable presence who is not afraid and who can run when she (the addicted adult) and her inner baby seek containment.

Some other concepts

At a higher conceptual level we can differentiate two theories:

1. Patients use drugs to feel they exist, because they confuse themselves with a dead object. A typical case is Philip, who confuses himself with his father, his brother, and his dead daughter. As we have already pointed out, these patients use increasing drug doses in order to feel they are alive and not dead. In these cases, drug use is due to pathological mourning.

2. Patients relate to drugs through links in which they confuse living and inanimate objects. In these cases, schizophrenic areas or actual psychotic episodes are found (Searles, 1960).

My experience has prompted me to suspect the existence of a third group of patients, but I need more extensive observations before going from a hypothesis to an explanatory theory. I think there are patients who use drugs to attain sensations similar to those of the autistic world. In treatments and supervisions I have been able to open a new line of research by detecting encapsulated autistic nuclei through drug use. In Philip's case, for example, there are two coincidental aspects: there is a pathological mourning, and drugs are used to attain autistic sensations.

3. In patients with a predominance of the primitive psychotic body image, the intravenous use of heroin is for the purpose of establishing blood bonds. They seek a close bond, almost like a blood pact, without worrying about the possibility of AIDS transmission. What is important is the blood-to-blood bond. To be alone, without a link, is even more dangerous than to risk being infected with AIDS.

Second thoughts

Today, in 1991, I think that drug-addicted patients do not necessarily fall into just one category. Under the title 'drug-addicted patient' we can include various structural varieties and different fantasies about the body image, and we can also suggest some hypotheses of the origin of this type of psychopathology.

Category A

In the first category we can group a variety of addicted patients, for instance, those who need the drug to obtain an envelope, such as a skin. We can also include under this classification those who use the drug as an anti-depressive, or in order to deny unbearable mental states; these would usually be patients who have suffered the loss of very important object relations and who are in mourning. The case of the patient Irene shows some of the characteristics of Category A.

If these patients are treated in time, in the early stages of their pathology, they usually accept the treatment and have the possibility of recovery.

Category B

Another type of drug-addicted patients, with different structures and fantasies, are those with a higher fantasy level of sexual hyperactivity and/or perversions, as well as a special psychopathology: their threshold for the reception of perceived stimuli and sensations from outside seems to be blocked or diminished. These types of patients search for powerful stimuli in order to feel alive and not be confused with dead objects. Some features of this category can be found in the case of the patient Philip, who had lost his father and his brother in automobile accidents. We can also include here the patient Horace, whose case is described in chapter eleven. The prognosis varies with these patients. Some of them may improve and adapt better to their external relationships; they may also lower their drug consumption.

With these patients, it is very important to be aware of the danger of an overdose or over-stimulus, especially as we may also find clear suicidal fantasies in them.

At times the drug provokes an isolation effect, as they wish to be encapsulated. When this happens, the relationship with the therapist becomes very disturbed.

Usually, however, these patients do accept treatment.

It is very difficult for an analyst to understand that a patient believes that he is not alive, that he is dead. This requires a very difficult technical handling of the transference. However, once we comprehend this psychotic logic, it becomes easier to understand why a patient such as Philip can race a car at 140 miles per hour without respecting traffic lights, or why he uses drugs: By their logic, fear and danger do not exist. However, if they survive this type of challenge, they believe that they have resuscitated themselves.

These patients have no concept of danger; they have no perception of risk. Their minds lack this notion, because they do not feel alive themselves; because of their identification with dead objects, they feel dead. At the most perilous point, they defy death, and if they survive, they feel they have come back to life for a moment. They can even convince the analyst of this, since drug abusers are habitual liars. But, if the analyst believes them, he is confirming to the patients that reality is such as they have constructed it through their delusions, and therefore the patients come to assume that they share the same 'drug' with the analyst, which makes them both see the same reality. In other words, when addicts lie, they erect a delusive working-out of reality, and they strive for the analyst to believe them.

This is the group of patients with whom I have had the highest rate of abandonment of treatment and/or treatment failure—especially in the case of individuals who live within reference groups that become primary groups, whose members are all drug addicts (Freud, 1921c). They prefer living with, or establishing links with those groups, rather then suffering from isolation and loneliness. Fighting against these group structures is sometimes impossible. At the same time, many of these failures have taught me lessons I have successfully applied to other patients, since failure is also a source of knowledge.

Perhaps only a poet can express in words the mental feelings of this type of patient:

Et nous sommes encore tout mêlés l'un à l'autre,
Elle à demi vivante et moi à demi mort.
Victor Hugo, 'Booz endormi'

[And here we are, mingled to each other,
She is half-alive, and I am half-dead.]

Category C

Into this third category I would put those kinds of patients for whom it is most difficult to effect a change for the better, and for whom it is unusual to expect a lessening in drug-taking. The psychopathological structure of these patients is different to that of the others. They are people who in their early childhood had mothers with severe depressive episodes.

One of my patients, Mr A, had a mother who suffered from a severe postpartum depressive state. She also had another depressive state after the death of her father, the grandfather of my patient, when A was five years old. During the first interview with him and one member of his family, it came to my patient's notice and mine that the grandfather had committed suicide. During the treatment, in one of the sessions patient A showed me a photograph album. The photographs showed the mental state of the mother very clearly. In one we can see the mother, lying on the floor in a depressive state, looking at nothing; A, a three-year-old child, is trying with one hand to reach the father, who is standing behind the mother.

These patients were children with a great hypersensibility— extraordinarily sensitive. Any type of object relation loss provokes in them a terrible psychic pain. To avoid suffering this pain, they create a protective shell—the same characteristics as those we find in autistic children. To be able to survive, these children create their own worlds, isolated, enveloped in the protective shell of their own bodily sensations. They may, for example, suck a piece of steel, or rub their anus against the door. In one case discussed in a clinical seminar, a five-year-old girl, diagnosed as a type of autistic, provoked bodily sensations by pressing her tongue around her lips. As she repeated this constantly, her lips became very sore, and it was difficult for her to eat. She also refused to eat because she preferred her own bodily sensations, with which she felt protected from the outside world.

In general, patients in Category C were children with some autistic features, who survived by creating their own sensation world. But the adaptation system of these children is very fragile. Faced with any kind of external or internal catastrophe, they try to repeat their early autistic functioning, this taking the form of drug consumption or other corporal activities that provoke bodily sensations.

In the case of Mr A, when he was 12 years old, his mother had died. One year later he began to experiment with drugs, apparently in an effort to deny this unbearably painful situation, but also to find in the drugs his bodily sensations and to live inside them, as in his early childhood. This seems to be their only and most primitive notion of identity. *They are not so much drug-addicts as survivors. They feel like autistic children who do not feel protected by their flayed skin; for this reason, each little breeze is transformed inside them into a terrible tempest. Against this, they search for autistic sensations as a defense mechanism in order to survive and to obtain a primitive mode of identity.*

Even with good treatment and some hospitalization one cannot always be successful with these patients. They are prisoners of one pragmatic paradox: They use drugs to obtain very primitive autistic sensations, which seem necessary for them to survive and be protected, as in a shell. They fear that if they cannot obtain these sensations through drugs, they will lose all notion of identity and disappear. However, if they continue with their level of drug consumption, they become more intoxicated each day, and finally they may die. This is the real pragmatic paradox: Whatever they may decide, whether to abandon drug use or to continue with it, will always be wrong for them.

CHAPTER TEN

Psychoanalysis of the impulsive character: a linguistic–communicative study

Psychoanalysis started with the investigation of neurotic symptoms—that is, with phenomena that are ego-alien, ego-dystonic, and that do not syntonically fit the character. Character is the ordinary, habitual ways of behaviour, and Freud's insight concerning anal character made it possible to study the habitual behaviour modes as motivated by unconscious tendencies.

In his work on Dostoyevsky, Freud (1928b) wrote of the compromises of the superego's morality as an organized mode that is used not to purify guilt, but to permit new murders. Freud presented the example of Ivan the Terrible. In Dostoyevsky there coincide contradictory and opposing features: selfishness, violence, gambling, raping, epilepsy on the one hand and, on the other, his immense capacity for love and manifestations of exaggerated kindness. However, a large part of this conflict could be sublimated, enabling him to live in society. 'Dostoyevsky's very strong destructive instinct, which might easily have made him a criminal, was in his actual life directed mainly against his own person (inward instead of outward) and thus found expression as masochism and a sense of guilt' (p. 178).

Here an attempt will be made to correlate the characteristics of Dostoyevsky within the present author's approach to the impulsive character. It is particularly significant that Freud should speak of the relationship in Dostoyevsky between 'his instinctual demands and the inhibitions opposing them (plus the available methods of sublimation)', classifying Dostoyevsky as an *'instinctual character'* (p. 179, emphasis added). In summary, Freud describes Dostoyevsky's general character traits, his masochism, his guilt feelings, his epilepsy, and his twofold attitude concerning the Oedipus complex, and then discusses his passion for gambling and his addiction to alcohol. All these features, so strikingly described and explained by Freud, are to be found in almost all the patients who can be included under the label of impulsive characters. The clinical case presented in this chapter can be said to include all the features and feelings attributed by Freud to Dostoyevsky. In this respect, the coincidence is sometimes striking. Both cases include addiction to gambling (the gambler is very attached to masturbation and to the mother's sexual nearness). The murder of the father is witnessed by Dostoyevsky and, in our patient, is carried out in oedipal fantasy with his mother's help (she castrated and murdered the father's moral standards). Regarding transference, Dostoyevsky's dream of the prison corresponds to the patient's dream of being tied up, afraid of the therapist's revenge. (In Dostoyevsky's case prison also appears as a triggering factor of his epilepsy.) Dostoyevsky identifies himself with a woman and adopts feminine attitudes, for example with his first wife's lover, as a reaction-formation against his hostility towards his father. Our patient also makes a feminine identification and tries on female clothes. The criminal component that leads to a search for punishment or masochism in Dostoyevsky appears in our patient's dream, in which there is a search for punishment and masochism is eroticized: it is a dream where the patient is searched by a policeman and receives 'blows he finds beautiful'. Dostoyevsky behaved impulsively towards women; on many occasions, our patient's intercourse with his wife implied raping her, or else he could have pleasure only if a rape were fantasied. Thus, Freud's work is perhaps the most important starting point for the study of this type of patient (Avenburg, 1975; Brudny, 1980).

Dynamic theory

At one pole the impulsive character acts through impulsive discharges, and then the weakening of a stable organization becomes obvious; at the other pole the same patient may resort to the repertoire of behaviours that are nearer the obsessive type. A psychoanalytic treatment, by modifying certain traits, gives rise to states where the patient fears that every change will lead to dissolution of the personality, to the point of psychotic fragmentation, and in that situation the most impulsive traits may emerge as a last defensive link against treatment, in order to expel or control the fear of mental confusion, the unbearable mental pain, or a psychotic transference.

At the pole of impulsive discharges, patients face the present with past experiences that never became historical, and thus they repeat similar acts. They display their inner world through their associations in transference, which take the form of acting out. With these characters there is an allo-plastic tendency. Impulsive neuroses in patients who are accident-prone are rather similar, insofar as they find it difficult to tolerate tension, do not distinguish between acting and thinking, and, as the clinical example illustrates, they sometimes try to avoid displeasure rather than look for pleasure.

Some fragments from the analysis of a patient, Horace, are presented in order to point out some of the motivations behind impulsive behaviour and to stress that impulsive acts are the result of the coincidence of the inner infantile world with the psychotic transference. The patient's inner world experiences object relationships as blows, violence, and torture, and therefore, genuine dependence is experienced as being tied up and diabolically possessed. If this inner world coincides with an intense transference experience concerning the therapist, the

patient finds a way out of that prison through an impulsive discharge that becomes the vehicle of his or her unconscious fantasies. The strength of dissociation is so pathological that the
acting out takes place far away from the consulting room.
Horace came to four sessions each week.

Clinical material: Horace

Horace is about 30 years of age, newly married, and has an older
brother. He remembers having tried on, as a child, women's hats
in the shop his mother ran, and having spied on the customers
when his mother helped them to try on clothes. There is reason
to believe that he engaged in some sexual play with his brother.
He has managed to acquire a considerable fortune by means of
behaviours at least partially motivated by his frantic madness
for possessing. On weekends he regularly drove at very high
speed towards gambling establishments or to a race-track far
away from the city; he then participated in a perverse sexual
activity with a married couple, in which he and the other man
tied up the woman with her arms and legs stretched apart,
Tupac-Amarú style, and then punished her and did things that
aroused her to the point of 'madness'. The purpose was to make
the woman reach orgasm. The patient described the situation,
saying that the whole thing ended up amidst disagreeable
smells, faeces, sweat, and semen, and that he felt a prisoner of it
all. In the third step of this sequence, his alcoholic addiction was
exhibited when, in a state of semi-consciousness, he came back
for his Monday sessions. Sometimes he started drinking alcohol
before his sexual activity. In the course of his analysis there was
a period during which he recounted many of his dreams, which
were very difficult to work on due to their overabundance and to
the absence of associations. The great number of dreams is a
proof of the strength of his dissociation and the power of his
impulses. However, their careful consideration after the sessions
led to an understanding of the motivating dynamism in his

impulses in connection with his transference and, therefore, to an ability to predict, especially towards the weekend, the occurrence of impulsive discharges (Freud, 1901b, 1905d, 1931a).

In order to show some aspects of his transference state on a Monday, the beginning of the session is described. The patient said:

> I disappeared from home on Friday and never saw my wife again until yesterday, that is, Monday. On Friday I went out for dinner with some people, then I had my 'little party' with the married couple, then I drove very fast to the race-track in X (another city), then I returned, went back to this couple's house, and had another 'party' between the three of us. Then I think I drank a lot and I think I met a girl. What I do remember is that when I was leaving the house, the husband was fucking with the woman and asked me what I was going to do afterwards.

Then he added something worth taking into account: 'Why is it that I do all this on weekends, when I have no session? I told my wife, "On the weekends I disappear, I have orgies, disasters."'

He is thus showing his omnipotent defense: on the weekends, he excludes and abandons somebody else, the analyst, and acts this out by abandoning his wife. He offered very detailed descriptions of his sexual activities with the tied-up woman, which 'drove her mad'. In transference, this was aimed at reversing the abandonment situation of the weekend. He believed that in this way he encouraged the therapist's voyeurism, arousing the therapist with his descriptions and also excluding the therapist from the primary scene, which he also did with the woman's husband during the acting out. On another occasion the therapist pointed out to him that he was projecting a part of himself onto the humiliated, violated woman, and that he made her feel the way he thinks the therapist wants him to feel, which in turn, represents his conception of having to depend on the therapist as a patient.

His response to this interpretation consisted in returning home and breaking an enormous mirror in which he was himself reflected while he was drinking alcohol. This was interpreted as his desire to break the therapist up into hundreds of pieces, to which he responded with intense anxiety and then with a second attack on the interpretation, recalling fantasies of perverse and sadistic sexuality: 'I have just remembered the last orgy, and I feel very aroused.' These words were interpreted as announcing a new impulsive discharge that would allow him to evacuate what he thought was to introject an interpretation. For him, to receive an interpretation meant being a woman ('I've just remembered that I told my wife I wanted to have intercourse with her as if she had a penis and I, a vagina').

Additional sessions are excerpted in order to illustrate the dynamics of the way in which transference feelings that coincide with the inner world are the cause of discharges in these impulsive characters. For example, one Thursday he dreamt that he ended up in jail, tied up with ropes, while the therapist enjoyed himself until Horace was driven mad. This is, besides, a projection onto the therapist of the jail in the patient's inner world. Only when transference (as the dream so clearly shows) coincides with the jail in his inner world (the prison of his continual reenactment of early object relationships), does an impulsive act occur. On the Monday following this dream he described an acting out: he undressed a girl, lay alone on the bed, and masturbated, saying, 'I can manage by myself, I don't need you'. Obviously, he was thus attacking dependency by means of perverse sexuality. After this type of murder of the analytic dependency by means of food, alcohol, and orgies, he turned up for his session feeling exhausted; sometimes he looked actually destroyed, that is to say, melancholically identified with the analyst he thought he had destroyed.

On Mondays he described episodes indicating a certain possibility of having a dialogue with the therapist (for example, 'I spoke with a friend until six o'clock in the morning; I told him about myself, about the analysis; I told him a lot about myself'). On the other occasions, after the weekend orgies, he spoke about having met a very old and sad person with whom he talked about his orgies. In this case, it was interpreted that he saw the therapist as an old and destroyed person, and that he was trying to arouse the therapist so as not to see him depressed and destroyed after the attacks implicit in his orgies. The patient answered, 'Just now, when you sighed, I thought you were tired, fed up with my stories about the old man', thus confirming the previous interpretation. Consequently he thought that the therapist was revengeful, violent, and murderous. That was the prison in which he lived. He had no symbolic possibility of establishing a certain distance, and, as usually happens at the psychotic levels of the personality, his terrifying image of the therapist, which coincided with his inner objects (attacked and destroyed parents who persecuted him in revenge), had become utterly concrete.

I will now include material corresponding to a Friday session and to the following Monday. On Friday the patient speaks of a book, *The Exorcist*. He says that in the book a woman forces her daughter to suck her vagina, in order to get rid of the devil, or else introduces a crucifix into it. He goes on talking about exorcism. The patient is thus displaying his transference psychotic fantasies, which reveal who the analyst is for him at that moment: someone like the devil, who tries to attain demoniacal possession of his body and his mind. *It becomes possible to formulate a predictive theory, in the sense that the patient was announcing an acting out designed to dissociate a terrifying and persecutory aspect of the therapist, which coincided with his primitive persecutory objects.* The patient offered clues on the basis of which we could predict the type of sexual activity in the following orgy; sucking the vagina, introducing objects into it and into the anus, etc. I took this as a predictive hypothesis in which he announced that the most terrified, psychotic, and omnipotent part of the self was going to be displayed during the following weekend.

After the weekend the subject of exorcism is taken up again on Monday, Tuesday, and Wednesday. On Tuesday he says that, after the 'little party' (which is what he called the three-person orgy) he slept with them, got up, stayed there to watch them having intercourse, and then he made love with the woman.

That Monday night he visited his parents. Then he tells a dream he had that same night.

He was at his parents' house, and his father told him not to do the exorcism with his body. Then he went to see a priest, who also told him not to do the exorcism with his body, but thinking, mentally. His mother said something similar. She asked him to lie down, and then she stood by the bed and told him so. But two other people came in and 'pierced' him (the patient used Spanish word that can mean either 'pierce' or 'lie across') one on his feet, the other on his chest. There were two others across the first two. Apparently, that was the method for the exorcism. Then he was at the apartment. Perhaps it was the same in which he had been before. Something coming from inside him was violently expelled, so much so that it—he did not know what it was—went through the walls, the glass, jumped out of the window and landed in the next-door apartment. That had to do with the exorcism.

All this was so vivid that, on waking up, he thought he had expelled it. He woke up trembling and sweating. He was afraid of going back to sleep and having the dream return. He put on all the lights in the house until morning came. He read or watched television for above five hours.

The first part of the dream seems to be related to his visit to his parents, from whom he takes those parts of the bond that help him by telling him to think, that he must not evacuate with his body, that he should remain in treatment. His analyst—in the dream, the priest—tells him the same thing. In this first part of the dream, the listener seems to be a part of his mind that wants to think, a part of himself with some faint signs of 'dependency'.

But dependency gradually became something terrifying, where the skin-to-skin contact between a baby and its mother turned into a primary scene of mixed-up, 'pierced' and overlapping bodies. The attempt at contact implied in the mother–analyst standing by the bed–couch became an orgiastic scene where it was impossible to tell whether the patient was pierced through with nails or knives or with a person in a perpendicular position. The way in which he described the scene made it possible to accept either of the possibilities. The mere glimpse of a certain degree of dependency evoked the primitive mental conception he had of the analytic bond: to be crushed, tied up, immobilized in a raping primary scene. It was as if I tried to crush him against the couch and thus find pleasure in possessing his mind and his body.

In the dream there was a third part in which he violently expelled something that came out from inside him and went through walls. This implied going back to the subject of exorcism of the previous week: a dissociated part of the therapist was seen in the psychotic transference as a demon. This time the patient could include in the dream, and also bring to his session, part of his evacuation and projection techniques. He showed the violence of fragmentation and a projective identification of an omnipotent type in order to evacuate the demon—analyst (which coincides with his primitive inner objects, as can be seen in the dream), even if that meant becoming fragmented and emptying his self.

However, he landed in the apartment next-door. It would seem that, even though in his orgies during that weekend and also in the dream he perforated, made holes, broke through, and destroyed the analytic container and the analyst, that apartment symbolized the hope of the Tuesday session that I might contain him and also prevent total fragmentation. The fact that he woke up trembling and sweating showed that the dream was not enough as a container. On the contrary, the number of fragments of himself, together with the analyst's fragmentation, all of which was projected, made him fear that all that would fall back revengefully upon himself. He was afraid I would do to him what he did to me in his fantasy, but then I would be so fragmented that the patient no longer knew where or how I could take revenge on him. When I gave the patient this interpretation, he answered in a way that confirmed the interpretative hypothesis: 'What frightened me the most last night, when I turned the lights on, was to look through the window and see something unknown coming back into the room, something I couldn't see or control, coming in through doors and windows.' Thus he confirms the interpretations, that is, the fear of a revengeful re-introjection of what he has projected.

Linguistic analysis of the dream content

It is useful to formulate this hypothesis: The characteristics of Horace's way of communicating become evident when one compares some dreams he recounted on pre-weekend sessions to other dreams corresponding to sessions at the beginning of the week, some time later. The Friday dreams reveal motivations and triggering factors, and the dreams after the weekend reveal the effects caused by patient's acting out.

Description of dreams

Dreams previous to the weekend   (Friday)

1. I was away from the city, in the Delta Islands. The houses were built on pillars, and there were two drunken boys. There was a bakery, and a wooden cabin, a bar. They were fighting, but they didn't hit each other. A couple of yards from my room there was a demonstration. It was a series of similar faces. They were below, saying something. The room had only one door. There were neither walls nor roof: I could see the sky.

2. I was in jail. I ran away to a hotel in Mar del Plata. I went to gamble at the roulette. Suddenly I was at the race-track and I was being chased. There was a guy standing on the subway stairs who said: 'Examine the liver, examine it with apparati.' I ran away from jail and they arrested me. I didn't know what was going on.

3. A car stopped in the middle of a tunnel. I got lost when coming out of the stairs. There were doors to go into the subway. I got lost in the labyrinth.

For the patient, depending on the therapist meant being in prison, immobilized, tied to the couch on which he was subjected to humiliations, to sadistic investigating behaviour that he could only suffer passively. The therapist was tyrannical, and

Horace had to submit, although all this saved him from becoming de-structured. When the end came he felt helpless, without any support. In dream 3, which shows his uncertainty, there is an indication that during the weekend he would try to find himself again and overcome his confusion by means of acting out.

In general terms, these interpretations were offered, as was the prediction that he was likely to resort during the weekend to a reversal, that is, that he would inflict upon someone else what he suffered during the sessions.

Dreams following the weekend   (Monday)

In one of the sessions, Horace unfolded a piece of paper on which he had written down his dreams. The therapist told him that he was trying to order and keep his dreams on a piece of paper so as not to become a victim of his suicidal and self-destructive part. He nodded.

4. I was on board a very beautiful modern yacht on my way to Europe. There was a violent wind-storm. Owing to the windstorm there were many fallen trees. I told the steersman to be careful, for the trees driven by the wind made it very dangerous. Suddenly there were violent, enormous waves. They were saying that the difficult thing was to cross the Gulf of Saint Catherine, which was the stormiest area, full of waves and where storms were more frequent than in any other part of the world. Suddenly I thought we were coming out of the Paraná river, but then I looked behind and saw that I was in the Riachuelo and didn't understand anything. Suddenly it seemed that the ship had fallen into the Riachuelo or was there. I was terrified of drowning.

The interpretation of this dream, together with those corresponding to the other dreams, was given to the patient at the end of his description. He was told that being on the yacht represented the vicissitudes of the weekend and the analytic journey in the consulting-room where he lay on a comfortable couch in expectation of an experience that he knew would be very long. It also represented his fear of windstorms, of being alone during the weekend, that is, his fear of what was mad, aggressive, and uncontrolled in him, which could only be overcome if the therapist remained a coherent, strong, and orderly steersman, which is what he was asking the therapist to be in the dream. There was the fear that everything that was chaotic in his mind would force him back into the mud (the Riachuelo).

5. In a street downtown a guy was running. He was wearing a white beret, and they were running after him. A friend who was with me said, 'That guy is always making trouble'. They got him, and they hit him terrible blows, beautiful, violent blows.

The patient had a lot of trouble associating in relation to this dream. He thought it had to do with his homosexuality and his fear of fights. He said that, in general, in other dreams he always disguised blows and turned them into caresses. The dream shows his fear of being persecuted. His head (beret) is the target against which aggression is directed, since it is in his head that the identification with the mother took place (he used to try on women's hats in childhood), which showed his homosexual disposition. He felt possessed by a maddening mother, like the ship in the Gulf of Saint Catherine. Likewise, he attributed to the therapist the ambition to control his mind.

6. I was at the bar with a friend. Then the police arrived, just when I was planning to leave. I think I was staying only to drink some glasses of water. They told me to undress because they were searching for drugs, and they took me to the bathroom to undress me. They wanted me to confess quickly. I was afraid they might knee me in the testicles. I was afraid they might hurry me and hit me. Finally I shouted that I was the president of the company L., and one of them told me, 'We can fix everything for a million pesos', and then added: 'All right, half of it now and the rest afterwards, when the trial is over.'

After the dream he said:

> Last night I got home very late to see my wife. That was because I had been with the married couple, having a 'little party'. We were driving and I told them I had mixed feelings, that I had felt terribly confused about my feelings that week, that I was very mixed-up about them. We went to have a drink and suddenly, I don't know whether because I was afraid of speaking up or if I became confused, the thing is I said goodbye and left (*he tried to find a word, but in vain (confusion at a linguistic level)—the word he could not find might have been 'abruptly'*) almost running, and arrived in time to be with my wife at the house of my partner's fiancée. Then I told my partner he should start his analysis because if he wasn't well, what was going to happen to the firm?

This was the first time in which he had abruptly left the couple with whom he shared his sexual orgies in order to be with his wife.

Thematic study of the dreams

Several elements are common to several of the dreams. Only a few aspects are considered here, though the analysis can be extended to many others. The patient feels himself the object of different actions performed by individuals of superior strength: the object of imprisonment, persecution, and searching (dream 2), natural forces (dream 4), searching and blows (dream 5), and at the mercy of others.

The helplessness inherent in this situation becomes manifest in the absence of walls and a roof in the room, in the fact that the house is built on pillars (dream 1), as well as in his nakedness (dream 6), in his ignorance of what is going on (dream 2), and in his feeling lost (dream 3). The illegal nature of certain activities is suggested in some scenes (dream 1), or more or less openly expressed in other dreams (dream 2 and dream 6). Another important aspect is the hypochondriacal anxiety (dream 2), which has to do with his confusional anxieties and his alcoholic addiction (dream 1). (In the acting-out of many alcoholics, the objective is not a splitting or dissociation of a state of confusional anxiety. Rather, the acting-out aims at recovering a confusional state—that is, a state of confusion–defense in the face of intolerable paranoid anxieties and persecutory objects.)

The hypochondriacal anxiety as a way of self-expression on the bodily level, confusional and persecutory anxieties, and castration anxiety, are experienced by the patient as a consequence of having carried out the fantasy of a homosexual, oral, primary scene: to drink with other men (dream 1). However, apparently this patient is not a manifest homosexual; rather, he shows another type of perversion that is the transformation of the previous one. This is one of the ways in which he defends himself from the risk of an ever greater de-structuralization: to use his economic resources to appease men and see to it that his belongings (especially his penis) may be used by a woman for a narcissistic type of gratification by possessing him.

What meaning did the bond with the therapist have for the patient? The therapist was someone who coveted his fortune and treated him out of selfishness and not altruism. The therapist's cognitive and interpretive activity amounted to a penetration that transgressed the patient's limits, thus evoking hypochondriacal anxieties as a result of the therapist's 'revengeful persecution' (dream 2).

The same happened whenever Horace had to recognize his own wish and establish a dependent relationship with someone else. This was impossible for him, particularly when his need was experienced as a humiliation, a submission (dream 6). He resorted then to the acting out already mentioned, in which he identified himself with a sadistic, tyrannical object, or else with its counterpart, a submissive masochistic object (i.e., he was a prisoner of his sadistic fantasies, which he compulsively displayed over and over again in the Euclidian outer space in the presence of other people who were also involved).

In the dreams before the weekend, where his language was of a more imperative nature—one can detect transference fantasies of attacks, hatred, blows, revenge, the omnipotent wish to be self-sufficient, getting lost in the emptiness of labyrinths. In the dreams after the weekend, one can detect the disastrous aftermath of his orgies: forcing someone else to feel humiliated and dependent; experiencing the chaos, the confusion, and the storms; and houses that cannot contain him.

Microlinguistic analysis

The microlinguistic analysis suggested here has as its clinical objective in this case the prediction of impulsive behaviours brought about by the loss of the equilibrium in the patient's psychic apparatus, on the basis of a systematization of the clues the patient may offer at a verbal and paraverbal level in the course of the session. In this patient's psychic apparatus there was a tendency to corrupt and bribe his father–superego–ego ideal in order to make it ego-syntonic, as is quite common in the impulsive characters.

The type of verbs used by the patient is significant, since this grammatical category expresses the characteristics of the impulse, and the conjugation may indicate the end of the impulse (active, passive, reflexive). Likewise, verbs may give some clues as to the qualities of the actions that the patient regards as specific for the fulfillment of a wish. These types of verbs are addressed to different characters in the patient's inner world, characters or psychic places to which one can give proper names or attribute more general characteristics, according to Freudian theory. Some verbs have to do with moving through space and habitually indicate the use of mobility as a means of attaining a specific action through contact with an object in a favourable position.

A higher degree of passivity is found in the Monday dreams. Sometimes the first Monday dream is the continuation of the last dream on Friday as regards its content—in both of them there is loss of orientation, for instance—but in the Monday dream the content and the verbs indicate confusion and loss of orientation. These thematic and linguistic clues allow one to predict whether the acting out during the weekends goes on within the patient's mind or if he can reorganize himself within the setting of the session—for instance, when a Monday dream indicates he has overcome his confusion or found a way out of it.

In the Friday dreams, verbs are in general more imperative, and this observation may be useful in detecting the impulsive acting out. In this respect, it should be remembered that in the Friday sessions the words and the verbs were 'they were fighting. . . . I want to go . . . they persecute me . . . search him.'

On the other hand, on Mondays verbs are in general less imperative and sometimes show linguistic elements that may indicate confusional anxiety and relationships with the super-ego, or the internalized model of Horace's father and his therapist before whom he tries to show off, and whom at the same time he tries to appease through his acting out during the weekend. This is equated to criminal action when the patient becomes aware of certain values in the infantile inner world, as experienced in transference.

The Friday dreams, characterized by a high percentage of imperative verbs, are the way in which his attempt to dominate or to give orders to take possession of another person becomes manifest at the linguistic level. Within the pathology of the impulsive character is the desire to take possession of the other person's mind and body—that is, as if his arm extended into the therapist's mind or his accompanying objects, and other people's minds become the extension of his own arm. The imperative verb also announces a quantitative amount of instinctual impulsive charge that is on the verge of uncontrolled discharge due to its increase as regards quantity and quality.

The types of verbs the patient used on Fridays are listed and compared with those used on Mondays; in both cases we categorize four items: (1) action having motor effects on the other, (2) punishment or avoidance of punishment, (3) actions aiming at possessing an object, and (4) space displacement.

Fridays

1. *action having motor effects on the other,* who then becomes an extension of the subject's activity or motor pole: this is related to the pragmatic distortions that appear with an epic

style in those patients known as psychopaths; sometimes there is a hidden delirious belief; verbs implying depriving the other of a material good or its equivalent: to fight, to ask, to order, to steal;

2. *punishment or avoidance of punishment* through action (relationship established with the ego ideal or the superego as a *model* of justice): to run away, to persecute, to arrest, to imprison, to search;

3. *actions aiming at possessing an object:* bond with the *object* of the wish (mother)—to have a drink, to gamble. Gambling and having a drink imply a search through the addiction for an idealized object (the mother's breast), and, at the same time, this action is put to destructive uses in the acting out;

4. *Space displacement* (verbs that are a means to an end): to go, to get lost (a failure in orientation due to lack of an objective);

Friday verbs are presented in the clinical material mainly in the imperative tense.

Mondays

1. *verbs of action:* to hit, to order, to confess;

2. *verbs in connection with punishment:* to bribe, to undress;

3. *verbs in connection with the object of desire:* to get hold of, to drink, to take;

4. *verbs of displacement:* to run, to get lost (dream of the windstorm), to find himself.

Monday verbs are presented in the clinical material mainly in the passive tense.

Conclusion

The systematization of the verbs presented in the sessions leads
to the conclusion that they are addressed to different characters
in the patient's inner world, characters or psychic places to
which one can give proper names or attribute more general
characteristics within the Freudian theory. Some verbs have to
do with moving through space and habitually indicate the use of
mobility as a means to attain the specific action through contact
with an object in a favourable position.

CHAPTER ELEVEN

Linguistics and psychosis

Alba

I n this chapter, I present the clinical history of a patient suffering a psychotic episode, which was characterized by delusions, cenesthetic hallucinations, and a particular way of speaking: very fast, without pauses or silences.

I present the beginning of her treatment, as well as her family and historical data. I also describe the clinical material, and I comment in detail on a session showing the transformations in the patient's language.

The patient was treated with medication from the beginning of her therapy, which began at a rate of four sessions a week; she then had three sessions per week during the last years of therapy. The treatment lasted for a total of nine and one-half years, and I supervised the case for part of that time.

I go on in my presentation to develop some hypotheses regarding the origin of the delusions, and I stress the importance of using countertransference with psychotic or very regressed patients. I also discuss how linguistics allows us to study the alterations of thought, detectable through the alterations of language.

277

Some delusion episodes concerning God or religious virgins, who at times harass the patient and at other times protect her, bear a striking similarity to the Schreber case.

The patient began to have delusions and psychotic ideas while she was attending a chemistry class at the University. She felt everyone watching her, and she thought the teacher was attracted to her; she then felt sexually excited by a female teacher. This is a self-reference delusion, in which the person feels she is at the centre of attention. Another interesting fact is her undifferentiated link to her family, especially to her sister. I want to mention here that she and her sister had been sharing a bed since childhood, and she often mixed up their names.

I shall now make the general presentation of this case, as I saw it when I first met this patient, who was then 23 years old, and whom I shall call 'Alba'.

The first contact with the patient was quite unusual. One day, while I was treating another patient, the door-bell of my consulting room rang. Given the insistent calls, I opened the door and found myself confronting a woman who had come to ask me if I had time to treat her daughter. When she came back to see me later, what she said was so ambiguous that at first I was unable to establish whether she was asking for an appointment for herself or for someone else. I had to put a series of questions to her to clear up the matter, and finally she said that she wanted me to treat her daughter, although at first she did not explain clearly why. Instead, she described the girl's close bond with herself, recounting how, as a mother, she would not let her daughter go out at night to see 'dirty and disgusting things' at the cinema. At most, they would go together to the cinema or to a dance. She claimed that it was right for her, as a mother, to control her daughter's life and to send her on errands, and then check up to see whether she had done what she set out to do.

The patient's mental void, through an exaggerated identification with an object, is revealed through one of her recollections: a school friend had asked her for half of her sandwich, saying that afterwards she would give her half of her own. The girl did not do as she had promised, and Alba cried and screamed, 'Why does this always happen to me? Why . . . why?'

She seemed to believe in a fantasy in which she lost half of herself, which was left inside an object that she appeared to be searching for, controlling; this tied up with what her mother had said, and was a manifestation of the symbiotic structure. Half of her head—the part that could think and make decisions—had been eaten, like the half of her sandwich, projected by her mother.

As we shall see, this difficulty to differentiate things was evident in the fact that she talked at the same time as the therapist, which represented an attempt to refuse to acknowledge the distinction between them, between her own self and the therapist's self.

During the whole first year of her analysis, the patient could not use words implying a meaning of union, nor any word meaning 'together', or 'togetherness'.

For the patient, in her psychotic logic, to say 'union', 'together', was a psychotic concretization instead of a verbal symbol. A psychotic concretization means that the patient believes that if she uses words meaning 'union' or 'togetherness', she is having sexual intercourse.

Early in the treatment, a psychotic fantasy of coitus came up, seen in terms of the total mixing of one person with another. Alba was a medical student, and she specifically made this comparison. Every time she mentioned a boy and a girl becoming involved in any way, she compared the situation with anastomosis.

The way in which she referred to boys showed a gradual change from regarding them as 'a bit unkind' to regarding them as 'rather beastly'. This was related to her fear of rape because of the drawing-pins some boys in her group had put on her chair. The rape fantasy was also evident in her conviction that they had stolen her handbag, the symbol of womanhood, thereby destroying her virginity. This is an expression of the idea that the 'man takes', so that he is transformed into a 'wicked person who, through rape, makes a woman spill out and lose her own identity'. A transformation of this fantasy, which was barely identifiable, appeared more clearly as a delusion some months after the interview. The earlier conception expressed by the comparison 'a bit unkind/rather beastly' assumes a new form in the delusion: the devil is a vampire who tries to attack her vagina to destroy her virginity. There was an antecedent to this in the form of a para-verbal element that appears throughout the material. In those six months, her short bursts of laughter had an element of the dramatization of this devilish character, which is later defined as an enemy. A complete transcript of this session is given at the end of this chapter.

We will see that there is a passage in the session at the end of the chapter which reveals quite clearly what the patient understood by a relationship; she saw it as the identification of the concepts of the two persons involved, as if the two minds became one in thinking and expressing the same idea. This is particularly noticeable at the point in the session where she continually interrupts the therapist to express, in almost the same words, the ideas stated by the latter in her interpretations. The conception of relationships as the identification of thought processes also presupposes the risk of scattering her mind, by merger with that of another person.

This fragmentation fantasy is mentioned in another passage of this same session, in which the words 'cerebral haemorrhage' are used. This is a way of expressing a fantasy involving the spillage, fragmentation, and emptying of her mind, in terms of bleeding, or the bursting of a container or of blood vessels.

I regard the fantasy of fear of haemorrhage and the bursting of blood vessels in the head, fingers, nose, or any other part of the body—including even menstruation—as an observational pattern from which psychotic emptying-out or possible fragmentation can be diagnosed at a very early stage. My own clinical experience, and that of many of my colleagues, is wide enough to confirm the usefulness of this observational model in diagnosis and in establishing a prognosis at the deepest, most regressive and psychotic levels (see chapter eight).

It is very important to bear in mind that sometimes fantasies involving fear of bleeding may indicate a different pattern of development and have a different meaning. If the blood or body fluids fall into a vacuum, into outer space, or into a bottomless crevasse, this indicates something more regressive than the fantasy that blood falls on a defined area, as in the case of a patient who hallucinated that he was bleeding all over the walls of the consulting room (Ahumada, 1989, 1990; Mordo, 1987).

Linguistic changes in Alba's speech

In the session given at the end of the chapter, when Alba refers to separation, she says: 'We each . . . we became separated . . . everyone is in different groups.' This is interesting on account of the difficulty experienced by the patient in saying: 'We became separated from one another.' Saying 'we became separated' transforms the fact of separation into a new reunion, thus rejecting the earlier 'each'. From this we can infer the patient's difficulty in referring to any sign of differentiation between people, as well as physical separation. This is based on her overall conception of interpersonal relationships, where she sees no differentiation between the persons concerned.

In the same passage she says that she never notices the reaction of the other person. She is unable to imagine or suppose that other people's thoughts or reactions would be different from the one she was expecting. This is evidence of a conception about interpersonal relationships that is similar to one that we were previously only able to infer: the 'other' is not someone different, but merely an extension of herself (Lowenstein, 1959).

On the basis of these statements, we can discuss the more general problem of the psychopathology of this patient. From the interpersonal point of view, we may regard it as symbiotic, and from the individual point of view, she appears to be suffering from the disintegration that is typical of acute psychotic conditions. In the final analysis it really amounts to a description and conceptualization of the same process from two different points of view, one referring to the individual and the other to the individual's relationship with other people.

At some point in the evolution of this patient (two or three years after the beginning of therapy), some optical illusions, delusions, or hallucinations became distonic—that is, she became capable of self-criticism about what she called 'those strange ideas I get about a man coming through the door, or raping men up in the trees'. Later on, it was interesting to study and analyse the evolution of her delirious ideas about a man being able to get her pregnant by just touching her or sitting close to her. In this patient we see an element that we find quite frequently in these delusional fantasies: she has a disturbed body image, and her feeling of skin-to-skin contact is perturbed; in her unconscious body image her bodies has no skin, no limits (no bounds) (see chapter eight). Thus, for her, being touched is the same as someone intruding into the hollow, inner part of her body. In other words, there is no concept of an inner space; anything that comes from the outside may enter her, fill her, invade her, make her pregnant. In cases of extreme delusion, and in paranoic patients, there is a predominance of the intrusive element, such as rape, as is the case at the beginning with this patient, when she tells about the nails or thumbtacks that the boys had put on her chair to prick her. This then evolves into fantasies in which she becomes pregnant by just being touched. This body image fantasy is more common than we usually believe, and quite frequent in women; in fact, fantasies about being made pregnant through a simple contact often appear in the dreams or fantasies of normal women, who are well adapted to reality (Mordo & D. Rosenfeld, 1976).

Evolution

After the session to which these comments relate, Alba's delusion related to the religious image of a virgin became more manifest: she thought the virgin could move her eyes and watched her constantly. The therapist discovered that the mother also had exaggerated fears of somebody breaking into the house, and she used to lock doors and windows with keys and padlocks; in other words, the patient was not the only one showing this symptom.

Her fantasy about a rapist was also a delusion transformation of the primal scene, in which her parents performed a sadistic coitus.

Some years after this session, Alba wanted to have sexual intercourse: she practically invited a fellow student, who was a married man, to have sex with her. In other words, she inverted the situation, as if she had become the active, intrusive person, the rapist of a man. The young man complied, in what he called an 'act of generosity'.

Some months after this sexual enacting, she began dating a young man and became his fiancée. She always said she had liked this boy for a long time, but she described him as someone who would never dare to make sexual overtures, because he was very shy and timorous, and, besides, he had never had any previous sexual experience. Thus, the patient played the role of the 'sexually experienced' one. This is the man she eventually married, after her therapy had been completed.

When we analyse this clinical history, and we see that a treatment can end after a good evolution such as this one, it becomes interesting to reflect about a differential diagnosis: a patient who is initially diagnosed as an acute psychotic may be confused with an irreversible schizophrenic. Of course at the outset, the clinical presentation may be very similar. We believe that an acute psychosis, treated rapidly and adequately, can change a process. In other words, by treating an acute psychosis early, with psychoanalysis, including medication and/or hospitalization, we may change some diagnoses and some evolutions, which might otherwise evolve into a chronic, irreversible schizophrenia.

Dreams

Before presenting some of the patient's dreams, it is important to emphasize a significant fact: it was only after two and one-half years of treatment that the patient was able to remain silent for a moment. As the transcript of the session shows, in the first sessions of her therapy Alba could not tolerate even one minute of silence, and there were no pauses between sentences.

During a session before her first dream, which occurred after three years of treatment, the patient was able to remain silent for 25 minutes. We think this means she is able to be with herself, to begin creating her own private space. We might note here that Winnicott (1965a and 1965b), has developed the concept of the intermediate space, and of its importance for the normal evolution of the child.

Some days later, Alba began the session by saying:

'I remember two dreams, one from last night, the other from a few nights ago. In the one from last night, I woke up, screaming: Mummy! mummy! I dreamt that my sister and I were sleeping one by the side of the other, very close to each other. I touched her without meaning to, in my sleep, and my sister was very angry. She pounced on me to strangle me. I screamed, and this is how I woke up. And I awoke in bed. We were sleeping just like in my dream. We slept together, glued together, until we were eighteen.'

And she repeated aloud:

'until we were eighteen. It was only after we moved into another house that we had separate beds.'

The therapist correctly interpreted the transferential fantasies and also used this dream to show Alba that it is a way of becoming aware of how traumatic it was for her when her sister left home to go to the University; she left her and the house and thus triggered her disease. It is possibly not necessary to repeat that the self-reference delusion and the homosexual overtures to a female teacher were delusive ways of searching for the lost link with her sister, in a fragile personality, without self-identity. When her sister went away, it was as if she had lost the sense of her own identity and was trying to recover it with her delusions.

In the same session, Alba continued:

'I told my aunt Inés about my other dream. I'm in a car with some girl friends. The one who is driving crashes into something like a barrier. I get out of the car to see what happened, and there is a boy, a young man, dressed in a uniform like a policeman's, but he also looks like a prince, because it's all white, with gold buttons.

This young man seems to think I'm responsible, and he takes me away, to some place. But he is considerate, he is nice to me.

There are other people in this place, and not enough chairs. He sits down, and I sit on his knees. We are looking at television, and at one point I tell him, 'there is something on the television which I think is wrong! The young man pays no attention to my comment, and I feel disappointed. After that, the scene changes; we are not looking at the television any more. We are in a sort of theatre, as if we were acting. In this scene I put a rope around my neck, as if I wanted to strangle or choke myself. There are other people present, who also pull the rope, helping to strangle me. Another person enters, who has come to save me, and I tell him to hurry up, because perhaps I would strangle and really die. At the end of my dream, I am saved and taken away, and I had almost passed out. I told this dream to my aunt Inés, and she said that perhaps I was being theatrical, exaggerating things.'

If we examine this dream sequence with the therapist, today, several years later, we believe it offers a great wealth of data about the patient's inner world, which unfolds in her dreams, and also in the transference, showing the quest for a symbiotic and undifferentiated relationship with her sister or her therapist, and also her fear of a symbiotic homosexual relationship (Laufer, 1989; Ogden, 1986; Treurniet, 1987, 1989).

We also see that in her first dream someone pounces on her to strangle her, while in the second one she is the one who tries to strangle herself. In the first dream we may suppose there is a projective identification of a murderous facet in her, which she projects on her sister, to kill her own yearning for intimate bodily contact and homosexual activity. In the second dream, on the other hand, she is the one who wants to strangle herself, thus killing her crazy sexual arousal, sitting on the knees of a handsome young prince. As a very important fact, we can note the presence of the therapist in the dream, when Alba says, 'another person enters, who came to save me', and she tells this person to hurry up. In this second dream, there is also, in the scene with the television, a projective identification on the television screen, where she sees something 'she thinks is wrong'. We believe it is herself on the screen, extremely erotized, sitting on a young man's knees, and at one point she says, 'this is wrong', and then wants to cut off her head, her thoughts, and her erotic fantasies.

The therapist worked for many months on this dream scene and showed the patient that, just as in the dream she wanted to strangle herself, in her inner world she always strangled or split off her thoughts and her feelings. At one point the therapist told her:

> 'This is how you lose your head and your ability to think, trying to get rid of some sexual thoughts, feelings, or ideas.'

Alba answered:

> 'Yes, it's true, I never think my opinion has any value. I always think that I know nothing, that I take everything from other people.'

This reply is very illuminating and highlights her mental functioning:

1. Alba cuts, strangles her head, and also splits off her ability to think.
2. She then uses other people's heads and thoughts to supplant her own, and the thoughts she lacks.

Final comments:
the father's role; technique and countertransference

During the last stages of the treatment, the therapist began to discover a hierarchy in the way the family structure of the patient operates. It became apparent that it was not true that they were all 'just the same', 'all small'. For instance, the mother used a very expensive soap and gave the rest of the family a cheap soap, of the kind used for laundering clothes. It was obvious that the mother created a hierarchy, a pecking order, which favoured her. It took years to uncover this, as well as other secret codes.

Another interesting aspect I want to include in this last part of the chapter is the evolution of the relationship between Alba and her father. Towards the end of the treatment, the father established a sort of alliance with his daughter, which worked in a subtle way to disobey the mother: for instance, when they were walking in the street, the mother always walked up front, like a captain in the army, and everyone else had to walk behind her. The father used to suggest to Alba to cross the street to the opposite pavement, so they would not have to go where the mother wanted. It was obvious to me and to the therapist that father and daughter were crossing to the other side of the street to avoid being dominated by the mother's codes. In this case, the father helped to establish a dividing line, and to separate the daughter from the mother, allowing her to achieve a total object relationship with her father. This small rebellion, with which the father helped Alba to differentiate from her mother, was in our opinion an important element in the improvement of this patient. (For the importance of the father's role in very disturbed patients see chapter three on cardiac transplant.)

All this secret link with the father was wordless; it was a deep complicity link, made of conniving and loving looks.

* * *

The therapist's holding capacity enabled her to receive and contain a fast, non-stop verbalization for several years. I want to stress the countertransferential capacity that enabled the therapist, in spite of the difficult condition of the patient, to interpret the basic elements in the delusions, particularly when they concerned the field of transference or appeared in it. Another important technique is the discrimination in the transference between the separate identities of the patient and the therapist, which helped discriminate on the days they had no session.

Acquiring this awareness of different spaces and the concept of absence and presence is a process that takes long years. It was also very important to help the patient to clarify confusions about her body and about her erogenous zones. For example, she used to say she leaked fluids through her anus; this was mixed up with vaginal erotization and masturbation: she confused the secretions of her vagina with what came out of her anus. At other, more primitive levels, this fantasy also represented a means of emptying herself of her body fluids, a sort of haemorrhage of her self. (This aspect is particularly developed in this book in chapter eight on the primitive psychotic body image.)

Concerning the technical use of countertransference, I emphasize that it is necessary to speak with a colleague or a supervisor, to help to decode the invasive projections of this type of patient (Boyer & Giovacchini, 1989; Maldavsky, 1991; Silverman, 1987).

I want to stress the importance of providing a firm framework, with regular, fixed hours, on regular, fixed days. This contributes to an adequate holding or containment, achieves stability, and helps to create a firm space in the transference, which in turn helps create in the mind of the patient her own firm mental space.

The reader can find other technical details on the use of countertransference in chapter four on 'Countertransference' (Green, 1986; Pines, 1986).

Transcript of the session

Let us now look in detail at one of Alba's treatment sessions—the key session, on which the above observations are based. The session took place in the first months of treatment.

ALBA (*clearing throat*): I wanted to tell you that perhaps this idea that I like girls because I am afraid of boys, among other things, you know, well, how it comes about. Because when I was younger, what I thought of boys in general . . . well, I told you that both my primary school and secondary schools were for girls only, so I didn't really know any boys. But when I was 11 years old—let's see if you can make anything of this—I went to this . . . they taught music, dancing, drama, drawing—a sort of . . . of . . . general corporal and manual self-expression, you know? Boys and girls seemed to me to be in groups . . . I mean, they were in age-groups. They put me in the biggest group, the one doing . . . people were put in groups according to what they wanted to do. One was a special drama group, doing plays, but really, everyone did a bit of everything. Perhaps those who were especially good at something spent more time on it in the morning, and they put me in the drawing group. Well, most of this group (*laughs*), you see (*laughs*), they were bigger than me. I was 11—no, 12—and there were kids who were a bit older than me, and as it was the last year, you know, some of them already knew each other well. I mean, they were already pretty well a group, so . . . er . . . so new arrivals were put through it a bit, you know. There was this boy, Martinez. He was the one I liked, anyway. I liked him because he danced very well. We . . . er . . . it was folk dancing, I mean. We did learn other dances too, but not really properly; it wasn't like taking a dance class—a sort of expression. . . . We had one hour a day. Well, he was the boy I liked best. Later there were two others. Well, there were about six or seven boys, perhaps more. I remember that these two didn't tease me, but the others were rather beastly, you know? They . . . er . . . caused a lot of trouble, but of course it wasn't that I was afraid of the boys. But . . . it wasn't an open fear, if you know what I mean, or that I didn't want to go to school because of how the boys went on, it wasn't that. Sometimes I didn't want to go to school, but for other reasons, or because I didn't enjoy the drama class. We acted plays, you know? But it wasn't for that . . . the boys . . . it wasn't because of them I didn't want to go, but anyway, I didn't like the boys . . . you know . . . because those boys used to put drawing-pins on the benches. (*Laughs.*) They did it on purpose to see what we would do. Of course (*laughs*), it made one jump. They didn't do it to everyone. They did it to newcomers, and they didn't bother those who were already in the group, or those they accepted from the start. I mean, if a new girl came who looked lively or who immediately (*laughs*) began chattering to everyone, you know, she was OK. They would pick on someone who was shy, like me.

(*Laughs.*) Then they made your life, well, not exactly impossible, but. . . .

Alba went on to recount how one day while she was doing clay modelling, they stole a little bag from her, in which she kept her keys. She hunted everywhere for it but could not find it, and when she went to the teachers crying for help, they paid no attention. Finally, she found it half-hidden. She thought the teachers were protecting the other children because they had been at the school for years.

ALBA: And then I met a friend from last year, one of the other boys, the one I liked best in the anatomy group, whom I hadn't seen for ages, not since the end of the term when we each . . . we became separated . . . everyone was in different groups, and I hadn't seen him in all that time. Because I liked him, and I'm an impulsive person, I showed how happy I was to see him and said, 'How are you? I haven't seen you for ages.' I hardly noticed how he reacted, because afterwards I discovered that . . . I don't now if they are engaged or anything, but . . . er . . . he is going out with one of the girls who . . . from last year's group, you know— they still go around together . . . er . . . they enrolled in the same class because in fact last year they had been going out together, I suppose. I know the girl because she was in my group. Er, well, the question, you know . . . I already knew that . . . you know . . . this boy was, well, I don't know whether he was going steady or what, but these affairs, I think they are pretty flimsy, I can't see anything very steady about them. Last year, too, at the beginning of the year, he was going with another girl. Then they quarrelled, and six months later it was all over, and now he's back with her again. . . . (*Laughs.*) . . . I don't think it's anything very serious, but the fact is . . . er . . . I worry a lot about these things, because I . . . er . . . well, any- way, I was talking about it with another friend of mine, this girl Delia, and I discovered she liked another boy. He was in the same group too, you know . . . also very nice. . . .

ALBA: Actually, I am very much afraid of acting, because if I can be myself, you know, and feel sure of myself, I don't give a damn if I react differently from the way someone else reacts, but as . . . er . . . I . . . that is, I think that if the way I normally act is all right, I mean if I behaved all right and then . . . you know . . . of course I . . . er . . . because of all these things . . . this confusion, that my feelings are not all . . . not all clear, even what I feel about the boy, er . . . and this girl said, when we were chatting, she said that . . . I mean, she is the girl, Delia is her name, and ever since she learned that he had another girlfriend, she says, 'That's it, she's put him right out of her head (*laughs*), because she says (*laughs*), 'I no longer have anything to do' she says, 'with him', so . . . and with Pancho, well, yes. As regards Jose Luis, but then Jose Luis . . . I mean . . . although he's got a girlfriend, sort of, what does it matter, when we see each other we're friends, and so forth. As for Pancho, well, that's why I said I didn't notice how he reacted, because I was saying to myself . . . er . . . I was so happy that I hardly noticed what he did . . . you know . . . and . . . er . . . she said Pancho didn't see her in the library, and she said to him, 'Hello, Pancho. How are you?' and he said to her, 'Yes, I have to go' (*laughs*) 'to Physiology right away', and off he went, she said.

ALBA: I mean, there is no reason to give up if one really likes him, I mean if one is really in love with the boy. I can't go chasing him or anything like that, if I am not really certain of my feelings, and I get worried thinking . . . er . . . not because I usually like them all . . . I don't know, I usually liked him better than the other, but really I usually find all boys nice, and I like them all, and I like being in their company, and I like one thing about one and another thing about another, and then it turns out. . . .

ALBA: I don't know, because I am very uncertain of my feelings, or perhaps if it is as I see it . . . what happens to me is that even if I do like all boys, I don't mean . . . I like him more because I like him better than the others, I . . . with another boy, I don't know, he's very polite, he . . . he . . . talks very nicely, well I also like this boy.

THERAPIST: It seems to me that you are terribly afraid. . . .

ALBA (*interrupting*):   What of?

THERAPIST: Because. . . .

(*Both talking together*)

ALBA: Yes, I am terribly afraid.

THERAPIST: Because you have found out that you like boys.

ALBA: What?

THERAPIST: Because you have found out that you like boys, and not only one, but all boys.

ALBA: So. . . .

THERAPIST: And it's not just that you like one boy. For example, you like Pancho's eyes, and in this other one, you like the fact that he is polite, so you have to regard yourself as a shameless hussy.

ALBA (interrupting):   But of course, yes, that's very good, er . . . no. . . .

THERAPIST: As if liking boys made you a bad girl.

ALBA: No, but the fact that I like them all . . . well, it's like biting off more than one can chew. And that fits in very well, you know, because the fact that I like them all is something which . . . well . . . it's quite natural, but if . . . I don't know, if it isn't very correct, not that there is anything improper about it, if I, for example. . . .

THERAPIST: So it would appear that the idea that you preferred girls was a refuge, to get away from thinking of yourself as someone who liked all boys . . . or could go out with every Tom, Dick, and Harry.

ALBA: Yes, people say I get things twisted. Yes, it could be that. Yes, because there is no doubt about it. I do like boys very much. (*Laughs.*) Anyway, I don't know why I came up with these ideas. But it's another matter, I mean, what I said is one thing, and it is quite another that I . . . I mean, of course, as I am . . . I mean, generally speaking, but as I am afraid, as you might say, of . . . well . . . (*all this in a very low voice*) of . . . going all the way . . . er . . . I am afraid of having sex, as I told you but . . . er . . . in the sense that it is because I believe that . . . er . . . the man takes . . . er, for example, what I told you about rape . . . er . . . that is, it could happen if he is a bad person, couldn't it? Then . . . er . . . of course, women like me can't hurt me, so it's the man, yes, that's it, and of course I'm not talking about all of them. . . . I mean, for me it's something which I am very . . . I mean, I'm not afraid of the boys, er . . . who study with me at Medical School. I like them, and I'm not afraid of them, or perhaps it's just that I don't know what I would do if I really had a boyfriend. Well (*laughs*), now (*laughs*) I don't know. . . .

THERAPIST: It seems to me that you are trying to calm yourself by telling yourself, 'Well, this is a lady doctor, not a man.'

ALBA: (*interrupts, laughing*):   Ah, that's another problem that I. . . .

THERAPIST: But I really think that today you have been talking very fast, as though you wanted to shut me up because what I said to you yesterday seemed to you like a violation.

ALBA (*interrupting*):   What?

THERAPIST: What I said to you yesterday.

ALBA (*interrupting*):   What do you mean?

THERAPIST: You're not letting me finish. . . .

ALBA (*laughs*):   You just draw any old conclusion.

THERAPIST: I am referring to your fear of finding that you are more sick than you thought you were.

ALBA: Ah, that's true.

THERAPIST: I think that really frightened you, and you regarded it as a violation that I should say such a thing in your face.

ALBA: No, yesterday I was. . . .

ALBA (*at the end of the session*):   Yes, I told you about the dream and I told you how long, because I really don't know, it is not as if it were something, well . . . if not, I would have said it . . . if it were something extremely serious, but since it it only one or two days that I haven't been able to sleep . . . well, er . . . and then, on top of that, you know. . . . We dealt with this matter in the . . . which to me . . . later I saw that it was . . . er . . . was not . . . I don't know, that the headache had nothing to do with the cerebral haemorrhage either, did it? And I was reading one day about (*laughs*), I am impossible. . . . I mean, I study all these diseases as if I was going to get them myself.

REFERENCES AND BIBLIOGRAPHY

Abraham, K. (1908). Psychosexual differences between hysteria and dementia praecox. In: *Selected Papers*. London: Hogarth Press, 1973. [Reprinted London: Karnac Books, 1979.]

————. (1911). Notes on investigation and treatment of manic-depressive states. In: *Selected Papers*. London: Hogarth Press, 1973. [Reprinted London: Karnac Books, 1979.]

————. (1916). The first pregenital stage of the libido. In: *Selected Papers*. London: Hogarth Press, 1973. [Reprinted London: Karnac Books, 1979.]

————. (1919). A particular form of neurotic resistance against the psycho-analytic method. In: *Selected Papers*. London: Hogarth Press, 1973. [Reprinted London: Karnac Books, 1979.]

————. (1924). A short study of the development of the libido. In: *Selected Papers*. London: Hogarth Press, 1973. [Reprinted London: Karnac Books, 1979.]

————. (1973). *Selected Papers on Psycho-Analysis*. London: Hogarth Press. [Reprinted London: Karnac Books, 1979.]

Abt, L. (Ed.) (1965) *Acting Out. Theoretical and Clinical Aspects*. New York/London: Grune & Stratton.

Ahumada, J. L. (1989). On the limitations and infiniteness of analysis. *International Review of Psycho-Analysis, 16*: 297–304.

———. (1990). On narcissistic identification. *International Review of Psycho-Analysis, 17*: 177–187.

Anzieu, A. (1986). Comment on parle aux enfants. *Journal de la Psychanalyse de l'enfant, 1.*

Anzieu, D. (1974). Skin ego. In: S. Lebovici & D. Widlocher (Eds.), *Psychoanalysis in France* (pp. 17–32). New York: International Universities Press.

———. (1975). Transfert paradoxal. *Nouvelle revue de Psychanalyse, 12.*

———. (1980). Sur la création. Conference of the Buenos Aires Psychoanalytical Society.

———. (1987). Formal signifiers and the ego-skin. In: D. Anzieu et al., *Psychic Envelopes*. London: Karnac Books, 1989.

Arieti, S. (Ed.) (1981). *American Handbook of Psychiatry, Vol. 7*. New York: Basic Books.

Aryan, A. (1985a). La adolescencia aportaciones a la metapsicología y psicopatología. *Psicoanálisis* (APdeBA), *4* (3).

———. (1985b). El proceso psíquico en el adolescente. *Psicoanálisis* (APdeBA), *7* (3): 445–478.

Aulagnier, P. (1987). Sources somatiques et discursives de nos représentations de la réalité. *Journal de la Psychanalyse de l'enfant, 3* (247): 70.

Avenburg, R. (1975). *El aparato psíquico y la realidad*. Buenos Aires: Nueva Visión.

———. (1976). The concept of truth in psychoanalysis. *International Journal of Psycho-Analysis, 57*: 11–18.

Baranger, W., & Baranger, M. (1969). *Problemas del campo psicoanalítico*. Buenos Aires: Kargieman.

Barros, I. Garcia de (1985). Problemas de identidade e identificação em psicanálise [Identity and identification in psychoanalysis] *Revista Brasileira de Psicanálise, 19*, 343.

Begoin-Guignard, F. (1986). Cadre et contre-transfert. Psychanalyse d'enfant. *Journal de la Psychanalyse de l'enfant, 2*: 66–85.

Bellak, L. (1965). The concept of acting out. In: L. Abt (Ed.), *Acting Out. Theoretical and Clinical Aspects*. New York/London: Grune & Stratton.

Berenstein, I. (1981). *Psicoanálisis de la estructura familiar*. Buenos Aires: Paidós.

Bergman, A. (1986). 'I and you': The separation–individuation process in the treatment of a symbiotic child. In: J. B. McDevitt & C. F. Settlage (Eds.), *Separation–Individuation: Essays in Honor of Margaret Mahler* (pp. 325–355). New York: International Universities Press.

Bettelheim. B. (1967). *The Empty Fortress*. New York: Free Press. London: Collier-MacMillan.

————. (1990). Children of the Holocaust. In: *Recollections and Reflections*. London: Thames & Hudson.

Bick, E. (1968). The experience of the skin in early object relations. *International Journal of Psycho-Analysis, 49* (3): 484–486. Also in M. Harris Williams (Ed.), *Collected Papers of Martha Harris and Esther Bick*. Perthshire: Clunie Press, 1987.

Bion, W. R. (1963). *Elements of Psychoanalysis*. London: Heinemann. [Reprinted London: Karnac Books, 1984.]

————. (1967a). Differentiation of the psychotic from the non-psychotic personalities. In: *Second Thoughts*. London: Heinemann. [Reprinted London: Karnac Books, 1984.]

————. (1967b) *Second Thoughts*. London: Heinemann. [Reprinted London: Karnac Books, 1984.]

Bleger, J. (1967). *Simbiosis y ambigüedad*. Buenos Aires: Paidós.

Bleichmar, S. (1982). Los origenes del aparato psíquico. *Trabajo del psicoanálisis, 1*: 305–326.

Boyer, L. B. (1983). *The Regressed Patient*. North Vale, NJ: Jason Aronson.

————. (1987). Countertransference and technique in working with the regressed patient: Further remarks. Presented at The Boyer House Foundation Symposium on the Regressed Patient, San Francisco.

Boyer, L. B., & Giovacchini, P. (Eds.) (1989). *Master Clinicians on Treating Regressed Patients*. North Vale, NJ: Jason Aronson.

Brudny, G. (1980). La represíon primaria en la obra de Sigmund Freud. *Psicoanálisis* (APdeBA), *2* (1): 401–486.

Canetti, E. (1978). *Le territoire de l'homme*. Paris: Albin Michel.

Carnap, R. (1942). *Introduction to Semantics*. Cambridge, MA: Harvard University Press.

Chasseguet-Smirguel, J. (1975). Perversion, idealization and sublimation: A reply to the discussion by Andrei Lussier. *International Journal of Psycho-Analysis, 56*, 233–235.

————. (1978). Reflections on the connections between perversion and sadism. *International Journal of Psycho-Analysis, 59*: 27–35.

————. (1984). *Éthique et esthétique de la perversion*. Champ Vallon: L'Or d'Atalante, Presses Universitaires de France.

Chomsky, N. (1965). Syntactic structures. In: *Aspects of the Theory of Syntax*. Cambridge, MA: M.I.T. Press.

Diatkine, R. (1972). *La psychanalyse précoce*. Paris: Presses Universitaires de France.

Dimsdale, J. (1979). *The Coping Behavior of Nazi Concentration Camp Survivors*. Stanford, CA: Stanford University School of Medicine.

Dufresne, R. (1985). Clinical Case: About identification problems in a patient survivor of the Nazi persecution. Paper presented to the Montreal Psychoanalytic Society.

————. (1990). La dame à imperméable et au petit bouton. *Revue Topique, 24*, 65–109.

Dupetit, S. (1985). *La drogadicción y las drogas*. Buenos Aires: Kargieman.

Erikson, E. (1968). *Identity, Youth and Crisis*. London: Faber & Faber.

Etchegoyen, R. H. (1978). Some thoughts on transference perversion. *International Journal of Psycho-Analysis, 59*: 49–53.

————. (1991). *The Fundamentals of Psychoanalytic Technique*. London: Karnac Books.

Fenichel, O. (1957). *The Psychoanalytic Theory of Neuroses*. London: Routledge. New York: W. W. Norton, 1966.

Freud, S. (1895d) (with J. Breuer). *Studies on Hysteria. S.E., 2*.

————. (1896b). Further remarks on the neuro-psychosis of defence. *S.E., 3*.

————. (1901b). *The Psychopathology of Everyday Life. S.E., 6*.

————. (1905d) Three essays on the theory of sexuality. *S.E., 7*.

————. (1905e [1901]). Fragment of an analysis of a case of hysteria. *S.E., 7*.

————. (1908b). Character and anal erotism. *S.E., 9*.

————. (1909a). Notes upon a case of obsessional neurosis. *S.E., 10*.

————. (1909b). Original record of the case. *S.E., 10*.

————. (1910a [1909]). Five lectures on psychoanalysis. *S.E., 11*.

————. (1911c [1910]). Psycho-analytic notes on an autobiographical account of a case of paranoia (dementia paranoides). *S.E., 12*.

————. (1912b). The dynamics of transference. *S.E., 12*.

————. (1914c). On narcissism: An introduction. *S.E., 14*.

————. (1914g). Remembering, repeating and working-through. *S.E., 12*.

————. (1915e). The unconscious. *S.E., 14*.

_____ . (1916–17). *Introductory Lectures on Psycho-Analysis. S.E.,* 15–16.

_____ . (1917c). On transformations of instinct as exemplified in anal erotism. *S.E., 17.*

_____ . (1917e). Mourning and melancholia. *S.E., 14.*

_____ . (1919e). A child is being beaten. *S.E., 17.*

_____ . (1919h). The 'uncanny'. *S.E., 17.*

_____ . (1920g). *Beyond the Pleasure Principle. S.E., 18.*

_____ . (1921c). *Group Psychology and the Analysis of the Ego. S.E.,* 18.

_____ . (1923b). *The Ego and the Id. S.E., 19.*

_____ . (1924b). Neurosis and psychosis. *S.E., 19.*

_____ . (1925d [1924]). *An Autobiographical Study. S.E., 20.*

_____ . (1926d). *Inhibitions, Symptoms and Anxiety. S.E., 20.*

_____ . (1926e). *The Question of Lay Analysis. S.E., 20.*

_____ . (1928b). Dostoevsky and parricide. *S.E., 21.*

_____ . (1931a). Libidinal types. *S.E., 21.*

_____ . (1937c). Analysis terminable and interminable. *S.E., 23.*

_____ . (1940a) [1938]. *An Outline of Psycho-Analysis. S.E., 23.*

_____ . (1940e) [1938]. Splitting of the ego in the process of defence. *S.E., 23.*

Gálvez, M. (1980). Identificación de los padres con sus hijos. *Psicoanálisis* (APdeBA), 2 (3).

Geissmann, C., & Geissmann, P. (1988). Croissance d'une pensée. *Journal de la Psychanalyse de l'enfant, 5:* 50/71.

Gillespie, W. M. (1956). The general theory of sexual perversion. *International Journal of Psycho-Analysis, 37:* 396–403.

Gioia, T., Lancelle, G., Rosenfeld, D., & Zac, J. (1976). *El Acting Out desde el pensamiento psicoanalítico Argentino.* Buenos Aires: Gamon.

Green, A. (1973). *Le discours vivant.* Paris: Presses Universitaires de France.

_____ . (1986). *On Private Madness.* London: Hogarth Press.

_____ . (1990). *La folie privée.* Paris: Gallimard.

Greenacre, G. (1965). In: L. Abt (Ed.), *Acting Out: Theoretical and Clinical Aspects.* New York: Grune & Stratton.

Greenson, R. (1967). *The Technique and Practice of Psychoanalysis.* London: Hogarth Press.

Grinberg, L. (1956). Sobre algunos problemas de técnica analítica determinados por la identificación y contraidentificación proyectivas. *Revista de Psicoanálisis, 3.*

————— . (1965). Contribución al estudio de las modalidades de la identificación proyectiva. *Revista de Psicoanálisis, 22*: 263–278.

Grunberger, B. (1971). *Narcissism: Psychoanalytic Essays*. New York: International Universities Press.

————— . (1967). En marge de 'L'Homme aux Rats'. *Revue française de Psychanalyse, 31*: 589–607.

Guiard, F. (1977). Sobre el componente musical del lenguaje en etapas avanzadas y finales del análisis. *Revista de Psicoanálisis, 34*: 25–76.

Heimann, P. (1990). *About Children and Children No Longer: Collected Papers, 1942–80*, edited M. Tonnesman. London: Routledge.

Houzel, D. (1987). The concept of psychic envelope. In: D. Anzieu et al., *Psychic Envelopes*. London: Karnac Books.

Hugo, V. (1961). In G. Pompidou (Ed.), *Anthologie de la poésie française*. Paris: Hachette.

Joseph, B. (1960). Some characteristics of the psychopathic personality. *International Journal of Psycho-Analysis, 41*: 4–5. Also in *Psychic Equilibrium and Psychic Change*. London: Routledge, 1989.

————— . (1971). A clinical contribution to the analysis of a perversion. *International Journal of Psycho-Analysis, 52*: 441–449. Also in *Psychic Equilibrium and Psychic Change*. London: Routledge, 1989.

————— . (1988). Projective identification: Clinical aspects. In: J. Sandler (Ed.), *Projection, Identification, Projective Identification*. London: Karnac Books.

Kafka, J. (1967). The body as a transitional object: A psychoanalytic study of a self-mutilating patient. Presented at the Thirteenth Annual Chestnut Lodge Symposium, Maryland.

Kanzer, M. (1952). The transference neurosis of the Rat Man. *Psychoanalical Quarterly, 21*: 181–189.

————— . (1965). Acting out and the creative imagination. In: *Acting Out: Theoretical and Clinical Aspects*. New York/London: Grune & Stratton.

Kernberg, O. (1984). *Severe Personality Disorders: Psychotherapeutic Strategies*. New Haven, CT: Yale University Press.

————— . (1988). Projection and projective identification. In: J. Sandler (Ed.), *Projection, Identification, Projective Identification*. London: Karnac Books.

Kijak, M., & Pelento, M. (1982). La labor analítica en época de crisis. *Revista de Psicoanálisis, 40*: 283–407.

Klein, M. (1948). *Contributions to Psycho-Analysis*. London: Hogarth Press.

————— . (1975a). *The Writings of Melanie Klein, Vol. 1: Love, Guilt and Reparation and Other Works*. London: Hogarth Press.

_____. (1975b). *The Writings of Melanie Klein, Vol. 3: Envy and Gratitude and Other Works*. London: Hogarth Press.

Klein, M., Heimann, P., Isaacs, S., & Riviere, J. (1952). *Developments in Psycho-Analysis*. London: Hogarth Press. [Reprinted London: Karnac Books & The Institute of Psycho-Analysis, 1989.]

Klein, M., Heimann, P., & Money-Kyrle, R. (1955). *New Directions in Psychoanalysis: The Significance of Infant Conflict in the Pattern of Adult Behaviour*. London: Hogarth Press. [Reprinted London: Karnac Books, 1985.]

Klein, S. (1980). Autistic phenomena in neurotic patients. *International Journal of Psychoanalysis, 61*: 395–402.

Klimovsky, G. (1971). *El método científico en psicología y psicopatología*, Zienzenski (Ed.). Buenos Aires: Nueva Visión.

_____. (1980). Estructura y validez de las teorías científicas. In: Zienensky (Ed.), *Métodos de investigación en biología y psicopatología*. Buenos Aires: Nueva Visión.

Lacan, J. (1966). *Écrits*. Paris: Éditions du Seuil.

Krakov, H. (1987). El paciente que daña: contratransferencia y autismo. Presented at the Conference of the Buenos Aires Psychoanalytical Society.

Lagache, D. (1961). La psychanalyse et la structure de la personnalité. In: *Oeuvres, Vol. 4: Agressivité structure de la personnalité et autres travaux*. Paris: Presses Universitaires de France, 1982.

_____. (1968). Acting out et action. In: *Oeuvres, Vol. 6: La folle du logis et autres travaux*. Paris: Presses Universitaires de France, 1986. [Also in *The Work of Daniel Lagache: Selected Papers*, London: Karnac Books, 1992.]

Laplanche, J. (1979). *Problematiques. Vol. 4: L'inconscient et le ça*. Paris: Presses Universitaires de France.

Laplanche, J., & Pontalis, J. (1973). *The Language of Psychoanalysis*. London: Hogarth Press. [Reprinted London: Karnac Books, 1988.]

Laufer, M., & Laufer, E. (1989). *Developmental Breakdown and Psychoanalytic Treatment in Adolescence*. New Haven, CT: Yale University Press.

Lebovici, S. (1987). Les psychanalistes et les psychoses de l'enfant. *Revue française de la Psychanalyse, 50*: 1545–1566.

Lebovici, S., & Widlocher, D. (Eds.), *Psychoanalysis in France* (pp. 17–32). New York: International Universities Press.

Levisky, L. D. (1987). Acting out na análise de criancas: un medio de comunicacao. *Revista Brasileira de Psicanalise, 21*.

Liberman, D. (1970-72). *Lingüística, interacción comunicativa y proceso psicoanalítico (1–3)*. Buenos Aires: Nueva Visión–Galerna.

————— . (1978). Affective response of the analyst to the patient's communication. *International Journal of Psychoanalysis, 59*: 335–340.

Limentani, A. (1966). Revaluation of acting-out in relation to working-through. *International Journal of Psychoanalysis, 47*: 274–282.

López, B. (1968). Técnica de trastornos del carácter. *Revista de Psicoanálisis, 4* (1).

————— . (1983). Los afectos y el narcisismo. *Psicoanálisis, 5*: 26–46.

————— . (1985). Una distorsión semántico-pragmática: el paciente del discurso ininterrumpido. *Revista de Psicoanálisis* (APdeBA), 7 (1–2): 279–300.

Lowenstein, R. (1959). Notes on the roles of speech in psychoanalytic technique. In: *Readings in Psychoanalytic Psychology*. New York. Appleton-Century-Crofts.

Lutenberg, J. (1983). Lo siniestro y el complejo de Edipo. *Psicoanálisis, 5* (2).

McDougall, J. (1985). *Theatres of the Mind: Illusion and Truth on the Psychoanalytic Stage*. New York: Basic Books.

————— . (1986). Identifications, neoneeds and neosexualities. *International Journal of Psycho-Analysis, 67*: 19–31.

————— . (1989). *Theatres of the Body: A Psychoanalytic Approach to Psychosomatic Illness*. London: Free Association Books.

Mahler, M. (1968). *On Human Symbiosis and the Vicissitudes of Individuation*. New York: International Universities Press.

————— . (1971). *Separation–Individuation: Essays in Honor of Margaret Mahler*, edited by J. B. McDevitt & C. F. Settlage. New York: International Universities Press.

Maldavsky, D. (1977). *Teoría de las representaciones*. Buenos Aires: Nueva Visión.

————— . (1991). *Procesos y estructuras vinculares*. Buenos Aires: Ediciones Nueva Visión.

Mauer, S., & Resnizky, S. (1991). *Acompañantes terapéuticos y pacientes psicóticos*. Buenos Aires: Editorial Trieb.

Mélega, M. P. (1984). Um jovem psicanalista trabalhando. *Revista Brasileira de Psicanálise, 18*: 357.

Meltzer, D. (1964). The differentation of somatic delusions from hypochondria. *International Journal of Psycho-Analysis, 45*: 246–250.

————— . (1966). The relation of anal masturbation to projective identification. *International Journal of Psychoanalysis, 47*: 335–342. Also in: E. Spilius, (Ed.), *Melanie Klein Today*, Vol. 1. London: Routledge, 1988.

_____ . (1973). *Sexual States of Mind*. Perthshire: Clunie Press.

Meltzer, D. et al. (1975). *Explorations in Autism*. Perthshire: Clunie Press.

Mordo, E. (1987). L'effrayante étrangeté et les survivantes de l'holocaust. Discussion on a paper presented to the International Psychoanalytical Congress, Montreal, on the Panel entitled 'Children of the Holocaust'.

Mordo, E., & Rosenfeld, D. (1976). Fusión, confusión, simbiosis e identificación proyectiva. In: *Clínica psicoanalítica*. Buenos Aires: Galerna.

Nagel, E., & Newman, J. (1958). *Gödel's Proof*. New York: New York University Press, 1958.

Nunberg, H. (1932). *Allgemeine Neurosenlehre auf psychoanalytischer Grundlage*. Bern: Huber.

Ogden, T. (1986). *The Matrix of the Mind: Object Relations and the Psychoanalytic Dialogue*. North Vale, NJ: Jason Aronson.

_____ . (1990). On the structure of experience. In: L. B. Boyer & P. Giovacchini (Eds.), *Master Clinicians on Treating the Regressed Patient*. North Vale, NJ: Jason Aronson.

Osório, L. C. (1984). Vicissitudes da aquisiçao do sentimento de identidade durante o proceso puberal. *Revista Brasileira de Psicanálise*, *18*.

Pao, P.-N. (1967). The syndrome of delicate self cutting. Presented at the Thirteenth Annual Chestnut Lodge Symposium, Maryland.

Piaget, J. (1926). *La representation du monde chez l'enfant*. France: Ed. Allan.

Pichon Rivière, E. (1970). *Del psicoanálisis a la psicología social*. Buenos Aires: Galerna.

Pines, D. (1986). Working with woman survivors of the holocaust. *International Journal of Psycho-Analysis*, *67*: 63–79.

Popper, K. (1965). *Conjectures and Refutations: The Growth of Scientific Knowledge*. New York: Basic Books.

Racamier, P. (1959). Psychotherapie psychanalytique des psychoses. In: *La psychanalyse d'aujourd'hui*. Paris: Presses Universitaires de France.

Racker, H. (1957). The meanings and uses of countertransference. *Psychoanalytical Quarterly*, *26*: 303–357.

_____ . (1960). *Transference and Countertransference*. London: Hogarth Press, 1968. [Reprinted London: Karnac Books, 1985.]

Radó, S. (1933). The psychoanalysis of pharmacothymia. *Psychoanalytic Quarterly*, *2*.

304 REFERENCES AND BIBLIOGRAPHY

Reich, W. (1950). *Character Analysis*. New York: Farrar, Straus & Giroux.

Resnik, S. (1973). *Personne et psychose*. Paris: Payot.

————. (1987). *The Theatre of the Dream*. London: Tavistock.

Ríos, C. (1980). Las representaciones del cuerpo en el aparato psíquico. Presented at the Symposium of the Buenos Aires Psychoanalytical Association.

————. (1985). Las identificaciones en la adolescencia. *Psicoanálisis* (APdeBA), 7 (3): 499–515.

Robertiello, R. (1965). 'Acting out' or working-through. In: L. Abt (Ed.), *Acting Out. Theoretical and Clinical Aspects*. New York/London: Grune & Stratton.

Rosen, J. (1965). The concept of 'acting-in'. In: L. Abt (Ed.), *Acting Out. Theoretical and Clinical Aspects*. New York/London: Grune & Stratton.

Rosen, V. (1967). Disorders of communication in psycho-analysis. *Journal of the American Psychoanalytic Association, 15* (3).

Rosenbaum, B., & Sonne, H. (1986). *The Language of Psychosis*. New York: New York University Press.

Rosenfeld, D. (1972). La obra de Daniel Lagache en el psicoanálisis francés. Algunas correlaciones con las ideas de J. P. Sartre y M. Klein. *Revista de Psicoanálisis* (APdeBA), *4*.

————. (1975). La lingüística en la clínica psicoanalítica con pacientes psicóticos. *Imago, 1*: 139. Buenos Aires: Letra Viva.

————. (1976). *Clínica psicoanalítica*. Buenos Aires: Galerna.

————. (1982a). Psychotic body image in neurotic and psychotic patients. Presented at the International Psychoanalytical Society Congress, Helsinki.

————. (1982b). La noción del esquema corporal psicótico en pacientes neuróticos y psicóticos. *Psicoanálisis, 4* (2): 383–404.

————. (1983). Hipocondrías, delirio somático y esquema corporal en la práctica psicoanalítica. *Revista de Psicoanálisis* (APdeBA), *40* (1): 175–189.

————. (1985). Distortion: sur un mode particulier de résistance. *Nouvelle revue de Psychanalyse, 31*: 191–199.

————. (1987). Freud: An imaginary dialogue. In: *Imaginary Dialogue on Freud's 'Analysis Terminable and Interminable'*. London: International Psychoanalytical Association. New Haven, CT: Yale University Press, 1991.

————. (1989). *Psychoanalysis and Groups*. London: Karnac Books.

_____ . (1990). Psychotic body image. In: B. Boyer & P. Giovacchini (Eds.), *Master Clinicians on Treating Regressed Patients*. North Vale, NJ: Jason Aronson.

Rosenfeld, D., & Luna, B. (1983). Inmovilidad del tiempo y esquema corporal. Presented at the Symposium of the Buenos Aires Psychoanalytical Society.

_____ . (1988). *Omnipotencia narcisista*. Paper presented at the Latin-American Congress, Brazil.

Rosenfeld, D., & Mordo, E. (1973). Fusión, confusión, simbiosis e identificación proyectiva. *Revista de Psicoanálisis, 30*: 413–457.

Rosenfeld, D., & Pistol, D. (1986). Episodio psicótico y su detección precoz en la transferencia. Presented at the XVI Latin-American Congress on Psychoanalysis, Mexico, July 1986.

Rosenfeld, D., & Schenquerman, C. (1977). Fracasos en el tratamiento psicoanalítico. La reacción terapéutica negativa: guia clínica y técnica. *Revista de Psicoanálisis, 35*: 463–486.

Rosenfeld, H. A. (1965). *Psychotic States: A Psychoanalytic Approach*. London: Hogarth Press. [Reprinted London: Karnac Books, 1985.]

_____ . (1987). *Impasse and Interpretation*. London: Tavistock.

Rubinstein, G. (1982). Algunas consideraciones acerca del acting out en adolescencia. *Psicoanalistas* (APdeBA), *3* (4): 669–697.

Ruesch, J. (1957). *Disturbed Communication*. New York: W. W. Norton.

Sandler, A.-M. (1988). Concluding discussion. In: J. Sandler (Ed.), *Projection, Identification, Projective Identification*. London: Karnac Books.

Sandler, J. (1983). Reflections on some relations between psychoanalytic concepts and psychoanalytic practice. *International Journal Psycho-Analysis, 64*: 35–45.

_____ . (1988). The concept of projective identification and concluding discussion. In: J. Sandler (Ed.), *Projection, Identification, Projective Identification*. London: Karnac Books.

Schafer, R. (1983). *The Analytic Attitude*. London: Hogarth Press. [Reprinted London: Karnac Books, 1992.]

Schilder, P. (1935). *The Image and Appearance of the Human Body*. London: Kegan Paul, Trench, Trubner.

Scott, C. (1980). Narcissism, the body phantasy, internal and external objects and the 'body schema'. Presented at a Meeting of the Advanced Institute for Analytic Psychotherapy, New York.

Scott, W. C. (1991). Discussion of the paper, 'Hypochondria, somatic delusion, body image'. Montreal, 4 February 1991.

Searles, H. F. (1960). *The Non Human Environment in Normal Development and in Schizophrenia.* New York: International Universities Press.

————. (1963). Transference psychosis in the psychotherapy of chronic schizophrenia. *International Journal of Psycho-Analysis, 44*: 249–281.

————. (1965). Transference psychosis in the psychotherapy of schizophrenics. In: *Collected Papers on Schizophrenia and Related Subjects.* London: Hogarth Press. [Reprinted London: Karnac Books, 1986.]

————. (1974). Les sources de l'angoisse dans la schizophrénie paranoide. *Nouvelle revue de Psychanalyse, 9*: 143–162.

————. (1979). *Countertransference and Related Subjects.* New York: International Universities Press.

Segal, H. (1950). Some aspects of the analysis of a schizophrenic. *International Journal of Psycho-Analysis, 31*: 268–278. Also in: *The Work of Hanna Segal.* Reprinted London: Karnac Books, 1986.

————. (1973). *Introduction to the Work of Melanie Klein,* 2nd ed. London: Hogarth Press. [Reprinted London: Karnac Books & The Institute of Psycho-Analysis.]

Sibony, D. (1988). *Écrits sur le racisme.* Paris: Christian Bourgois.

Silverman, M. (1987). The analyst's response. *Psychoanalytic Inquiry, 7* (2): 277–287.

Tabak de Bianchedi, E. (1989). De Bion a Meltzer. Presented to the Buenos Aires Psychoanalytic Association (APdeBA).

Treurniet, N. (1987). On transference neurosis. The structure and the process. A clinical study. *Psychoanalytical Inquiry, 7* (4): 511–533.

————. (1989). On Having and Giving Value.

Tustin, F. (1972). *Autism and Childhood Psychosis.* London: Hogarth Press.

————. (1981). *Autistic States in Children.* London & Boston: Routledge & Kegan Paul.

————. (1984). Autistic shapes. *International Review of Psychoanalysis, 11*: 279–290.

————. (1986). *Autistic Barriers in Neurotic Patients.* London: Karnac Books.

————. (1990). *The Protective Shell in Children and Adults.* London: Karnac Books.

Watzlawick, P., Beavin, H., & Jackson, D. (1967). *Pragmatics of Human Communication*. New York: W. W. Norton.

Wilson, C.P., & Mintz, I. L. (1989). *Psychosomatic Symptoms: Their Underlying Personality Disorders and the Technique of Psychotherapy*. North Vale, NJ: Jason Aronson.

Winnicott, D. W. (1958). *Collected Papers: Through Paediatrics to Psychoanalysis*. London: Hogarth Press. [Reprinted London: Karnac Books & The Institute of Psychoanalysis, 1992.]

———. (1960). Countertransference. *British Journal of Medical Psychology, 33*: 17–21. Also in: *The Maturational Processes and the Facilitating Environment*. London: Hogarth Press. [Reprinted London: Karnac Books & The Institute of Psycho-Analysis, 1990.]

———. (1963). Dependence in infant care, in child care, and the psychoanalytic setting. *International Journal of Psycho-Analysis, 44*: 339–344.

———. (1965a). The capacity to be alone. In: *The Maturational Processes and the Facilitating Environment*. London: Hogarth Press. [Reprinted London: Karnac Books & The Institute of Psycho-Analysis, 1990.]

———. (1965b). Communicating and not communicating leading to study of certain opposites. In: *The Maturational Processes and the Facilitating Environment*. London: Hogarth Press. [Reprinted London: Karnac Books & The Institute of Psycho-Analysis, 1990.]

———. (1971). *Playing and Reality*. London: Tavistock.

Zac, J. (1968). Relación semana—fin de semana. Encuadre y acting out. *Revista de Psicoanálisis, 25* (1).

———. (1973). *Psicopatía*. Buenos Aires: Kargieman.

Zetzel, E. (1966). *An Obsessional Neurosis: Freud's Rat Man*. London: Hogarth Press, 1987. Also in: *The Capacity for Emotional Growth*. London: Hogarth Press, 1970. [Reprinted London: Karnac Books, 1987.]

INDEX

Abraham, K., 6, 11, 149, 164,
   178, 188
acting out
  and *agieren*, 142
  as communication, 141, 143
  definition [Freud], 141
  in impulsive character, 261–
    62, 264, 265
  neurotic vs. psychotic, 142
  in psychosis [clinical
    example], 152–54
  and psychosomatic illness,
    141–55
    [clinical example], 144–
     49
  recovering, 155
  and repetition compulsion
    [Freud], 143
  and schizophrenia, 142
  and verbal symbols, 155
addiction equivalent, 204, 240
  see also drug abuse
aggression
  as communication, 134
  drug abuse as, 205–6
agieren, and acting out, 142
Ahumada, J. L., 281
air
  dealing with, and drug abuse,
    242–43
  use of, and drug sniffing, 249–
    52
Alba [clinical example], 277–
    94
analysis, child, 101–37

analyst, role of, in treatment of
  psychotic transference,
  14
anti-drug medication, role of,
  221–28
anxiety
  castration, 232, 272
  hypochondriac, 272
  hysteria, and fundamental
    rule, 80
  separation, 124–27, 136, 214,
    218
Anzieu, A., 107
Anzieu, D., 60, 197
armour, autistic, and drug
  abuse, 248
Aryan, A., 83, 155
Aty [clinical example], 101–37
Aulagnier, P., viii, ix, 133
Auschwitz, 55, 58–60
autism
  encapsulated, ix, xi, 23, 100,
    112
  secondary, x–xi, 133
  infantile, 192
autistic mechanisms, and
  hypochondria, 188–90
autistic shell, and drug abuse,
  256–57
Avenburg, R., 8, 12, 60, 83, 152,
  161, 191, 261
axiology, 178

Baranger, M., 83, 161, 189, 207,
  208

308